Strategic Choices in Reforming Public Service Employment

Strategic Choices in Reforming Public Service Employment

An International Handbook

Edited by

Carlo Dell'Aringa

Giuseppe Della Rocca

and

Berndt Keller

Editorial matter and selection © Carlo Dell'Aringa, Giuseppe Della Rocca and Berndt Keller 2001
Chapters 1–9 © Palgrave Publishers Ltd 2001

All rights reserved. No reproduction, copy or transmission of this publication may be made without written permission.

No paragraph of this publication may be reproduced, copied or transmitted save with written permission or in accordance with the provisions of the Copyright, Designs and Patents Act 1988, or under the terms of any licence permitting limited copying issued by the Copyright Licensing Agency, 90 Tottenham Court Road, London W1T 4LP.

Any person who does any unauthorised act in relation to this publication may be liable to criminal prosecution and civil claims for damages.

The authors have asserted their rights to be identified as the authors of this work in accordance with the Copyright, Designs and Patents Act 1988.

First published 2001 by
PALGRAVE
Houndmills, Basingstoke, Hampshire RG21 6XS and
175 Fifth Avenue, New York, N.Y. 10010
Companies and representatives throughout the world

PALGRAVE is the new global academic imprint of
St. Martin's Press LLC Scholarly and Reference Division and
Palgrave Publishers Ltd (formerly Macmillan Press Ltd).

ISBN 0–333–92162–3

This book is printed on paper suitable for recycling and made from fully managed and sustained forest sources.

A catalogue record for this book is available from the British Library.

Library of Congress Cataloging-in-Publication Data
Strategic choices in reforming public service employment : an international handbook / edited by Carlo Dell'Aringa, Giuseppe Della Rocca, Berndt Keller.
    p. cm.
    Includes bibliographical references and index.
    ISBN 0–333–92162–3
    1. Employee–management relations in government.
    I. Dell'Aringa, Carlo. II. Della Rocca, Giuseppe. III. Keller, Berndt.
HD8005 .S78 2001
331.88'11351—dc21
                                                                    2001032124

10 9   8   7   6   5   4   3   2   1
10 09 08 07 06 05 04 03 02 01

Printed and bound in Great Britain by
Antony Rowe Ltd, Chippenham, Wiltshire

Contents

List of Figures	viii
List of Tables	ix
Notes on the Contributors	xi
Preface and Acknowledgments	xii
List of Abbreviations	xiv

1 Reforming Public Sector Labor Relations 1
  Carlo Dell'Aringa

Introduction	1
Privatization and labor cost reductions	4
The New Public Management	9
Administrative decentralization and collective bargaining	12
Trade unions' responses to increasing flexibility	17
Concluding remarks and open questions	21

2 The New Public Management in Europe 24
  Stephen Bach and Giuseppe Della Rocca

Challenges and problems	24
Traditional organization and practice in the public services	25
Management practice in Europe: toward a New Public Management?	28
Comparative evidence	32
Market-type mechanisms	37
Exploring national variations in management practice	39

3 Collective Bargaining in Western Europe 48
  Lorenzo Bordogna and David Winchester

Introduction: common pressures, diverging solutions?	48
A framework for comparative analysis	50
Unilateral versus joint regulation: the coverage of collective bargaining	52
Centralization versus decentralization: the level of bargaining	57

The coordination of collective bargaining	62
Concluding remarks	65

4 Employer Associations and Unions in the Public Sector 71
Berndt Keller, Jesper Due, and Søren Kaj Andersen

Introduction	71
Public sector employers and their associations	72
Centralized control versus decentralized flexibility	74
Initiating change and modernization	78
Trade unions	83
Coping with change	87
Outlook	91

5 United States Public Sector Employment 97
Jonathan Brock

Overview of public sector employment	97
Organizational structure	100
Qualitative employment and wages	102
Civil service systems and employer associations	109
Unions	111
Bargaining and negotiations	114
Reform efforts	121
Conclusions	123

6 Canadian Public Sector Employment 127
Mark Thompson

Introduction	127
Organizational structure, employment and wages	129
The actors: employers and employer associations	135
The actors: trade unions	138
Public sector labor relations	140
Labor conflict and regulation of strikes	146
Labor management cooperation	149
Conclusions	150

7 Japanese Public Sector Employment 155
Kazutoshi Koshiro

Introduction	155
Organizational structure, employment and wages	157

	Employers and employer associations	169
	Trade unions	174
	Public sector labor relations	178
	Conclusions	181
8	Public Sector Industrial Relations in New Zealand *Pat Walsh, Raymond Harbridge, and Aaron Crawford*	185
	Introduction	185
	Organizational structure, employment and wages	186
	The actors: employers and employer associations	193
	The trade unions	198
	Public sector labor relations	204
	Conclusions	210
9	Employment Relations in the Australian Public Sector *Russell D. Lansbury and Duncan K. Macdonald*	216
	Introduction	216
	Organizational structure, employment and wages	217
	The role of employers in the public sector	223
	Trade unions	229
	Public sector industrial relations	232
	Conclusions	240
Subject Index		243

List of Figures

7.1	Number of public employees (1995)	158
7.2	An international comparison of the number of government employees	162
7.3	Changes in the average pay differentials (Laspeyres Index) between national and local government employees, 1963–1997	168
7.4	Distribution of pay differentials (Laspeyres Index) between the national and local public services in 1974 and 1997	168

List of Tables

1.1	Total public employment	8
1.2	Compensation costs in the public sector as a percentage of GDP	9
6.1	Government final consumption as a percent of GDP, current prices	128
6.2	Public sector employment, 1980–1995	131
6.3	Public sector employment share of labor force, 1980–1997	132
6.4	Membership, major public sector unions, 1980–1998	139
6.5	Public sector union membership and density, 1980–1992	140
6.6	Cumulative negotiated wage change, private and public sectors, 1980–1996	146
7.1	Budgetary fixed number of national government employees	159
7.2	National government employees by employment status	160
7.3	Local government employees, 1975–1997	161
7.4	Average straight-time monthly earnings of the national public service, 1988–1997	166
7.5	Number of organized workers classified by the applicable laws, fiscal year 1953–1997	176
8.1	Public sector employment, 1980–1998	187
8.2	Public service organizations by size, 1984 and 1998	188
8.3	Staffing in selected SOEs, 1987–1991	188
8.4	Employment in public health and education sectors, 1984–1998	189
8.5	Gender breakdown of employment, 1980–1998	190
8.6	Public sector union membership, 1990 and 1997	203
8.7	Labor cost index by sector, 1992–1998	208
8.8	Work stoppages, involvements and days lost by sectors, 1990–1996	209
9.1	Changes in numbers of government employees, 1990–1997	219
9.2	Employment in the Australian public service, 1988–1997	219

9.3	Employment in the Federal Department of Health, 1990–1997	220
9.4	Employment in the State Department of Education in New South Wales, 1988–1996	220
9.5	Major public sector unions in Australia	236
9.6	Industrial conflict in Australia: comparison of public and private sectors	236
9.7	Industrial conflict in Australia: selected industries	238

Notes on the Contributors

Carlo Dell'Aringa, Department of Economics, Catholic University of Milan

Stephen Bach, The Management Centre, King's College, London

Giuseppe Della Rocca, Department of Sociology, University of Calabria

Lorenzo Bordogna, Professor of Organizational Sociology, Department of Social Sciences, University of Brescia, Italy

David Winchester, Industrial Relations Research Unit, Warwick Business School, University of Warwick

Berndt Keller, Department of Political Science, University of Konstanz

Jesper Due, Industrial Relations Research Group (FAOS), Department of Sociology, University of Copenhagen

Søren K. Andersen, Industrial Relations Research Group (FAOS), Department of Sociology, University of Copenhagen

Jonathan Brock, "Daniel J. Evans" School of Public Affairs, University of Seattle

Mark Thompson, Faculty of Commerce and Business Administration, University of British Columbia

Kazutoshi Koshiro, Yokohama National University and University of the Air

Pat Walsh, Human Resource Management and Industrial Relations, Victoria University of Wellington

Raymond Harbridge, Employment Relations, Victoria University of Wellington and Management, La Trobe University of Melbourne

Aaron Crawford, Industrial Relations Centre, Victoria University of Wellington

Russell D. Lansbury, Department of Industrial Relations, University of Sydney

Duncan K. Macdonald, School of Management, University of Newcastle

Preface and Acknowledgments

The idea for this book arose from a research network of scholars with an established interest in public sector employment relations. The motivation in common was to understand and discuss the most significant trends in the rationalization and changes in employment relations in the public sector in quite a representative number of OECD countries. The aims of the book are twofold. First, it puts forward a number of interpretative hypotheses on this phenomenon and investigates why the public sector was once regarded as a model for "good employer" practices in the private sector, and why, instead, it has now taken a different direction. These questions are answered by discussing the main factors of change beginning with global competition, trade liberalization and the restructuring of economic systems. The second aim is to provide a comparative analysis of the changes in the organization of public service management and in employment relations. Across different countries we can see not only common political and economic pressures but also a diversity of constraints and solutions. The differing approaches occurring in different countries have also been explained.

The focus of the research is on core public services, which include national and local governments and their provisions for health, education and social services. The research network has been progressively enlarged. Initially (1996–97), it involved researchers and practitioners from Europe who often met to discuss their countries' respective contributions. The primary result of the network was a systematic and authoritative set of national case studies, published (Routledge, 1999) under the title: *Public Service Employment Relations in Europe: Transformation, Modernization or Inertia?* The book was edited by Stephen Bach, Lorenzo Bordogna, Giuseppe Della Rocca, and David Winchester. Each chapter of the book provides an up-to-date analysis of the restructuring of public service employment relations in six European countries (Britain, Italy, Germany, France, Denmark and Spain). The introduction previews its principal findings and draws some comparative conclusions.

A second stage resulted in several studies that were presented at the Eleventh World Congress of the International Industrial Relations Association in Bologna, Italy (September, 1998). One of the forums was dedicated to a comparative analysis of industrial relations in public employment. Immediately prior to, and during the congress, the European group of researchers met to define a more enhanced interpretative contribution (presented in this second book). The interpretative contributions were organized focusing on a comparative overview of the development of the structure of collective bargaining, the role of management and administrations, and the role of state employer associations and trade-unions.

Discussions were also extended to encompass non-European cases. The enlarged group included researchers and practitioners belonging to countries such as USA, Canada, New Zealand, Australia and Japan. The overall framework (based on the previous European one) for each country study was discussed during the world congress of the IIRA in Bologna. Consequently, each chapter considers the same agenda and conforms to a common format. It includes discussions on the key components of the public service sector: labor market and employment characteristics, administrative and management development and collective bargaining structure and its main changes. The structures, organization and membership of trade unions are reviewed and their response to new management initiatives is evaluated with the distinctive aspects of each country highlighted. All the national case studies were not only based on the author's main research interest in the area, but also focused on secondary sources of data and analysis. The choice of criteria was based on including countries that have a large and representative experience in administrative and employment relations.

The book would not have been possible without the administrative and financial support of the Catholic University of Milan. We have benefited greatly from discussions with contributors on different occasions. We are also grateful to the authors for responding to our requests and to Carey Bernitz, Lorraine Nicholson, Lucia Ricci and Alessandra Sabino for the editing of this book.

Carlo Dell'Aringa
Giuseppe Della Rocca
Berndt Keller

List of Abbreviations

ABS	Australian Bureau of Statistics
ACTU	Australian Council Trade Union
AEU	Australian Education Union
AFL-CIO	American Federation of Labor-Congress for Industrial Organization
AFSCME	American Federation of State, Country and Municipal Employees
AFT	American Federation of Teachers
AgV	Arbetsgivar Verket (Sweden) (Swedish agency for government employees)
AHBs	Area Health Boards (New Zealand)
AHEIA	Australian Higher Education Industrial Association
AIRC	Australian Industrial Relations Commission
ALP	Australian Labor Party
APS	Australian Public Service
ARAN	Agenzia per la Rappresentanza Negoziale della Pubblica Amministrazione (negotiates Italian pay levels)
ASMs	Association of Salaried Medical Specialists (New Zealand)
ASTE	Association of Staff in Tertiary Education (New Zealand)
ASU	Australian Services Union
AT & MOEA	Australian Tram and Motor Omnibus Employees Association
AUS	Association of University Staff (New Zealand)
AWAs	Australian Workplace Agreements
AWIRS	Australian Workplace Industrial Relation Service
BCA	Business Council of Australia
CCMAU	Crown Company Monitoring Advisory Unit (New Zealand)
CDC	Center for Disease Control (USA)
CEC	Collective Employment Contract (New Zealand)
CEOs	Chief Executive Officers (Australia–New Zealand)
CEPU	Communications, Electrical and Plumbing Union (Australia)
CFDT	Confederation Française Du Travail

CLC	Canadian Labor Congress
CLRC	Central Labor Relations Commission (Japan)
CPSU	Community and Public Sector Union (Australia)
CSC	Civil Service Commission (USA)
CSSO	Combined State Service Organization (New Zealand)
CTU	Council of Trade Unions (New Zealand)
CUPE	Canadian Union of Public Employees
DGB	Deutsher Gewerschaftsbund (German Trade Union Federation)
DIR	Department of Industrial Relations (Australia)
DWReSB	Department of Workplace Relations and Small Businesses (Australia)
ECA	Employment Contracts Act (New Zealand)
EEOC	Equal Employment Opportunity Commission (USA)
EIRO	European Industrial Relations Observatory
EIRR	European Industrial Relations Review
EMU	Economic and Monetary Union
EPAC	Economic Planning Advisory Commission (Australia)
FEN	Federation de l'Education Nationale (France)
FLRA	Federal Labor Relations Authority (USA)
FOL	Federation of Labor (New Zealand)
FSU	Federation Syndacale Unitarie (France)
FTE	Full Time Equivalents (New Zealand)
GBEs	Government Business Enterprises (Australia)
GDP	Gross Domestic Product
GEW	Trade Union for Education and Science (Germany)
HRM	Human Resource Management
HSC	Higher Salaries Commission (New Zealand)
IAFF	International Association of Fire Fighters (USA)
IHIs	Ishikawajima Harina Industries (Japan)
ILO	International Labor Office
IRC	Industrial Relations Conference
IRRA	Industrial Relations Research Association
JETRO	Japan External Trade Organization
JIL	Japan Institute of Labor
JR	Japan Railways
JT	Japan Tobacco
KGSt	Kommunale GemeinSchaftstelle (Germany)
LDP	Liberal Democratic Party (Japan)
LGA	Local Government Association (UK)
LGMB	Local Government Management Board (UK)

MSPB	Merit System Protection Board (USA)
NDP	New Democratic Party
NEA	National Education Association (USA)
NHK	Nihon Broadcasting Corporation (Japan)
NHS	National Health Service (UK)
NPA	National Personnel Authority (Japan)
NPM	New Public Management
NPR	National Performance Review (USA)
NSM	Neue Steuerungsmodelle (Germany)
NSW	New South Wales (Australia)
NTEU	National Territory Education Union (Australia)
NTT	Nippon Telegraph and Telephone
NUPE	National Union of Public Employees (New Zealand)
NUPGE	National Union of Provincial and General Employees (Canada)
NZEI	New Zealand Educational Institute
NZNO	New Zealand Nurses' Organization
OPM	Office of Personnel Management (USA)
OSHA	Occupational Safety and Health Administration (USA)
OTV	Gewerkschaft Oftentiche Deutsch, Transport und Werker (Public Services, Transport and Communication Union) (Germany)
PASA	Police Association of South Australia
PERBs	Public Employee Relations Boards (USA)
PERCs	Public Employee Relations Commissions (USA)
PHS	Public Health Service (USA)
PPTA	Post-Primary Teachers Association (New Zealand)
PSA	Public Service Association (New Zealand)
PSAC	Public Service Alliance of Canada
PSMPC	Public Service and Merit Protection Commission (Australia)
PSU	Public Sector Union (Australia)
PTU	Public Transport Union (Australia)
PUMA	Public Management
QES	Quarterly Employment Survey (New Zealand)
RDA	Resident Doctors' Association (New Zealand)
SEIU	Service Employees' International Union (USA)
SES	Senior Executive Service (Australia-New Zealand-USA)
SIPs	Strategic Incentive Plans (New Zealand)
SMOSS	Six Monthly Staffing Survey (New Zealand)
SNALS	Sindacato Nazionale Autonomo Lavoratori della Scuola (Italy)

SOEs	State Owned Enterprises (New Zealand)
SPSF	State Public Services Federation (Australia)
SSC	State Service Commission (New Zealand)
SSCE	State Services Conditions of Employment (New Zealand)
SUD	Solidaire, Unitaires et Democratique (France)
TUF	Trade Union Federation (New Zealand)
TWU	Transport Workers' Union (USA)
UFUA	United Firefighters' Union of Australia
USPS	US Postal Service (USA)

1
Reforming Public Sector Labor Relations

Carlo Dell'Aringa

Introduction

The aim of this book is to analyze in a comparative framework the main features and problems of the employment relations system of the public sector in the industrialized countries. In the last twenty years there has been great pressure to reform public sector labor relations in many countries. The stimulus for this change has arisen from the need to contain public expenditure and to reduce the tax burden on families and firms in a time of macro-economic constraints.

Important changes first occurred in employment relations in the private sector, the pressure coming from global competition, trade liberalization and fast technical change leading to an inevitable restructuring of economies. A large part of the labor force was involved in this process and employment relations also changed in the workplace with the introduction of more labor flexibility. This involved wage moderation and a sharp increase in atypical contracts such as part time, temporary, and fixed term.

After the two oil shocks monetary policy became more restrictive in order to keep inflation under control. At the same time, fiscal policy had to be more severe than previously in order to cope with the problems of huge public deficits and debts. It became more and more difficult to solve these problems by increasing taxes, first, because of the political opposition from taxpayers and, second, because of the fear that high taxes would negatively affect private investment and more generally, the supply potential of the economies. Public spending has been placed in an even more competitive role with the creation of jobs in the private sector of the economy.

The effects of budgetary pressures have been particularly important for the member countries of the European Union due to the Maastricht Treaty and the convergence criteria imposed on those countries wanting to join the Union. Among the criteria were the requirements that government deficit should not exceed 3 percent of GDP and the total debt should not be more than 60 percent of GDP. These have been clearly difficult targets to meet for member states and there are some countries which are still far from reaching this debt–GDP target ratio.

The main outlay of total government expenditure is government consumption and transfer payments which represent more than three quarters of the total spending in most Western countries (OECD, 1995). A significant part of the increase in total government expenditure has been due to transfer payments resulting from a combination of factors – recessions, sluggish economic growth, low levels of income and employment and unfavorable demographic trends. This has resulted in governments placing even more importance on controls in public spending in all possible budget areas. It was inevitable that some of the burden of adjustment would be carried by the public sector and their employees.

In addition to concerns about the cost of public services and the need for reducing it, there was another pressure arising from the demand to improve the quality of the services themselves. Consumers have become more selective in their demands for goods they buy in the market and so, for the same reasons, they have become increasingly concerned about the quality of services for which they are paying taxes (Flynn and Strehl, 1996). The widespread introduction of public service charters has met this demand for a better quality in the public services. Most reform proposals have focused on several interconnected dimensions which have been summarized in many publications of the Public Management Service (PUMA) of the OECD. They include, first, redrawing the boundaries between the private and public sector, involving the transfer of public organizations into private hands. Furthermore, different forms of restructuring have been adopted by introducing market or market-like mechanisms of governance into the financing and provisions of the public services. A second line of development has been to import private sector human resources management practices and to encourage a range of corporate management techniques whose adoption is aimed at improving efficiency and effectiveness. A third element has been to move decision making on employment conditions away from the central level to a lower one. Administrative decentralization has been introduced in a number of countries and issues regarding working conditions and pay determination have been decided on either at the local level or at the level of the single administration. In countries with strong traditions of collective bargaining and where unions maintain a strong presence, we have observed a decentralization in negotiations and practices of pay fixing. These aspects in the evolution of employment relations in the public sector will be examined later in this chapter. As well, a general overview will be outlined describing the main differences between these employment relations across countries.

Comparative analysis requires that similar phenomena should be examined in each country, although there are significant differences in the size, scope and role of the public services among the industrialized countries.

This book has been organized into two parts. After the introduction (Chapter 1) the first part is devoted to the European experience and is made up of three chapters each dealing with a specific theme. The first analyses the problems of transferring human resource management practices of the private sector to the public sector (Chapter 2); the second focuses on collective bargaining and the process of decentralization that has taken place in a number of European countries (Chapter 3); the third concentrates on the changing role of employers, employers' associations and unions in the collective bargaining arena of the public sector (Chapter 4).

This first part of the book deals with problems and issues, not following individual country cases but thematic lines, and takes advantage of previous findings of research on single countries conducted by a network of scholars with an established interest in public service employment relations in Europe. The research focused on the core public services: central and local government, health and education excluding public utilities and nationalized industries (see Bach et al., 1999). This part represents a second step in an ongoing program of research work on the same themes and issues.

The analysis has then been extended from the European countries to non-European ones and in the second part of the book single-country cases are presented. Chapter 5 describes some of the features of the US public sector; Chapter 6 presents the Canadian system of industrial relations; Chapter 7 deals with the Japanese case; Chapter 8 describes the evolution in New Zealand; and Chapter 9 analyses both the basic structure and the more recent reforms in Australian public service employment relations.

The present introduction tries to draw together the experiences of all the countries examined, European and non-European, by focusing on

4 Strategic Choices in Reforming Public Service Employment

the following common problems and issues that all of them face, although to different degrees and in different forms:

- the process of privatization and the problem of keeping labor costs under control
- the new management practices and their impact on the efficiency and the effectiveness of public services
- centralization versus decentralization in employment relations
- the role of unions and their reaction to the increasing need for flexibility, performance and better quality in public services

A few concluding remarks will be addressed to the problem of the convergence of employment relations in the public sector across countries. This issue has given rise to widespread scientific debate, the question being whether pressures for change, which have been common to many countries, have produced similar reactions. A similar, though different, problem is whether the gap between public and private sector systems of labor relations in each country has narrowed or not. The experiences of different countries described in this book can be of some help in providing preliminary answers to these questions.

Privatization and labor cost reductions

In a number of countries there has been a shift in political thinking in whether the state should directly provide a wide range of services to citizens, or whether the private sector should take over the role, at least partially. This shift in political thinking has led to a radical change in the size and the nature of government involvement in the economy and society.

In this new scenario governments have been forced to restrict operating expenditure through significant employment cutbacks and through the privatization of public services. They have also adopted alternative models of public service delivery. Bringing the public sector into line with the private sector has been one of the main goals of many governments. The term "privatization" has been bandied about although not always correctly (see Chapter 4). Strictly speaking, the term implies a transfer of services or administrative units into private hands. There are several ways of effecting this transfer of ownership; for example, if, following privatization, the state maintains a minority shareholding, this is often enough to keep the company under full public control. The consequence of privatization is a definitive solution to the problem of introducing private efficiency into the public sector. It has been the path taken by those countries which have undergone a more severe fiscal crisis and where the role of the state, both as a direct employer and as an owner of public enterprises was more pronounced.

Apart from countries with large problems of budget constraints, the transfer of public sector activities into private hands has been quite noticeable in the UK where in the last fifteen years about a million jobs have been reallocated to the private sector (Belman et al., 1996). Throughout Western Europe, telecommunications, postal services and public transport, have been among the main targets for privatization and marketization.

The scope of privatization differs significantly from country to country. While, for example, the UK has taken a definite lead, the Scandinavian countries, on the other hand, have been reluctant to adopt these policies (Chapter 4). The "credo" of "let the market lead" has found ground also outside of Europe, for example, it was the policy of the Australian government in the 1990s. Over the last fifteen years the number of employees in the federal government has been continuously cut back from 408,300 in 1983 to only 285,000 in 1997. Government business enterprises have been substantially downsized, while public service cuts also took place in many states, especially in New South Wales which accounted for more than half of the overall reductions (Chapter 9).

This is also the case in Canada where the government has completely withdrawn from some of its previous functions. The most common examples are the shift of physical infrastructures, such as telecommunications, railways and airports, to the private sector or to quasi-government agencies (Chapter 6). Also, in Japan important plans are underway to reduce public sector employment. In 1999 the prime minister announced a reduction in national public service employment by 25 percent over the next ten years. To achieve this goal a number of public organizations will be privatized or abolished while others will be transformed into agencies, following the lines of the British reforms (Chapter 7).

The anti-tax and anti-big government sentiments were also felt in the US in the 1980s, strongly influencing federal government policies. Coupled with public pressure to provide better, more cost-effective services, these sentiments have resulted in the smallest US federal workforce in nearly three decades. State and local governments have also been subject to these pressures and in some areas privatization has been a politically popular response. However, on the whole, it must be observed that privatization has not been as widespread as the level of discussion has led us to believe (Chapter 5). In fact, we should not forget that in many situations the rhetoric has exaggerated the scale and scope of privatization. This, however, is definitely not the case in New Zealand where effective and substantial changes have taken place over the last twenty years. New Zealand and the UK are probably the two main countries where the restructuring of the public service has been the most sweeping. In New Zealand the state-owned enterprises have been the target for privatization since 1988. Substantial numbers of staff were laid off with staffing levels in some enterprises reduced by as much as 65 percent during the first years of corporatization.

In addition to the privatization of corporations, various forms of contracting out and competitive tendering must also be considered among the instruments used to bring the public sector more into line with the private one. The normal practice being that the public sector authority concludes contracts based on bids/tenders from a number of potential suppliers. In England, for example, a new legislation has been introduced to require local authorities to seek competitive tenders for many activities such as building work, school catering, vehicle maintenance, refuse collection and so on (Beaumont, 1996). Similar practices have been introduced in almost every country and in New Zealand and Australia they are particularly widespread. Competitive and private factors have also been introduced into the organization of public administration by creating a form of "internal markets" where the demand and the supply of public services are distinct and separate so as to imitate the workings of a competitive market.

The health sector has been restructured in this way in a number of countries. Health services are a labor-intensive sector; however, the introduction of new technology has not led to a reduction in staff as in other sectors of the economy. At the same time, the increased demand for health care has resulted in increasing expenses.

The creation of internal markets in the British NHS, the *aziendalizzazione* (hospitals run as companies) in Italy and the "contractualization" of the financial relations between the single hospitals and the regional health authorities in France, are all typical examples of how competition as well as market-like mechanisms have been introduced in this sector.

The need "to do more with less" in public health has also been felt outside Europe as is the case in Australia and New Zealand. In Australia, in order to cope with the increasing costs, initiatives of output-based funding have been adopted and an increasing number of services are provided on the basis of a user-pay policy (Chapter 9). In the health sector purchasing and providing functions were split and it was clearly envisaged that private sector providers would compete with government-owned providers for public funding.

In New Zealand the introduction of a user element into public service management practices, stressing service quality and responsiveness to "customers," has been extended to schools. Each school is governed by a board of trustees which is made up of a parent majority elected as representatives of the local community: each board is responsible for the management of the school and for developing school policies (Chapter 8).

All these developments, stressing the role of incentives and external forces, have broken down the traditional uniformity of public organizations and have replaced them with smaller competing units. Devolution has been pursued for the same reasons, to empower service users, but also, and primarily, to allow managers to use resources more efficiently and facilitate competition between separate organizational units.

Not all countries have shared with the UK and New Zealand this strong market-oriented restructuring of the public service, at least not to the same extent. Policies used to reduce the size of public expenditure have varied across countries. Broadly speaking, governments had the options of either diminishing the scope of state action or simply and directly reducing the labor costs. Some governments have adopted both policies, while others have more frequently followed the latter and, at the same time, retained direct responsibility for traditional activities. In these countries public education at all levels, health care, social assistance and public safety have not been abandoned or even radically changed.

Many governments were successful in reducing labor costs by cutting back on employment. In Sweden a public employment reduction plan aimed at a cut of 23 percent was applied in the early 1990s. In Canada the government decided to reduce staffing levels in the public service by 15,000 persons over a five-year period. The US plan to downsize federal employment began in 1993 while the federal administration adopted a major program to reform government activity (OECD, 1995). Since 1983 France has adopted not only a strict pay policy but also the target of stabilizing public employment by placing a freeze on most vacant positions. Italy and Spain adopted similar measures in the 1990s.

Table 1.1 illustrates employment trends in the public sector over the periods 1985–90 and 1990–96 in a number of OECD countries.

During the first period, jobs were created in the public sector in most countries; however, there are a few exceptions. Four countries showed falls in public employment: the UK, for well-known reasons, and

8 Strategic Choices in Reforming Public Service Employment

Table 1.1 Total public employment

	1985	1990	1995	1996	1997
Australia	—	1,279,200	1,208,000	1,238,000	1,244,200
Canada	2,376,942	2,663,060	2,643,612	2,593,319	2,538,470
Denmark	682,000	692,200	699,000	—	—
Finland	617,000	580,487	518,291	531,094	541,386
France	4,466,518	4,568,768	4,347,067	4,366,481	—
Germany	4,118,000	4,305,000	5,409,000	—	—
Ireland	217,424	195,678	215,366	218,362	218,701
Italy	3,439,000	3,628,000	3,474,798	—	—
The Netherlands	763,603	730,740	713,000	—	—
New Zealand	—	209,900	207,000	211,300	207,400
Spain	1,532,000	1,809,500	1,981,600	1,979,100	2,009,300
Sweden	1,210,000	1,275,083	1,044,087	—	—
United Kingdom	4,469,000	4,354,000	3,947,000	3,847,000	3,793,000
United States	15,888,338	17,752,051	18,592,120	18,693,947	—

Source: PUMA, OECD, 1999

Ireland, the Netherlands and Finland which imposed a freeze on hiring in the public services. During the later period, a combination of various measures led to a reduction in employment in public services in over half of the countries. Many countries have also tried to contain public salaries (Elliot, Lucifora, and Meurs, 1999). Some have sought to do so by imposing direct controls on across-the-board wage increases while others, as well as responding in the short term with general restraints, have sought longer-term solutions in how public sector wages are fixed. In Canada (Chapter 6) pay restraints were introduced by the federal government suspending the bargaining rights for all its employees, requiring them to accept a wage freeze. This suspension of bargaining rights lasted for seven years. The provinces followed suit in reducing public sector payroll costs, adopting basic policies restricting compensation through centralized bargaining.

Japanese authorities have decided to freeze wage increments several times over the last twenty years. Many European countries, with France and Spain at the forefront, have behaved likewise (OECD, 1995), and a few countries have introduced more radical reforms in pay fixing. This is the case for Italy which abandoned the previous mechanism of linking salaries to seniority, for England where pay review bodies were set up to regulate wages in some sectors in place of collective bargaining and for the US where wages of federal employees were differentiated across states according to the movements of the local employment cost index.

Table 1.2 Compensation costs in the public sector as a percentage of GDP

	1990	1995
Australia	9.5	8.3
Canada	11.1	10.9
Denmark	18.7	17.7
Finland	14.2	15.6
France	10.8	10.9
Germany	8.9	10.3
Ireland	11.9	11.6
Italy	12.6	9.1
The Netherlands	8.6	8.4
New Zealand	11.2	9.4
Spain	11.0	11.6
Sweden	21.0	16.1
UK	12.3	11.3
US	8.1	7.9

Source: PUMA, OECD (1999)

All these different measures and policies – privatization, public employment reduction plans, changes in pay determination systems, freezes or ceilings placed on increases in public sector pay – have affected the trend of total compensation costs in the public sector. Averaged over the 1990–95 period, the proportion of these costs as a percentage of GDP shows significant reductions in many OECD countries (Table 1.2). This is the case in Australia, Canada, Denmark, Finland, Ireland, Italy, The Netherlands, New Zealand, Sweden, the UK and the US. There was a slight increase in Germany, France and Spain, the same three countries which underwent in the same period a rapid increase in total government outlays as a percentage of GDP. On the whole, one can say that the policies and the different measures adopted to keep the wage bill of the public sector under strict control have been quite successful in the majority of OECD countries.

The New Public Management

The traditional model of public sector employment has often been criticized for not being flexible enough to deal with the more sophisticated demands of public sector clients or to deliver services with efficient methods of production. This criticism has been most persistently expressed in the publications of the OECD Public Management Unit

(PUMA) which is also the main source of comparative information on public sector reforms in industrial countries.

PUMA suggests that the traditional public service approach to human resources management is a major impediment to improved performance as the administrations are "highly centralized, rule-bound and inflexible organizations that emphasize process rather than results" (OECD, 1995). Public administration has been associated with a Weberian model of administrative structures and rules (Chapter 2) based on three specific characteristics.

First, the public administration is associated with a highly centralized structure and uniform rules. These allow for the equal treatment of all citizens, ensure political and social accountability and prevent corruption, favoritism and discrimination. In this framework there is little scope for autonomous management action. Second, the integration and control of human and economic resources mainly takes place hierarchically. Only the highest level of administration is aware of the results and costs. By nature this control is slow, often delayed and is unable to deal with unexpected events and problems. Third, and most important from the point of view of the employment relations issues, public employment is seen as a peculiar kind of employment. Staff identity and motivation cannot be based on purely economic incentives. For their commitment to the general well-being of the community, the public employee is attributed with certain privileges such as a guaranteed job, improved retirement benefits and reduced performance control and discipline.

According to the German constitution, the *Beamte* (the civil servant) has the duty to do his best to serve the public interest and, at the same time, he has the right to be paid enough to live decently. Thus, no link is established between work performance on the one hand and remuneration and economic benefits on the other.

Moreover, in the public administration the impersonal nature of evaluation and promotion processes must be guaranteed by the management. The choice of staff, both incoming and those applying for internal promotion, takes place by means of open public competitions. In most cases career advancement is based on seniority rules which impede the incursion of management in the functioning of the internal labor market.

Currently, a new cultural approach is gaining ground and the term "New Public Management" dominates discussions on these issues. It is used to underline the need to move toward a system where efficiency and effectiveness are taken as the main objectives for public organizations, and in order to carry this out a wide range of different management reforms have been labeled as New Public Management. A disparate set of management tools have been put into place. A common denominator of all these initiatives has been to imitate private sector best practices.

In many countries human resources management has been most obviously impacted by the new "managerialism." In Australia, New Zealand, Sweden and the UK, fundamental reforms are being pursued which are transforming the nature of public sector employment by focusing on performance in terms of efficiency and effectiveness rather than compliance with rules and regulations. Wide-ranging changes are also underway in The Netherlands, the European Nordic countries, and, to a lesser extent, in Canada and the US.

PUMA has conducted many studies following a comparative approach on this issue.

For example, in response to economic pressures, New Zealand, as is reported in Chapter 8, began the process of radical reforms in the public service in the 1980s. The 1986 State-Owned Enterprises Act radically altered the management framework for government-owned trading organizations as managers were delegated power comparable to their private sector counterparts, while the 1991 State Sector Act extended many of the same principles to the management of the non-commercial activities of the public service.

In the same period the new managerialism gained force in Australia (Chapter 9). It was argued that the public sector needed to have more flexible and responsive organizations involving flatter structures, greater devolution of authority, multiskilled jobs and greater focus on performance and output measures. One of the most significant examples of restructuring aimed at greater flexibility in management was the establishment of the Senior Executive Service (SES). It was introduced in the Australian federal government in 1984 and in the New Zealand state sector in 1988. This reform was intended to create an elite corps of senior, experienced managers who were expected to guarantee flexible organization, personal mobility and efficiency in the delivery of services.

Devolution of HRM responsibilities from central government agencies to line departments has been an important component of recent reforms. Management devolution has for the most part concerned the operational aspects of HRM, with responsibilities of policy making retained by the central government. Areas which still tend to remain under the control of the central government are those affecting personnel costs, basic terms and conditions of employment, selection and management of senior public servants, rules and management procedures.

However, budgeting for human and administrative resources, traditionally an area of tight central control, is being increasingly devolved to the agency and even to the line managers level. Several countries (Canada, Finland, Ireland, New Zealand, Sweden) are using devolved budgeting and eliminating detailed control over staff numbers and, in some cases, even over pay and classification of workers. However, central budget policies continue to set budget frames and ceilings. On the whole, the OECD reports state that delegation of financial management appears to function as a powerful incentive for more effective people management.

At the same time, other countries such as Japan, Switzerland, France and Germany, among others, are engaging in more specific reforms of the public sector in line with changes which occur in the labor market in general, with emphasis on greater flexibility. Often, however, they are leaving their traditional structures and principles of labor organization in the public service relatively unchanged for the present (Chapter 2).

Administrative decentralization and collective bargaining

One of the policies adopted in order to increase efficiency and effectiveness in the public service is the decentralization of the institutional level at which pay and working conditions of employees are determined. The policy is not new and the debate on this issue has been around for a long time. For some decades economists and political scientists have tried to identify the advantages and disadvantages associated with the decentralization of the industrial relations system. However, until now the debate on the economic and social benefits of decentralized systems has focused mainly on the private sector of the economy while very little attention has been paid to what happens in the public sector.

As a matter of fact, the framework of analysis used in the literature dealing with the private sector, though useful as a reference, must be modified in the context of the public sector situation. First, we must consider different institutional features of the two sectors in the analysis of the merits of the various systems of pay determination.

A first aspect which is to be considered in the public sector is the relation between different levels of government. The question of where the focus of power lies is of paramount importance. For example, while in some countries there are three levels of government (federal, state, local) – this being the case in countries such as the US, Canada and Australia – in others (the majority) there are only two levels. A critical point on this issue is whether the local administration, or the lower level of government in general, has some degree of autonomy from the higher level in determining pay and working conditions for its own employees. While in some countries the constitutional law recognizes the right for local governments to determine autonomously the working conditions of their employees, in other countries this is not possible. This is the first and most important limitation that single and local administrative units have to face.

It is worth stressing that this question has nothing to do with the type of industrial relation system prevailing in each country, but rather this reflects the legislation which is in force, and which can differ substantially from one country to another. The degree of decentralization depends on current legislation and not, as happens in the private sector, on the free decision of the social parties, unions and employers.

A second issue, directly linked to the first, is the degree of decentralization which is applied within each level of government. In the central administration, for instance, decentralization implies that authority and responsibility are delegated to single ministries or single agencies. However, even in those countries where decentralization of this kind is most pronounced, as in the UK and New Zealand and, to some extent, also in Sweden, the delegation of responsibility is necessarily limited because of the often imposed financial constraints and budget controls. Local authorities can also devolve responsibility to lower-level administrative units and this often happens where they are large enough to make devolution convenient.

A further point is important in the case of local administrations. In fact, the delegation process is likely to work also in the reverse, that is, towards centralization. In some countries (the UK and Germany are typical examples) single administrative units (regions, municipalities, and so on) pass on some of their authority for setting pay and working conditions to a representative body or an association which can negotiate on their behalf with the unions. The delegation process is in this case bottom up and is similar to what happens in the private sector.

The impact and the importance of industrial relations and, more specifically, that of collective bargaining has to be analyzed in this more general institutional framework. Moreover, the legal framework is paramount not only because it sets the rules that govern the devolution of administrative responsibilities from the central to the local level, but also because it determines the limits of trade union actions.

In fact, it should be made clear that collective bargaining is neither the only nor the most common way of determining pay in the public sector. Collective bargaining in the public sector emerged only after the rise of unionism and flourished where the institutional framework was more conducive to its development (Freeman, 1986). However, there are other mechanisms for setting pay in the public sector which are equally or more important and, in most countries, they often coexist with collective bargaining (Yemin, 1993). The existence of collective bargaining is still likely to be an important element for differentiating between the various national systems of pay determination and it must be taken into consideration when analyzing differences in national experiences and performances (Treu, 1987).

The system of collective bargaining is made up of many important aspects. One is the scope of bargaining, that is the aspects of the employment relationship which are the object of the negotiation. While in many countries bargaining covers quite a number of these aspects, in others, the scope is rather limited. In Japan, for example, and also in the US federal government, wages of employees are not even bargained over. Collective bargaining may also be viewed as either a mechanism for consultation or more fundamentally as a mechanism to ensure that the negotiated agreement is binding on the parties and that they must respect the terms of the contract. In some countries bargaining is nothing more than a procedure for consultation between the administration and the unions where the government has the last word, as is the case in France and Spain. Instead, in other countries there is a real negotiation binding the parties which sign the contract.

A further important element to consider is the categories of workers covered by the collective bargaining. In all countries studied some categories are excluded, such as judges, the armed forces and officials of the highest ranking. In some countries the categories excluded are many and important ones. In the UK important groups of workers are covered by review bodies while in Germany the *Beamte*, corresponding to 40 percent of the entire public service, are excluded from negotiations. There are significant exclusions also in the US although important differences occur across states, each state regulating the system of industrial relations to be applied to its own employees and to those of its internal local governments.

The scope, the binding character and the categories covered by collective bargaining reveal the importance of the negotiation in the public service of different countries and the presence of unions.

Foremost, we find the North European countries having unquestionably a larger and more solid tradition of industrial relations not only in the private but also in the public sector. At the other end of the spectrum we find countries such as France, Spain and Japan, characterized by a strong central government power which often unilaterally sets pay and working conditions. However, we also find countries such as the UK and the US which, although more decentralized than the above-mentioned countries, do not have a very strong union presence and important collective bargaining traditions (Dell'Aringa and Lanfranchi, 1999).

In comparing the experiences of different countries one does not find a significant correlation between the degree of centralization of the system for determining working conditions, which depends on the institutional framework, and the importance of the industrial relations system which depends on different social and historical factors.

These are the actual features different in the public service which, although influencing one another, must be kept conceptually quite distinct.

Going back to decentralization we observe that OECD countries offer a range of experiences on this issue, as thoroughly described in Chapter 3. On the one extremity we have highly centralized countries with no or very limited delegation of authority to the local level and a common national pay policy for all public sector employees. Belonging to this group we have France, Spain and Germany and, while the same can be said for Japan and The Netherlands, these two countries are now taking the first steps towards decentralization. In The Netherlands negotiations have been organized separately for each of the eight functional sub-sectors of the public service (ministries, education, police, defense and so on) since 1993. In Japan, as noted before, an important reform of the central administration is in progress and it envisages a devolution of authority to specialized agencies (Chapter 7).

In other countries there are two levels of bargaining. In Ireland, for example, public sector pay negotiations are divided into two steps. First, a centralized agreement determines the across-the-board rate of increase of salaries and then a second round of negotiations organized by groups of occupations provides for further and differentiated wage increments. In Denmark a new system has officially been put in place to ensure that part of the pay determination process occurs at the local level. The government sets aside a certain percentage of the pay bill to be locally distributed among workers or groups of workers. A similar system works in Italy, and in both these countries we observe a significant move toward decentralization.

Among the most decentralized countries we find those of the Anglo-Saxon tradition: Australia, Canada and the USA. They are characterized by a federal administrative structure that is reflected in the pay determination system (Preiss, 1993). The US, the Australian states and the Canadian provinces enjoy a substantial degree of administrative autonomy. There is only a limited degree of horizontal coordination between the state authorities and between the states and the national governments. Yet, even in these countries there are some elements of centralization in decisions over pay. There are cases where, contrary to the general trend, steps towards centralization have been taken. In Canada, for example, the autonomy of local authorities in the field of education and health care has been reduced by provincial policies tending to centralize administration and collective bargaining for purposes of reducing inefficiencies and controlling costs (Chapter 6).

The most radical reforms towards decentralization have been taken in New Zealand and the UK. In England the reform of the civil service has been significant and agencies and departments now have a wide measure of autonomy. Subject to rigid budget constraints, the agencies and the departments can autonomously decide their own pay scales and the classification system of their workers. New Zealand has moved in the same direction. Since the State Sector Act of 1986 chief executives are employers of their staff and service-wide occupational systems have been replaced by departmental agreements as the primary means of determining pay and other working conditions. Although the picture since then has been one of increased fragmentation in the bargaining units (as in the UK civil service), funding of the whole public sector has remained under tight, centralized control through the principle of fiscal neutrality (that is, the principle according to which any new expense would need to be funded out of the existing budget) (Chapter 8).

An important point to make is that pay determination systems not only vary between, but also within, countries. In some cases a description of the system which is limited to the civil service gives only a partial picture of what takes place in other parts of the public sector. This is the case, for instance, for the UK where pay reform has focused on the civil service and on the health sector, on the other hand much less has happened in local government. In the USA and other federal countries, systems differ according to occupational groups, states and localities.

In general, however, over the last twenty years we have observed a general trend towards some form of decentralization, even if a number of countries have not abandoned their traditional and rather centralized systems. The question one could pose is whether this process has achieved the expected results. However, not much information is available in this area.

One conclusion we could come to (see Dell'Aringa and Lanfranchi, 1999) is that the countries which have a rather decentralized system adopt pay determination methods which, at least in principle, are not so rigid as the ones adopted by the more centralized countries. As a matter of fact, the former makes less use of the traditional automatic pay increases related to the cost of living and to seniority in favor of more flexible systems such as "performance related pay" and more generally, pay "individualization" and pay merit. Closely related to this difference in the use of more flexible pay determination criteria is the way of determining internal pay differentials. Pay differentials are wider in decentralized systems due to a more fragmented system of fixing wages. In these countries, not only are pay methods more flexible, but also the wages themselves which are usually more compressed in the public sector than in the private one, are more differentiated and probably, more suited to reacting to external labor market pressures. Moreover, one of the latest studies of the OECD (1997) shows that the countries with a higher degree of centralization have actually succeeded in cutting down the proportion of labor costs in total public expenditure.

However, all these studies stress the need for more information in order to reach more definite conclusions on these issues.

Trade unions' responses to increasing flexibility

Pressures on the public sector have led to pressure on public sector unions. In the public sector of almost every country the proportion of employees who are union members is very high, significantly higher than in the private sector. Moreover, while in the private sector of most countries unionization decreased in the 1970s and in the 1980s, it remained at a high level in the public sector. In the meantime general conditions of employment have also changed drastically in the public sector, as we previously noted. Privatization, contracting out, "new managerialism," decentralization of administrative responsibility and bargaining are among the new conditions that unions have to face. Furthermore, plans and initiatives have been taken to deregulate major features of employment relations, such as employment security or even lifelong employment security. These different strategies of qualitative as well as quantitative forms of flexibility include, among others, more use of part-time working, different forms of contingent work such as fixed-term contracts, or temporary work. The UK, New Zealand and Australia are among the countries which have introduced with more clout these private sector-like strategies of labor flexibility.

In Chapter 4 of this book Keller, Due and Andersen have raised a relevant question that we should attempt to answer. How have the unions tried to cope with these new conditions and circumstances? Have they rejected reform plans? Have they, in one way or another, participated in the decision-making processes regarding modernization and restructuring in the public sector or even tried to take the lead? Significant differences between countries are obvious. Not only because there are wide national differences in the structure of the public sector and wide differences also existing in the intensity and speed of the process of reform, but also because the union movement has different traditions, culture and ideology in different countries.

Confronted with a reform that someone has called "neo-Taylorist," unions in the UK and in New Zealand, for example, felt they were being marginalized and so opposed (unsuccessfully) any kind of "modernization" of the public sector.

Conservative governments introduced major reforms in the British public services. The unions, however, took no part in planning or implementing these reforms. On the contrary, in that period it was an integral part of government polices to reduce and curtail the influence and power of trade unions. The picture was similar in New Zealand: a number of ideological precepts of managerialism were fundamentally hostile to collective bargaining and unionism in the workplace and these found expression in the behavior of industrial relations (Chapter 8). The Employment Contracts Act itself has been inimical to union representation because of its implicit preference for individualizing employment relationships. The increasing use of individual employment contracts in the public sector of New Zealand has drastically reduced the number of employees for whom union membership is relevant. Also in Australia, unions in the public sector were not only opposed to this on the economic grounds that they interfered with the achievement of maximum efficiency and caused artificially inflated wage costs but also on ideological grounds, especially in more recent years. The coalition governments have been anxious to ensure that their policies minimizing the role of unions in the industrial sector were also zealously implemented regarding their own public areas of employment (Chapter 9).

In a number of European countries unions interpreted terms such as "modernization, quality development, decentralization, restructuring" as nothing less than synonymous to cuts in spending (Martin, 1996). In many cases unions perceived that these terms were not used in any technical way but only with the aim of meeting budgetary constraints. Many unions felt that renewing the public service was not a political priority. Instead, the political priority was to reduce taxes and expenses. Moreover, in some countries unions opposed the demand for more labor flexibility.

French unions, for example, wanted to defend the status of the government civil servant for all public sector employees because they wished to maintain job security and other kinds of benefits. The same is true in Japan where unions fear that the transformation of a number of public organizations in autonomous agencies might lead to a loss of employment security and of basic labor rights for the employees involved in the restructuring process (Chapter 7).

However, this kind of defensive and conservative strategy is not followed by all unions in every country. For example, in Germany, OTV, the major national union, has been arguing for the need to modernize the public sector service since the late 1980s. A campaign called "shaping the future through public services" was enshrined in the idea of unifying the interests of public service users, staff and unions. Effects of the campaign have been rather limited but in spite of this it was re-launched in 1995, although in a more decentralized version (Chapter 4).

Other examples can be provided here. Italian unions have to a large extent supported the new legislation implemented since 1993 which placed employment contracts in the public sector on the same legal basis as those in the private sector. Italian unions are in favor of a "privatization" of the employment and industrial relations of the public sector. The unions are strong not only on a national level but also in the workplace and, for this reason, they are in favor of the decentralization of bargaining and the industrial relations system that goes hand in hand with the process of political and administrative decentralization which is taking place in this country.

Trade unions in the Scandinavian countries have taken part in reforms of the public sector in different ways. Martin (1996) characterizes the responses of Scandinavian trade unions as a "twin-track-approach." On the one hand, they seek to preserve their presence in the workplace and to promote reasonable development in pay and working conditions, while on the other hand, they concede to the reforms proposed by the governments. In Finland, unions are involved in a research program on methods of improving efficiency and quality. Denmark provides another example similar to Sweden where decentralization in bargaining and a reform of the pay system have been accepted by the unions. The introduction of performance-related pay which has been perceived as a threat by British public sector unions is accepted and in some circumstances even promoted by the same Danish unions.

In some countries various forms of participation appear to have gained importance. This is the case, for example, in the USA, where recent experiences of cooperation appear to be successful (Chapter 5). In recent years the most useful movement seems to be the advent of cooperative, service-oriented relationships that can be developed within most existing legislations by the simple agreement of the parties involved.

The recent report "Working Together for Public Service" (see Chapter 5) that was submitted in 1996 to the US Secretary of Labor shows that cooperative relationships have reduced costs, improved service, facilitated conflict resolution, reduced grievances and improved the quality of working life by increasing job security, improving skills and advancement opportunities and raising wages and bonuses (Chapter 5).

However, participation does not seem to lead to the same positive results everywhere. In Australia, for example, while formal consultative committees have spread in the public sector, their impact has been poor in terms of management practices. The movement for employee participation and industrial democracy that was growing in the 1980s in Australia, particularly in the public sector, was largely dissipated by the mid 90s (Chapter 9). The same applies to Canada where legislative restrictions on the subjects of bargaining inhibit more extensive efforts at cooperation. Those initiatives frequently involve joint efforts to deal with the effects of technological change, for instance, and employers are unwilling to cede authority over those issues. For their part, labor unions are reluctant to participate in cooperative programs where their role is restricted (Chapter 6).

The experiences of these countries show that cooperation and partnership taken in the context of restructuring is not at all easy to maintain and develop further, even in countries where the trade union movement is regarded as being well organized and in favor of non-adversarial industrial relations.

Indeed, the issues involved in the process of restructuring such as labor mobility and flexibility, internal reorganization and performance-related pay are difficult to reconcile with traditional attitudes of unions and workers in the public sector. Progressively moving towards a situation where competition, efficiency, individual performance and adaptability are becoming more and more important can meet resistance from those who were traditionally used to stability in employment, income and general working conditions.

Concluding remarks and open questions

The last decades have seen major developments in the public services of the industrialized countries. As well as macro-economic concerns about "fiscal crisis," the need to improve the quality of those services led many governments to try to reform the employment relations of this sector. What can be said about the impact of these "common pressures" on the responses of the different states?

OECD's PUMA has offered an interpretation of state responses to the challenges facing the public sector. PUMA views all public sector developments as converging towards a single framework of reforms. On the one hand, governments adjust the size and structure of the public sector by seeking to make it more efficient, less centralized and able to provide a better quality service. On the other hand, they try to improve public sector management (the New Public Management) by stressing the effectiveness of human resource management. All countries have realized that overall goals for improvements in the efficiency and effectiveness of public services are closely linked with the management of public employees (for example, pay and employment practices, working methods and incentives, organizational culture and worker satisfaction).

From the many reports on this issue produced by PUMA it emerges that many OECD countries have at least started down the path towards major reform and that, although not all of them have faced pressure for change to the same degree, nevertheless a certain linearity of trends seems to emerge and that the main difference between national policies is not the approach, being quite similar, but the speed at which reforms are implemented.

That interpretation has been questioned by different authors who argue that there are, instead, distinct country patterns in relation to reform strategies. Naschold (1996), for example, distinguishes between the neo-Taylorist approach of New Zealand and the UK from a more genuine devolution of decision making to the civil society which takes place in some of the Nordic countries in Europe. Others stress the fact that different approaches can be identified even in the same country.

Ferner (1994), for example, differentiates between different patterns of change in the UK where it is also possible to find, side by side, a model of participation evolution and a model of dictatorial transformation. These authors seem to suggest that the analysis of change in the public sector cannot be done by using only technical tools of interpretation, but by incorporating also political and cultural contextual factors.

The political explanation is a familiar one. It is true to say that Conservative governments have shown ideological hostility to the public sector and its trade unions as has happened in New Zealand, the UK, Australia and, more recently, even in Japan. However, this is only a part of the explanation. National governments have been continuing to shape their approach to the public service within a particular national configuration not only of political, but also of economic, legal, institutional, social and historic factors and features.

On the whole, the national experiences and the comparisons presented in this book suggest that a strong version of the convergence theory cannot be easily accepted. All countries share a common concern to increase efficiency, to control labor costs and to ameliorate the quality of services, but policies aimed at changing the employment relations, the role of bargaining and unions, and the level at which decisions over pay and working conditions are taken, vary widely. Not only the pace of change but also the direction of change has been, in some circumstances, different from country to country.

There is, instead, some support for the idea that there is a growing convergence of practices between public and private sector systems of employment relations (Bach, 1999). The relationship between corporate strategy, organizational structure and employment relations which has been explored for the private sector helps us to understand better the way in which the management of human resources and industrial relations in the public sector are changing.

To conclude, the reading of this book seems to suggest that there is clearly no strong evidence of convergence between the different systems in the Western countries analyzed here, although some common developments can be detected, it is also clear that some parts of the public services – in some, though not all countries – are moving closer to private sector systems of employment relations (Chapter 8).

References

Bach, S. (1999) 'Europe, Changing Public Service Employment Relations,' in Bach, S., Bordogna, L., Della Rocca, G., and Winchester, D. (eds.) *Public Service*

Employment Relations in Europe: Transformation, Modernization or Inertia?, London: Routledge.
Bach, S., Bordogna, L., Della Rocca, G., and Winchester, D. (eds.) (1999) *Public Service Employment Relations in Europe: Transformation, Modernization or Inertia?*, London: Routledge.
Beaumont, P. B. (1996) 'Public Sector Industrial Relations in Europe,' in Belman, D., Gunderson, M., and Hyatt, D. (eds.), *Public Sector Employment in Time of Transition*, Madison WI: IRRA Series.
Belman, D., Gunderson, M., and Hyatt, D. (eds.) (1996) *Public Sector Employment in Time of Transition*, Madison WI: IRRA Series.
Dell'Aringa, C., and Lanfranchi, N. (1999) 'Pay Determination in the Public Service: An International Comparison,' in Elliot, R., Lucifora, C., and Meurs, D. (eds.), *Public Sector Pay Determination in the European Union*, London: Macmillan – now Palgrave.
Elliot, R., Lucifora, C., and Meurs, D. (eds.) (1999) *Public Sector Pay Determination in the European Union*, London: Macmillan – now Palgrave.
Ferner, A. (1994) 'The State as Employer,' in Hyman, R., and Ferner, A., (eds.), *New Frontiers in European Industrial Relations*, Oxford: Blackwell.
Flynn, N., and Strehl, F. (eds.) (1996) *Public Sector Management in Europe*, London: Prentice-Hall.
Freeman, R. (1986) 'Unionism Come to the Public Sector,' *Journal of Economic Literature*, (24).
Martin, B. (1996) *European Integration and Modernization of Local Public Service*, Bruxelles: EPSU.
Naschold, F. (1996) *New Frontiers in Public Sector Management: Trends and Issues in Local Government in Europe*, Berlin: de Gruyter.
OECD (1995) *Trends in Public Sector Pay in OECD Countries*, Paris: OECD – PUMA.
OECD (1997) *Trends in Public Sector Pay in OECD Countries*, Paris: OECD – PUMA.
Preiss, B. (1993) 'From Centralized to Decentralized Pay Bargaining in the Public Sector: Lessons from the Australian Experience,' in OECD (ed.), *Pay Flexibility in the Public Sector*, Paris: OECD.
Treu, T. (ed.) (1987) *Public Service Labor Relations: Recent Trends and Future Prospects*, Genève: ILO.
Yemin, E. (1993) 'Labor Relations in the Public Service: A Comparative Overview,' *International Labor Review*, CXXXII (4).

2
The New Public Management in Europe

Stephen Bach and Giuseppe Della Rocca

Challenges and problems

Since the turbulent economic conditions of the early 1970s, policy makers have become increasingly preoccupied with re-appraising the size and scope of the public sector. Pay determination systems, working conditions and personnel policies have come under increasing scrutiny. Persistent concerns about the growth of public expenditure, which almost all countries had started to address by the early 1990s, encouraged a more comprehensive approach to public sector reform. This phenomenon was reinforced by the process of economic and monetary integration. In some countries, such as France and Italy, the requirements for participation in EMU have been used – not always successfully – to justify unpalatable and politically sensitive proposals for expenditure controls and public service reform. Furthermore, there has been persistent criticism of the quality of public service provision. Increasing levels of prosperity and improvements in private sector customer service have encouraged citizens to make unfavorable comparisons with service delivery in the public sector (Flynn and Strehl, 1996).

These criticisms have been expressed most forcefully by the OECD's Public Management Service (PUMA), which suggests that the traditional public service approach to personnel management is a major impediment to improved performance as "highly centralized, rule-bound and inflexible organizations that emphasize process rather than results impeding good performance" (OECD, 1995: 7).

This type of critique has led to an emphasis on a "new public management" in which public sector managers are encouraged to mimic private sector best practice (Hood, 1991; Ferlie et al., 1996; Ridley, 1996; Pollitt and Summa, 1997). These authors suggest that there has been a shift from public administration based on stable rules, equal opportunities and a politically-guided decision-making process, to an approach governed by strategic choices and private sector preoccupations for efficiency and competition.

This analysis and prescription suggests that the public sector is in a similar process of transition to that of the private sector where institutional structures have been challenged and flexibility increased in response to international competition. Most significantly, while in the past both private and public sector employers reacted relatively passively to trade unions, the initiative has now shifted to employers. In some countries such a strategic shift is visible, at least at the level of policy, while in others its broad implementation and usage requires further investigation. This chapter examines these changes in employer policy drawing on the findings of research conducted by a network of scholars (Bach et al., 1999). It analyses traditional approaches to public sector management practice, before going on to consider the pressures for reform which have led to a more detailed consideration of employer practice than in the past. Drawing on evidence from Britain, Denmark, France, Germany, Italy and Spain it assesses management practice reform in the public services. It concludes by considering the limitations of interpreting changing public service employment relations in terms of a convergence toward New Public Management, and outlines an alternative interpretation of such developments.

Traditional organization and practice in the public services

It is difficult to make a convincing case for current public service management strategies without having a clear idea of what preceded it. Public administration has been associated with a Weberian model of administrative structures and rules. According to Weber, legal power exists by virtue of an agreement between the various actors in the community, which can only be modified in accordance with predefined procedures and laws. Legal power cannot exist without being ratified by the community representing, for its members, an egalitarian system of rules which may not be changed by any form of personal authority. When defining the characteristics of legal power, Weber focused on distinguishing the constitutional state from previous forms of European monarchic absolutism, that were based on personal authority (Bendix, 1962).

These legal and administrative principles had important implications for the organizational forms and characteristics of public administration.

First, organizational structures were highly centralized and operated according to uniform rules to enable all citizens to be treated equally. The assumption was that the implementation of government policies in a uniform manner, with formalized rules of conduct, would ensure political accountability and prevent corruption. There was little scope for autonomous managerial action and the overriding impression was that differences in operating goals did not require separate administrative procedures, but could be dealt with in the same way (Giannini, 1986; Zan, 1989).

Second, the integration and control of human and economic resources was based on hierarchical principles. Only at the highest level were results and costs examined and the form of control used – based on annual statements of accounts – was slow and often delayed. Furthermore, such an approach was unable to take into account variations that occurred during the year. Employees were covered by similar arrangements with uniform personnel rules established centrally and, in many cases, decided unilaterally by the government. These rules, based on administrative regulations or laws, were not concerned with organizational efficiency and by definition were rarely established by means of collective bargaining. Other forms of control and integration were fairly weak in comparison to the private sector where integration between functions and roles was obtained through the presence of structures and technical staff roles as well as the development of methodologies capable of programming, allocating and controlling resources and results. In terms of work organization, the distribution of tasks was relatively haphazard and the large numbers of professional staff had a wide discretionary power arising from professional values of autonomy and self-regulation.

Third, the literature on organization and management has considered public employment as a "different kind of work," due to its distinctive mission, and its specific employment characteristics that arise from state employment policies whereby the state was traditionally considered a "model employer" (Fredman and Morris, 1989; Treu, 1987). Staff identity and motivation have never been exclusively based on a cash nexus relationship. According to the Weberian model, public employees are employed to serve society and not to satisfy personal interests or interests that are limited to a single organization (Rusciano, 1990). To sustain the individual's commitment to the community's general well-being, public employees were granted certain privileges such as job security, favorable retirement benefits and weaker forms of performance control. Services directed at the community, linked to specific terms and conditions, reinforced the motivational model of the public servant – as a representative of the common good (Crozier, 1987) or what has also been termed the public service ethos (Pratchett and Wingfield, 1996).

On the basis of these characteristics, the aim of personnel management has been to guarantee equal access to employment, to create opportunities for both existing and potential employees. The role of personnel management in individual organizations has been largely administrative. In contrast to market-regulated contexts where the individual employer defines personnel management rules and regulates the paybill, in the public sector these decisions are made by the state, delegating often minor aspects of the employment relationship to individual organizations (Dell'Aringa, 1997). Moreover, personnel practice must guarantee the impartial nature of assessment and promotion with staff selection and promotion occurring through open public competition. In general, selection is delegated to special committees, consisting of members not involved in the organization in question; executives are traditionally excluded, and the task of personnel management, when present, is to provide administrative support to selection and assessment initiatives (Della Rocca, 1995, 1996).

In Britain, this public administrative tradition has been associated with specific values and industrial relations policies whereby the state was considered a "model employer," although its application has been partial and uneven (Bach, 1999a; Carter and Fairbrother, 1999). The "model employer" tradition has been associated with a willingness to recognize trade unions and to institutionalize their position through collective bargaining mechanisms underpinning the type of procedural arrangements which governed employment, such as an emphasis on training, equal opportunities and joint consultation. In other countries, even in those characterized by limitations on collective bargaining and a stronger tradition of unilateral state decision-making (such as in France), trade unions and professional associations are none the less involved (through participation procedures) in many aspects relating to the determination of working conditions.

Although it cannot be said that this Weberian tradition precluded all vestiges of management, it nevertheless assumed specific forms. In many European countries, a number of professional staff were "managed" by their colleagues, and even when this was not the case, public service managers – especially in the welfare services – endorsed unitary values supportive of the professional staff which dominated public services (Winchester, 1983). In contrast to their private sector counterparts, managers were frequently members of a trade union or professional association, showing that they retained many of the same values as the staff that they managed. In France, for example, the state and its élite civil servants have played a central and privileged role in the national political economy. The ideology of a technical élite acting in the national interest limited the incursion of management into the French state. The features of the French public sector which have sustained this tradition include: the highly centralized character of the French state; the dirigiste tradition of state-directed growth; the political and social influence of the élite who form the grand corps; and the rigid and hierarchical structure of these different corps – with their own specific terms and conditions of employment and precise rules governing career advancement based primarily on seniority (Clark, 1998).

In many other countries, a similar type of tradition has existed irrespective of the specific administrative form it has taken (which has differed from state to state). Although not always explicit, the focus of attention is usually on civil servants who, on account of the essential functions performed, are governed by specific statutes frequently precluding the right to strike. The strongest version of this governance structure is the special legal status of *Beamte*, whose position in society is enshrined by a precisely defined set of legal rights and obligations (Keller, 1999a).

Management practice in Europe: toward a New Public Management?

The term "New Public Management" dominates discussion on public sector management. While a wide variety of different management reforms have been labeled as New Public Management, three key dynamics none the less underscore an apparently disparate set of management practices. The first is efficiency orientated. It emphasizes reforms of public sector management practice resulting in a more businesslike "value-for-money" approach with stronger managerial and financial controls. It involves the development of professional managerial roles and encourages the use of a range of corporate management techniques whose adoption is aimed at improving efficiency and effectiveness.

These roles are not necessarily new. What distinguishes them from earlier reform initiatives, however, is the commitment to endowing these managers with more responsibility in terms of results and expenditure, placing pressure on them to exercise greater control over staff. Whereas in traditional bureaucracies executive staff were essentially responsible for the legality of administrative acts, the emphasis of the new managerial paradigm is primarily based on service objectives and resource utilization. The new management model, thus, incorporates the establishment of discretionary powers which may challenge longstanding professional and trade union influence. Associated changes in employment practices include tighter control of staff through clearer performance targets and appraisal, sometimes linked to individual performance-related pay, as well as more interventionist management of issues such as mobility and the direct recruitment of staff without recourse to public competition. In order to complement these changes, decentralized pay determination is often advocated; this would be more responsive to managerial demands for flexibility and more sensitive to employee performance and labor market conditions.

A second key element concerns changes in organizational structures with the division of monolithic public service organizations into separate units with more devolved management practice. It is important to distinguish between the delegation of responsibility for budgetary and personnel management practices from higher to lower tiers of government, from the decentralization of pay determination, which is linked to broader features of industrial relations practice. The break up of large organizations is intended to produce smaller units with a clear focus on the services they deliver; enable more transparency in results and costs; improve flexibility; and reduce the number of hierarchical levels. Devolution of management responsibility, however, can be accompanied by forms of centralization. Indeed this is a logical consequence of the break-up of public sector organizations into more fragmented and independent units; the responsibility for implementation of policy is delegated downwards, while responsibility for making and monitoring policy resides with politicians at the center.

A third element is market-orientated and concerns the degree to which public sector management practice has shifted from management by hierarchy to management by contract. Market regulation can be seen as the most radical choice in transforming management roles and attitudes in an administrative organization. Market regulation has expanded in most European countries through the privatization of state-owned firms and services, for example, rail and postal services (Feigenbaum, et al., 1999). They are broken down into different enterprises and some of them have been sold to private owners or transformed into public companies. Conversely, within core public services, incentive structures based on systems of competitive tendering and internal markets have been introduced. These developments fragment traditional uniform organizational structures, replacing them with competing units linked by a series of contracts. This permits the redrawing of public service boundaries, where they need not directly employ their own staff but retain a core of staff who identify and buy services from a range of outside public and private sector agencies.

The development of the New Public Management paradigm presupposes a radical change in the social status and labor market position of public administrators. This shift is especially advocated for the top tier of management, as well as for those who are responsible for autonomous administrative units. The new public manager is, in this case, usually hired directly (bypassing public competition) by political authorities on the basis of personal preferences. The manager may typically have had some experience in the private sector and be employed on a fixed-term contract, its renewal dependent on targets being achieved. In so doing, advocates of the new managerialism suggest, the executive labor market becomes more competitive and is no longer characterized by life-time employment, while educational qualifications and seniority are not the sole criteria for promotion. Salaries may fluctuate and are performance linked, promotion can be more rapid and turnover is higher than in traditional public administration. In addition, central to New Public Management is an emphasis on a more strategic approach to the management of the employment relationship. It is suggested that this requires the establishment of an influential personnel function, alongside greater involvement of all managers in personnel management; greater use of forms of flexible working; and the development of employee involvement initiatives which extends beyond consultation with trade unions (see Bach, 1999b).

It is evident that New Public Management, and its "strongest" variant (which focuses on strategic choice), figure strongly in recommendations by the OECD (1995, 1996a, 1996b), and these studies have been very influential in establishing the public sector reform agenda (Andersen et al., 1997). PUMA's interpretation of state responses to the challenges facing the public sector suggest a three-fold process (Premfors, 1998). First, recognition of the welfare state crisis in the 1970s; second, the introduction of piecemeal reforms in the 1980s which concentrated on strengthening management and third, the unleashing of more radical reforms in the 1990s which provided market incentives (internal markets, performance-related pay, and so on) and altered management priorities.

There are a number of problems, however, with the PUMA account of recent public sector developments. First, it may be criticized for viewing all public sector management developments as converging towards the New Public Management approach and so systematically ignoring evidence of variations between countries and sub-sectors. Although it is recognized that policy makers in some countries have proceeded more rapidly than others, these developments are viewed as an essentially temporary phenomenon. It is assumed that the "laggards" will catch up – and will be forced to do so even against their will because of the pressures for change. Moreover, little consideration is given to the specific characteristics of each country, especially the legal, institutional and industrial relations structure that impact on the capacity and willingness of governments to endorse the prescriptions advocated by the OECD. Second, the PUMA account is not sensitive enough to the gap between the espoused policies of governments and the actual practice in terms of the extent to which reforms are implemented and their effectiveness.

A more general issue may be raised about the use of strategic choice frameworks in understanding public sector management reforms. It is necessary to bear in mind that strategic choices do not arise automatically from a turbulent environment. The role of the different actors, the decisions that they make and the function of other factors occurring in different national institutional contexts should be highlighted. For example, the emphasis on choices available to managers may exaggerate their discretionary powers while underplaying the structural constraints that they have to confront. The emphasis on structural constraints is particularly relevant when the range of legal, political, economic and labor market characteristics of the public sector are considered. This is not to say that managers have no discretionary powers, but merely suggests that an over-simplified use of strategic choice frameworks may exaggerate the scope for autonomous management action. The same applies to the effects on employment relationships and industrial relations; changes in management structure, such as those mentioned above, do not always have the same effects on employment conditions and industrial relations in every country. At both a national and local level workers, trade unions, professional associations and employers may find different solutions based on the opportunities available to them.

As advocated by PUMA, it might still be worthwhile for policy makers to pursue reforms associated with the New Public Management. However, in the absence of a more precise analysis of management practice in different countries, there is a risk of over-simplifying reforms, thus, making it difficult for policy makers to ascertain the right conditions for a sustainable and effective reform agenda. The next section examines the reform agenda in Europe focusing on whether a professional management function has been developed; the extent of decentralization; and how these aspects have changed the role and status of executives and conditions of employment. Particular attention will be focused on the changes that have taken place in personnel management roles and policies.

Comparative evidence

Professional management development

The first aspect of the New Public Management concerns the development of a stronger management function with managers being accountable for their performance. The role of the professional manager is different from that of the civil servant operating within traditional bureaucracies. The civil servant is constrained by legal regulations and works within an administrative rather than a managerial system. The role is to support policy makers and to ensure that the law is implemented fairly and consistently. Civil servants have little control over financial and human resources.

The distinguishing feature of the British experience is that it has attempted to alter the composition and practice of public sector management within radically restructured public services. Chief executive roles – often challenging powerful professional interests – have been developed. To facilitate this change, private sector managers were appointed to high-profile positions in the anticipation that they would introduce best private sector practice into the public service environment. These senior managers are increasingly recruited through open competition and, more generally, recruitment procedures have been delegated to departments and agencies (Winchester and Bach, 1999). The altered expectations of managers were clearly signaled by the introduction of individual performance-related pay and more articulated performance management systems. This process has been most extensive in the civil service with the abolition of age-related incremental pay scales (Marsden and French, 1998).

The most far-reaching managerial innovations have arisen less from the delegation of pay bargaining to executive agencies than from the discretion that managers have exercised in reforming patterns of work organization and working time, making use of temporary workers and ensuring tighter monitoring of sickness absences. These managers are empowered with rationalizing the labor process, establishing and changing the work organization, designing new roles, recruiting, retaining, promoting and motivating their staff. A prominent issue has been the introduction of human resource management practices: appraisal systems, payment by results, new forms of communication, with an increased focus on the individual employee. The aim of the changes introduced by the new management role has been to curb the power of interest groups, not only trade unions, but also professionals such as doctors and schoolteachers. Professional staff were believed to be indifferent to the need to use resources more cost effectively and were insufficiently accountable for their performance.

In no other country within Western Europe have there been such fundamental public service reforms, although in Italy considerable attention has been paid to the development of more professional management practices since the early 1990s. This has occurred within a context where there has traditionally been very limited separation of political and bureaucratic responsibilities, with politicians being wholly involved in detailed personnel management issues, thus providing little scope for the development of a strong public administrative function (Bordogna et al., 1999).

Although still within a context of relatively dense legal regulations, the 1993 reform created the basis for substantial change in management practices within the public services (Dell'Aringa and Della Rocca, 1999; Bordogna et al., 1999). The 1993 reforms included three key elements. First, a clear distinction was made between political and managerial decisions. Public sector managers, instead of simply complying with the law, were held responsible for achieving measurable results. Managerial salary structures were reformed to allow greater pay differentiation. Second, public sector managers were granted more autonomy in terms of financial and human resource management. Directors were provided with new budgetary control instruments and granted more discretionary powers over personnel policy, including the organization of work in their departments. Third, the managerial role was strengthened by eliminating the mandatory participation of unions in issues such as recruitment, internal mobility, career development and training. This scope for unilateral senior manager decision-making at the local level has been seen as an important change from past practices, when local representatives were involved in such issues. This type of involvement enabled union representatives to exercise a degree of informal co-determination with management. The 1993 and subsequent 1997–98 reforms replace the informal co-determination practice with collective bargaining procedures for specific issues, such as productivity bonus and merit payment, at national and local levels. These reforms established ambitious goals, not all of which could be met within the existing management structures and administrative culture. Difficulties arose in establishing forms of assessment based on results and introducing suitable tools to gauge performance. The control and distribution of financial resources remains centralized at a national level, although with their new responsibilities, managers have new powers regarding human resources. In some sectors, including the national health service and the municipalities, the local government may appoint a general manager. None the less, the majority of managers are recruited from the internal labor market by means of public competitions; those from outside employed on temporary contracts account for only a small percentage. The vast majority of managers still have a special employment status: long-term contracts, job security and special pension schemes. Their employment conditions remain covered by collective negotiations.

In Denmark there are also signs of the emergence of a more prominent managerial role, together with strong elements of continuity whereby most senior managers are usually given civil servant status. But this status no longer confers total job security and managerial dismissals are becoming more and more common. The use of short-term contracts, increased managerial salaries and more discretion *vis-à-vis* staff recruitment, promotion and remuneration are further indicators of a changing managerial role (Andersen et al., 1999). Unlike in Britain, government and senior managers have sought consensus for reform; there is no question of managers exercising unfettered discretion. Management decision making is influenced by various forms of employee participation at national and local levels – especially through works' councils (contained within public sector cooperation committees), which play an important role in personnel and strategic decisions.

In France, Germany and Spain the change in the role of managers has not been the main focus of reform. There has been some use of management techniques (for example, total quality management) similar to those in the private sector, but these have usually been grafted on to existing (usually highly centralized) administrative structures. In both France and Germany, although somewhat differently, a degree of ambivalence exists over the usefulness of adopting the tenets of the new managerialism. In marked contrast to Britain, most French commentators defend the job security of civil servants as integral to civil service modernization, rather than as an impediment to reform (Mossé and

Tchobanian, 1999). None the less, the defense of the classical model of French public administration has not precluded official support for the new managerialism. At decentralized levels, especially in the health sector, a more forceful cadre of hospital directors is emerging that has started to assert their influence within the hospital sector. In Germany, tentative steps have been taken toward the development of stronger managerial roles, and there is some interest in the New Public Management debate. But a dense network of administrative and legal regulations, together with fairly elaborate rights regarding co-determination, have stifled such developments. As Keller (1999b) notes, the problem of management prerogatives has basically been solved by legal enactment. The distinctive feature of Spain is that the transition to democracy has been accompanied by the development of the welfare state (stifled under Franco). The establishment of formal, transparent management systems has been of lower priority (Jódar et al., 1999).

In these three European countries, the internal labor market is still based on a strictly hierarchical system of different grades for different groups or professional corps. All these groups have their own careers, basically following criteria of seniority, rather than individual performance. Access to top executive positions is governed by public selection procedures and little emphasis is placed on the direct recruitment of management from the private sector. The implementation of performance-related pay was supposed to supplement, but definitely not replace, the traditional system of seniority and job-rank based principles of remuneration. Different performance indicators are being discussed for performance-related pay, but have not yet been introduced on a very large scale. The crucial questions are, first (as in many other countries), how to measure output for a number of different sub-sectors and for rather uniform jobs in an objective way; and, second, who has the power to define and, hence, to implement performance indicators whereby the discretionary power of managers is linked to legal rules of equity and objectivity, as well as to the value and negotiation power of the professional corps. As highlighted by Meurs (1999), in France, the term individual salary denotes the career advancement of each individual in the professional remuneration scale through mechanisms based mainly on seniority, rather than on performance and result-linked remuneration methods.

Devolution of managerial responsibilities

The second important component of reform has been the devolution of managerial responsibilities. In Britain, this devolution of responsibility for personnel practice has been accompanied by the establishment of separately constituted business units; each of these units has been designed according to the product or service supplied. By drawing on private sector practice, the Conservative government invoked the model of a multi-divisional company, with strict head-office monitoring of financial performance and service standards across a proliferating number of "business units". At the same time, central government has accrued unprecedented levels of influence over the funding and management of these nominally independent service providers. This model partially explains the apparent paradox of increased central control as set against government support for devolution (Winchester and Bach, 1999).

Budgetary constraints, performance indicators and, in some cases, competition have forced managers to rationalize working practices. Managerial scope for innovation has been strengthened by the lightly regulated labor market, government exhortation and the greater willingness of professional associations and trade unions to accept working practice reforms rather than concede to the decentralization or individualization of pay. Managers have experimented with changes in working time arrangements (in hospitals, for example), and made greater use of temporary workers – altering the composition of the workforce and the tasks undertaken by workers, a process termed "reprofiling" (Arrowsmith and Sisson, 2000; Grimshaw, 1999).

At the beginning of the 1970s in Denmark, the administrative structure reform delegated administrative functions to municipalities and counties. This process of change included both the strengthening of lower government tiers, budget reform and management devolution. In the case of budgetary reform, the government did not define a priori each item of expenditure for the administrative units; this means that management has wide margins of flexibility. The responsibilities delegated to the municipalities has increasingly been linked to more responsibility for expenditure and local taxation (Andersen et al., 1999). Consequently, Denmark exhibits strong elements of administrative devolution for financial and human resources alongside an elaborate system of coordinated coalition bargaining.

In France, Germany and Spain institutional changes took place with the shifting of some functions from central to local government. In France, although the influence of central government remains strong, the 1982 decentralization laws transferred a number of responsibilities to local government level. In Spain, the creation of autonomous committees or regions has been the major structural change in the post-Franco period, altering the responsibilities of civil servants and incorporating elements of budgetary devolution (Jódar et al., 1999). In Germany, the state's federal character incorporates a highly developed regional tier and there are fewer signs of organizational restructuring and managerial devolution – either at central or regional administrative levels, although the situation differs at the local level (Keller, 1999a).

In Italy, the greatest degree of financial and personnel autonomy has been granted to hospitals. Since 1992, funding has been more directly linked to patient activity, but managerial discretion remains within strict limits. Since 1997, schools have been delegated greater organizational powers to negotiate, for example, agreements with outside suppliers, but it is too early to assess whether the rationale of greater managerial and legal autonomy will result in significant change in management practice. Formidable constraints remain, and the reorganization of the central government has not occurred to support increased managerial responsibilities (Bordogna et al., 1999).

Market-type mechanisms

The final aspect of the implementation of New Public Management practices has been linked to the adoption of market-type mechanisms designed to alter the behavior of managers and employees. The most developed and widespread form of marketization is through the privatization of publicly-owned firms and nationalized industries and within the core public services the use of competitive tendering and internal market mechanisms.

From the early 1980s, compulsory competitive tendering for manual services was introduced into the health and local government sectors in Britain. In local government compulsory competitive tendering was extended in stages to other services, including professional white-collar services, such as personnel and information management. In the civil service, a policy of "market testing" has prevailed. This has given departments and agencies greater discretion to decide which activities to subject to tendering. In contrast to health and local government, in-house bids have usually been excluded, ensuring that a higher proportion of work has been contracted out than in other public services. Regardless of whether a service is retained in-house or is outsourced, this policy has led to substantial reductions in the workforce, and accompanying pay-roll savings (Colling, 1999). The imposition of mandatory tendering has provided managers with an opportunity to alter working practices, erode national terms and conditions of employment and improve service standards. This positive endorsement has influenced the Labor government's proposals for a framework of "best value" (IRS, 1998).

In other countries, competitive tendering has not been compulsory and has not been vigorously pursued. In Denmark, at the municipal level, there have been experiments with contracting out services such as street cleaning and transportation. Information technology has been put out to tender and some trials have been made in terms of contracting out services to the elderly (Andersen et al., 1999). Furthermore, particularly in sectors such as schools and health care, so-called consumer councils have been formed, the aim being to give consumers more market power.

In Italy, contracting-out has been applied to some functions without reducing employment levels or employee wages (Bordogna et al., 1999). In France, there is increased interest in contracting-out services in the hospital sector, with non-medical services such as catering and cleaning being outsourced (Mossé and Tchobabanian, 1999). In Spain, highway maintenance and many social programs have been contracted out to private companies, with employees losing their civil service status (Jódar et al., 1999). In Germany, at federal level, and especially at local level where budgetary problems are the most acute, only services such as rubbish collection and street cleaning have been contracted out. In general, these measures were introduced rather late in Germany; they have been fairly small scale and were negotiated with the trade unions in a consensual–corporatist style (Keller, 1999a).

Only in Britain and, to a lesser extent, in Denmark, have internal market mechanisms been introduced in a substantial way. In Britain, from the late 1980s onwards, a system of internal markets was established, intended to simulate competitive relationships in the private sector. In health and local government (particularly schools), the provision of services has been separated from funding by purchasing authorities. Service providers, particularly NHS trusts and grant-maintained schools, have to compete for the funding allotted to treating patients or educating pupils. Uncertainties about revenue have led managers to reduce the payroll and make greater use of temporary and fixed-term contracts to link employment costs with fluctuating income levels. In the civil service, an internal market model is less applicable, but many agencies face competition from the private sector and all agencies have to adhere to strict performance standards established by their parent department. In Denmark, the distinction between the financing of services and the provision of services has been clearly defined, and is concerned with a number of initiatives taken with outside or internal providers. By separating these roles, the aim is to respond directly to supply and demand factors, thus reinforcing the logic of competition (Andersen et al., 1999).

Exploring national variations in management practice

The evidence from Western Europe has confirmed that there has been considerable experimentation with reform initiatives that embrace aspects of the New Public Management. Nevertheless, the change in the original model of public administration has not always followed its guiding principles. All the countries analyzed have specifically insisted on introducing professional management roles and tools while less attention has been focused on the principle of creating autonomous business units and introducing quasi-market forms.

In many cases, attempts have been made to overcome the use of centralized and uniform rules of administration (inherent in the Weberian model), because it is necessary to handle extremely diverse economic situations, functions and types of employment. This complexity requires greater scope for managerial discretion and development of their competencies to enable organizational and personnel reforms, leading to output and cost efficiencies. In some cases, considerable emphasis has been placed on giving public employment a different identity and image; an image no longer only based on the idea of public service conducted in the general interest, but also employment that has to fulfill performance requirements that will be awarded appropriately.

Nevertheless, the debate regarding strategic models of public administration reform continues. If the expectation of implementing more efficient forms of management and services exists in all countries, this expectation does not however mean that the development of innovation is always guided by a New Public Management model. It can be suggested that comparative evidence obtained from our research network allows us to differentiate between two main patterns of reform. In broad terms some countries are shifting towards the New Public Management while others are retaining a commitment to an administrative system of governance that is trying to revitalize, but not overturn, the key elements of the classic Weberian model. In addition, as noted below, in some countries attempts at a synthesis between these two distinct reform patterns is also emerging. These patterns do not completely capture the experience of any one country – and within almost all countries differences may be found in the pattern of change between sub-sectors. None the less, this framework may be employed as an heuristic device to explore national variations.

The first approach corresponds most strongly to the practices associated with the New Public Management – a market-orientated system of governance placing a premium on cost-effectiveness criteria. To achieve these outcomes, administrative and legal regulations have to be modified to allow for managerial autonomy, altering the relationship between the political and administrative sphere and, at the same time, greater emphasis is placed on reducing the size and scope of the public sector. In this case, recourse to outside tendering, the establishment of autonomous units, fixed-term contracts for executives and assessment of their performance is very widespread. Selection, development and remuneration of employees is no longer carried out solely based on administrative criteria of qualifications or seniority, but according to potential assessment, experience and performance.

The second approach corresponds to an administrative system of governance. This is more than merely a re-labeling of traditional public administration to disguise the status quo but, instead, reflects measures to reform the public sector. This pattern of reform, however, tries to adapt rather than overturn existing institutional systems of governance because it continues to view state employment as fundamentally different from the private sector and the wholesale adoption of private sector "best practice" is inappropriate. The reform process may endorse improvements in management skills and less cumbersome administrative structures but these reforms are aimed at renewing traditional forms of public administration, not least to forestall the adoption of more radical forms of the New Public Management. The administrative structure remains centralized and recourse to sub-contracting and the use of forms of competition among various internal administration units does not constitute a significant strategy. The autonomy and responsibility of management for results is significantly constrained by the power of professional organizations and trade union involvement in employment regulation. The development and selection of most employees and executives takes place by means of the application of administrative rules. Determination of the employment relationship for executives and other personnel takes place by means of internal promotion in terms of professional job classification through certifiable criteria such as seniority and by means of public competition. Cost containment and increased flexibility are achieved through part-time jobs, the introduction of fixed-term contracts for newly hired employees, temporary work and a limited use of payment for performance, personnel mobility and more flexible patterns of work organization. As regards the manner in which reforms are introduced, much greater emphasis is placed on gaining the support of social partners and other political stakeholders than in the more authoritarian patterns of reform found amongst some New Public Management advocates.

Reforms in some countries have tried to blend elements of both approaches in a system of governance that emphasizes decentralization accompanied by strong local participation of key stakeholders. This approach aims to increase cost effectiveness, but is more sensitive to outcomes and the priorities of service users than either of the other two patterns of reform. Managerial initiatives are promoted as long as they do not jeopardize principles of consensus and inclusiveness. Thus the development of autonomous and decentralized public agencies, the improvement of central and peripheral control of resources and results and forms of tendering are present but within strict limits. The administrative legal status of managerial roles does, however, remain public. Strong emphasis is placed on participation in monitoring results and resources not only for trade unions and professional associations, but also for political and social institutions, representing consumers and citizens.

Comparative evidence suggests that a pure version of the New Public Management does not exist in Europe. According to our three criteria (stronger management, devolution of managerial responsibilities and market-style reforms) not surprisingly, Britain comes closest to this model of reform. First, there has been a sustained effort to develop a group of public sector managers committed to a different set of values than the traditional public service ethos. The absence of a grandees corps as in France and Spain, or the equivalent prestige and legalism of the German public service tradition has made this task easier. Second, the devolution of managerial responsibility has taken place. Although much attention has been focused on pay bargaining reform, more substantive change has occurred in terms of work reorganization and performance management. Third, there has been extensive experimentation with forms of contracting out and the establishment of internal markets in health care and social services. None the less, doubts persist about the degree of change; for example, the scope of management to exercise strategic choice has been questioned, national systems of pay determination remain important and market-style reforms have fallen short of establishing a competitive market for health and education services. What accounts for this pattern of management restructuring?

The most familiar explanation is political and derives from the radical reforms undertaken by the Thatcher government from 1979 onwards – a New Right administration ideologically hostile to the public sector. As witnessed by the subsequent experience of the Labor government – which continues with most of these policies – this is only a part of the explanation. As noted by Flynn and Strehl (1996), it is important to examine the differing constitutional arrangements and the nature of the industrial relations system. The Conservative government benefited from the first-past-the-post electoral system which gave it complete parliamentary supremacy. In addition, the lack of a written constitution, no tradition of administrative law capable of constraining political interference and the absence of a codified system of union and management co-determination within the public sector (possessed by Denmark and Germany), or formal practices of workplace participation (such as in France) ensured a virtually free hand for successive Conservative governments to unleash a radical program of reform.

In the Italian case there has been a strong emphasis on the development of more professional managers, more autonomy of civil servants from political influence and the recruitment of managers from the private sector. There have been forms of managerial devolution and the development of personnel practices. Especially in the hospital sector, elements of market-style reforms are apparent. None the less, attempts to "empower" the New Public Management approach have been constrained by a burdensome framework of administrative and legal regulations.

Organizational structures have been slow to change (creation of independent decentralized units, either in competition with each other or with private agencies) and, for this reason, devolution of managerial responsibilities has been limited. Furthermore, the development of performance indicators is only just commencing. The focus of the change is more in the privatization of employment relations and in the diffusion of collective bargaining than in new organizational and personnel management practice. The employment relationship governed by national collective agreements has been privatized and no longer falls within the ambit of public law, while administrative rules defining personnel policies such as recruitment and promotions remain prominent. This change has taken place thanks to trade union support and consensus. In fact, the latter continue to have strong political and contractual power both inside and outside the bureaucratic system in a context, such as the Italian one, that has always been characterized by the presence of weak governments.

France, Germany and Spain are indicative of the administrative system of governance. Attempts to reform the public sector have emerged from within this tradition. In these countries, there is limited emphasis on either introducing professional managers to modernize the state or on fundamental restructuring. Although some new management techniques have been introduced, their implementation is slow and uneven. These techniques are introduced within a very different context: highly centralized decision-making structures; well-developed systems of co-determination; and very limited, if any, commitment to market-style measures. In the case of France and Germany, this reform pattern reflects a deep suspicion of the values and relevance of the New Public Management within a highly codified system of legal and administrative regulation where civil servants enjoy considerable status and have been socialized into a particular style of public administration (Ridley, 1996).

Denmark represents a decentralized strategy, targeted at improving efficiency and the quality of public services. More than recourse to a hierarchical, centralized bureaucratic model, the aim of the reform is to define the number of service organizations, which – though possibly in competition with each other – are nevertheless democratically regulated. This case is representative of an empirical approach based on the hypothesis that the production of goods and services in the public sector must have a managerial autonomy but, at the same time, be governed by the political process operating on a different basis from that of the market economy. This approach is achieved through the introduction of internal market mechanisms, with decentralization of organizations and managerial practices and through tendering and grants. The result is often competition between public and private companies for service management. The criteria and standards resulting from this market-type pattern are government regulated. In Denmark, the restructuring process takes place through the participation of trade union organizations according to a strategy whereby the social partners regard the improving of efficiency and effectiveness of public services as an important attempt in developing and maintaining the welfare state. Consequently, this strategy is measured in terms of service efficiency, maintenance and the development of good public sector working conditions, as well as through consumer feedback.

This approach is generally representative of Scandinavian countries. In the case of Sweden, this reform process – oriented towards achieving better organizational functionalism – is targeted at transforming the state into a federation of welfare communes (Premfors, 1998). In this case, there is a division between government and ministry regulation and control, and that of execution, entrusted to decentralized independent agencies. In particular, this change has occurred within the sectors of education, health care and social services. It is maintained that in sectors where there is strong citizen pressure, the government and the administration representing it should not be directly responsible for service implementation. This new system has been made possible thanks to the State Financial Control reform, a prestigious institution similar to the Italian or French National Audit Office, to check the legality and conformity of the accounts of all public administration bodies. Its activity has been transformed, from the legal control of each individual item of expenditure, to a general budget control and to a system of monitoring throughout programs and results (Crozier, 1987). This system offers broad margins of flexibility in the management of each single agency. For example, in the case of industrial relations and personnel management, each agency has greater autonomy in allocating the resources to be spent for their own employees, in accordance with: the type of objectives, the total resource assigned by the government and by the national contract and the results desired (Schagger and Andersson, 1996, 1999).

To return to where we started, there is evidence that in all the countries assessed, fiscal and other pressures are challenging the traditional characteristics of public management practice. The New Public Management has been the dominant reform approach advocated, especially by the OECD, to modernize public service employment practices. Evidence suggests that within Europe, however, this has not been the only, or dominant, approach to management reform. In many countries, policy makers are trying to go with the grain of their legal, political and institutional traditions and modify – rather than overturn – existing employment practices and regulations.

References

Andersen, S. K., Due, J., and Masden, J. S. (1997) "Multi-track Approach to Public-sector Restructuring in Europe: Impact on Employment Relations; Role of Trade Union," *Transfer*, III(1).

Andersen, S. K., Due, J., and Masden, J. S. (1999) "Denmark. Negotiating the restructuring of public service employment," in Bach, S., Bordogna, L., Della Rocca, G., and Winchester, D. (eds.), *Public Service Employment Relations in Europe: Transformation, Modernization or Inertia?*, London: Routledge.

Arrowsmith, J., and Sisson, K. (2000) "Managing Working Time," in Bach, S. and Sisson, K. (eds.), *Personnel Management: A Comprehensive Guide to Theory and Practice*, Oxford: Blackwell.

Bach, S. (1999a) "From National Pay Determination to Qualified Market Relations: NHS Pay Bargaining Reform," *Historical Studies in Industrial Relations*, (8).

Bach, S. (1999b) "Personnel Managers: Managing to Change?," in Corby, S. and White, G. (eds.), *Employee Relations in the Public Services*, London: Routledge.

Bach, S., Bordogna, L., Della Rocca, G., and Winchester, D. (eds.) (1999) *Public Service Employment Relations in Europe: Transformation, Modernization or Inertia?*, London: Routledge.

Bendix, R. (1962) *Max Weber. An Intellectual Portrait*, New York: Anchor Books.

Bordogna, L., Dell'Aringa, C. and Della Rocca, G. (1999) "Italy: a case of coordinated decentralization," in Bach, S., Bordogna, L., Della Rocca, G. and Winchester, D. (eds) *Public Service Employment Relations in Europe: Transformation, Modernization or Inertia?* London: Routledge.

Carter, B. and Fairbrother, P. (1999) "The Transformation of Public Sector Industrial Relations: From Model Employer to Marketized Relations," *Historical Studies in Industrial Relations*, (7).

Clark, D. (1998) "The Modernization of the French Civil Service: Crisis, Change and Continuity", *Public Administration*, LXXVI(1).

Colling, T. (1999) "Tendering and outsourcing: working in the contract state?," in Corby, S. and White, G. (eds.), *Employee Relations in the Public Services*, London: Routledge.

Crozier, M. (1987) *Etat modeste etat moderne. Strategie pour un autre changement*, Paris: Fayard.

Dell'Aringa, C. (1997) "Pay Determination in the Public Service: An International Comparison," *Quaderni dellIstituto di Economia dell'Impresa e del Lavoro*, (16), Milano: Università Cattolica.

Dell'Aringa, C. and Della Rocca, G. (1999) "La Riforma della Contrattazione Collettiva e le Prerogative della Dirigenza nell'Amministrazione Pubblica Italiana," in Dell'Aringa, C. and Della Rocca, G. (eds.), *Razionalizzazione e Relazioni Industriali nel Pubblico Impiego in Europa*, Milano: Angeli.

Della Rocca, G. (1995) *La Differenziazione Retributiva nel Pubblico Impiego, il Caso degli Istituti della Produttivà-Indennità di Funzione nel Settore degli Enti Locali*, Milano: Angeli.

Della Rocca, G. (1996) *Lavoro Pubblico Lavoro Privato. Imprese e Amministrazioni nella Regolazione Sociale*, Soveria Mannelli: Rubbettino.

Feigenbaum, H., Henig, J., and Hamnett, C. (1999) *Shrinking the State: The Political Underpinnings of Privatization*, Cambridge: Cambridge University Press.

Ferlie, E., Ashburner, L., Fitzgerald, L., and Pettigrew, A. (1996) *The New Public Management in Action*, Oxford: Oxford University Press.

Flynn, N., and Strehl, F. (eds.) (1996) *Public Sector Management in Europe*, London: Prentice-Hall.

Fredman, S. and Morris, G. (1989) *The State as Employer: Labour Law in Public Services*, London: Mansell.

Giannini M. S. (1986) *Il Pubblico Potere. Stati ed Amministrazione Pubblica*, Bologna: Mulino.

Grimshaw, D. (1999) "Changes in Skills-mix and Pay Determination among the Nursing Workforce in the UK Work," *Employment and Society*, XIII(2).

Hood, C. (1991) "A Public Management for all Seasons," *Public Administration*, LXIX(1), 3–19.

IRS (1998) "Goodbye CCT", *Employment Trends*, (647).

Jódar, P., Jordana, J., and Alos, R. (1999) "Spain: The Modernization of Public Service Employment Relations Since the Transition to Democracy," in Bach, S., Bordogna, L., Della Rocca, G., and Winchester, D. (eds.), *Public Service Employment Relations in Europe: Transformation, Modernization or Inertia?*, London: Routledge.

Keller, B. (1999a) "Germany. Negotiated Change, Modernization and the Challenge of Unification", in Bach, S., Bordogna, L., Della Rocca, G., and Winchester, D. (eds.), *Public Service Employment Relations in Europe: Transformation, Modernization or Inertia?*, London: Routledge.

Keller, B. (1999b) "Tra Unificazione e Europeizzazione. Continuità e Discontinuità nelle Relazioni Sindacali del Settore Pubblico," in Dell'Aringa, C., and Della Rocca, G. (eds.), *Razionalizzazione e Relazioni Industriali nel Pubblico Impiego in Europa*, Milano: Angeli.

Marsden, D., and French, S. (1998) *Performance Management Reforms in the UK: A Study of the Effectiveness of Performance Related Pay in the Civil Service, Public Hospitals and Schools*, London: Centre for Economic Performance, London School of Economics.

Meurs, D. (1999) "Occupazione e salari nel settore pubblico: l"esempio francese," in Dell'Aringa, C., and Della Rocca, G. (eds.), *Razionalizzazione e Relazioni Industriali nel pubblico impiego in Europa*, Milano: Angeli.

Mossé, P., and Tchobanian, R. (1999) "France. The restructuring of employment relations in the public service," in Bach, S., Bordogna, L., Della Rocca, G., and Winchester, D. (eds.), *Public Service Employment Relations in Europe: Transformation, Modernization or Inertia?*, London: Routledge.

OECD (1995) *Governance in Transition: Public Management Reforms in OECD Countries*, Paris: OECD.

OECD (1996a) *Performance Auditing and the Modernization of Government*, Paris: OECD.

OECD (1996b) *Performance Management in Government: Contemporary Illustrations*, Paris: OECD.

Pollitt, C., and Summa, H. (1997) "Trajectories of Reform: Public Management in Four Countries," *Public Money and Management*, XVII(1).

Pratchett, L., and Wingfield, M. (1996) "The demise of the public service ethos," in Pratchett, L., and Wilson, D. (eds.), *Local Democracy and Local Government*, London: Macmillan – now Palgrave.

Premfors, R. (1998) "Reshaping the Democratic State: Swedish Experience in a Comparative Perspective," *Public Administration*, LXXVI(1).

Ridley, F. (1996) "The New Public Management in Europe: Comparative Perspectives," *Public Policy and Administration*, XI(1).

Rusciano M. (1990) "Lavoro pubblico e privato: dalla separatezza all"unificazione normativa," in AA.VV. *Stato sociale, servizi, pubblico impiego*, Napoli: Jovene.

Schager, N. H., and Andersson, P. (1996) "Recent reforms within the Central Government Sector in Sweden with respect to Employment and Pay policies," discussion paper at ARAN Conference, Rome. Edited in Italian (1999), "Recenti riforme del governo centrale delle politiche del lavoro e delle retribuzioni nell'amministrazione pubblica in Svezia", in Dell'Aringa, C. and Della Rocca, G. (eds.), *Razionalizzazione e Relazioni Industriali nel pubblico impiego in Europa*, Milano: Angeli.

Treu, T. (1987) "Labor Relations in the Public Service: A Comparative Overview," in Treu, T. (ed.), *Public Service Labor Relations: Recent Trends and Future Prospects*, Geneva: ILO.
Winchester, D. (1983) "Industrial Relations in the Public Sector," in Bain, G. (ed.), *Industrial Relations in Britain*, Oxford: Blackwell.
Winchester, D. and Bach, S. (1995) "The State: The Public Sector," in Edwards, P. K. (ed.), *Industrial Relations: Theory and Practice in Britain*, Oxford: Blackwell.
Winchester, D., and Bach, S. (1999) "Britain. The transformation of public service employment relations," in Bach, S., Bordogna, L., Della Rocca, G., and Winchester, D. (eds.), *Public Service Employment Relations in Europe: Transformation, Modernization or Inertia?*, London: Routledge.
Zan, S. (1989) "Teoria dell'organizzazione e Pubblica Amministrazione", in Freddi G. (ed.), *Scienza dell'amministrazione e politiche pubbliche*, Firenze: La Nuova Italia Scientifica.

3
Collective Bargaining in Western Europe

*Lorenzo Bordogna and David Winchester**

Introduction: common pressures, diverging solutions?

It is widely recognized that in many European countries public sector labor relations in the 1980s and 1990s have been exposed to two conflicting pressures. On the one hand, at a time of high public sector deficits and severe macro-economic constraints, national governments have sought ways to contain public expenditures, of which the wages and salaries of public service employees are one of the main components. Such constraints, of course, became even more severe after 1992 for many countries, because of the Maastricht eligibility criteria for admission to the third stage of the Economic and Monetary Union (EMU). The provisions of the Pact on Stability and Growth, approved at the Amsterdam European Union Council of June 1997, suggest that these fiscal constraints are bound to continue.

On the other hand, there have been pressures on behalf of the consumers of public services and citizens at large for increasingly differentiated, more efficient and better-quality services, in sharp contrast to the uniform and bureaucratic forms of provision which prevailed in the past.

These pressures have generated a widespread academic and political debate on the most effective ways to deal with them, and to achieve the double goal of keeping the public sector wage bill under control while at the same time improving the quality of services. Most reform proposals

---

*This paper is the result of a common work. However, the Introduction, the Unilateral versus Joint Regulation section and the Centralization versus Decentralization section have been written by Lorenzo Bordogna and the A Framework for Comparative Analysis section, The Coordination of Collective Bargaining section and the Concluding Remarks by David Winchester.

designed to solve this problem have focused on several, more or less interconnected, dimensions (as well summarized in many OECD Public Management Studies, for example OECD 1993; 1995). They include the redrawing of the boundaries between private and public sector and the transfer of services from the state or public ownership to private hands; various forms of restructuring aimed at introducing market, or market-like mechanisms of governance into the financing and provision of public services; the devolution of managerial authority to the level of an individual administrative unit; the strengthening of "managerial" criteria typical of the private sector in the internal organization of public services; and the reform of labor relations and personnel policies.

With reference to the latter dimensions, the need has often been stressed for a weakening of the special status of civil servants and public employees in general; for an extension of "free" collective bargaining (that is, on a voluntaristic basis) as the main method of regulation of the employment relationship; for a decentralization of the bargaining structure to the local level; and, to some extent, for an individualization of pay. These measures have been proposed as a means to make pay and conditions of employment more responsive to variations in local market conditions, organizational requirements and individual employee performance.

These interconnected proposals for reform cannot be described accurately as "privatization", although the term is used frequently in the current debate. Taken together, the above-mentioned processes do not necessarily constitute privatization in its complete form, since many of them do not imply a transfer of services or administrative units to private owners. It is, however, indicative of the broad meaning underlying this ideal picture of the process of change. That is, a reform aiming to profoundly modify the system of constraints and opportunities, of incentives and controls governing the entire functioning of the public services; to reduce the differences between the public and private sector of the economy by importing into the former the methods of management and the "best practices" of the latter; and to promote a logic of behavior on the part of the actors and a type of governance of labor transactions in the public services, significantly closer to those prevailing in the private sector of the economy.

To what extent does this ideal picture fit the actual experience of public service reform in European countries? Have all, or the majority of, countries followed that sequence of privatization of services – the introduction of market-like mechanisms, devolution of managerial authority, decentralization of bargaining and individualization of pay – as the only way to achieve a lasting reconciliation between the need to control public deficits and the need to improve the quality of services? There are no simple answers to these questions. The impression is that while changes along these lines can be observed in several cases, they have not only been pursued with varying degrees of intensity and completeness in different countries, but also the process of reform in some countries has taken rather different directions, while in others significant change has been resisted or avoided. Even in the case of Britain – the West European country which has most actively pursued the process of reform – the rhetoric has often exaggerated the scale and scope of change.

In the following pages we will address these and related questions in a comparative perspective. The primary focus of the analysis will be limited, however, to the structure, process and outcomes of collective bargaining, while broader strategies of reform on the part of governments, employers and trade unions will be taken into account only to the extent they impinge on our main topic.

A framework for comparative analysis

The general and comparative literature on the structure, process and outcome of collective bargaining is based mainly on private sector institutions an practice. None the less, it is useful in identifying the most important dimensions of collective bargaining structure; that is, the coverage, level, depth, scope and forms of bargaining (Windmuller, 1987; Clegg, 1976). In the private sector these dimensions describe the regularized patterns of interaction between trade unions and employers which, in turn, "establishes the framework for the exercising of power within the labor market" (Bean, 1994:79). In the case of the public sector, however, the analysis is complicated by the distinctive and variable role of the state.

In each country, the constitutional form of government, political values and electoral systems and administrative traditions and cultures – each of which is subject to a unique pattern of legal regulation – impact on the structure and process of collective bargaining. They also influence the concrete solutions that can be found to the above-mentioned pressures within each national context. This chapter will, thus, first explore the degree to which the boundary between joint regulation of employment relations and the unilateral decisions of politicians, state agencies or public employers has been redrawn in recent years. It will also consider the extent to which the related legal and practical distinctions between collective bargaining and various forms of consultation have become less distinct, and the ways in which different forms of political pressure typically supplement conventional collective bargaining procedures in the public sector.

This latter issue arises from a fundamental difference between public and private sector collective bargaining: in the public services, the employers' side exhibits a considerable dispersion of power among government ministers, state officials, politicians and the managers of public services. As Kochan (1974) argued many years ago, negotiations should be viewed as a form of multilateral bargaining in which the resolution of internal conflict on the employers' side complicates negotiations and invites political pressure from trade unions and professional associations. These pressures are most intense in the public services that have the highest political profile in each country (for example, aspects of health, education, law and order), and at the time in the electoral cycle when politicians and government ministers are most sensitive to public opinion. Such pressures still persist, even if they have been partly attenuated by the increasing separation between political authorities and managerial functions and by the privatization processes in some countries.

The peculiarities of the public sector extend beyond the issue of the collective bargaining process and its coverage to other dimensions identified in the literature. In considering the crucial and widespread debate on changes in the level of pay bargaining; for example, Dell'Aringa (1997a) has shown that the concepts of "centralization" and "decentralization" have a quite different meaning in the private and public sectors. In the private sector, individual firms, having previously delegated the responsibility for collective bargaining to an employers' association, may later choose to "decentralize" the process by rejecting multi-employer bargaining in favor of complete – or partial – enterprise autonomy in setting wages and conditions of employment. In contrast, in the public sector the process is usually reversed. The state invariably had the collective responsibility for pay determination and setting working conditions and, in some cases, it has chosen to delegate partially this responsibility – especially in relation to working practices – to the direct employers in individual administrative units. Thus, the logic and consequences of changes in the level of bargaining may be very different between countries – and within different parts of the public services within each country. This is because of variations in the degree of autonomy or dependence expressed in the constitutional and legal relationships between central government and various forms of local or devolved administration.

Comparative analysis of the scope of collective bargaining in the public services also raises questions that are largely absent in discussions of the private sector. A number of conditions of employment affecting recruitment, promotion, job security and pensions for some groups of staff may be determined by legislation and thus, be beyond the scope of collective bargaining in many countries. More generally, the distinction between the determination of pay and non-pay issues may be sharper than in the private sector; pay and conditions of employment may be negotiated in different bargaining arenas, or some employment conditions may be excluded from the bargaining agenda altogether. While this paper will explore comparative variations in substantive scope of collective bargaining, the analysis will focus on pay determination in particular.

The institutions and principles of public service pay determination attempt to resolve a number of seemingly intractable problems. For example, how can the relationship between public and private sector pay levels and movements be justified as "fair" to different groups of public service employees and their union representatives (internal and external relativities) and to taxpayers and elected governments responsible for fiscal policies? How can the responsibilities of public service managers for the recruitment, retention and motivation of staff and for the organizational imperative to improve efficiency and the quality of services within restricted budgets, be reconciled with pay determination systems often characterized by a high degree of centralization? Can collective bargaining procedures – and other forms of mediation – effectively resolve conflict over the above issues and prevent the disruption of politically sensitive "essential services?" The answer to these questions in each country depends partly on the degree of centralization or decentralization of the system of pay determination, but also on the differential impact of formal and informal mechanisms of collective bargaining coordination.

Unilateral versus joint regulation: the coverage of collective bargaining

The first, and in a sense preliminary, issue to address is that of the extension or the coverage of collective bargaining; that is, the proportion of public employees whose pay and working conditions are determined via collective agreements rather than through different methods – either unilaterally and directly on the part of the employer (the government, or a public agency to which the authority has been delegated), or through the evaluation of an independent authority.[1] The presence and scope of an area excluded from collective bargaining, and subject to unilateral regulation, is important because the larger it is the higher is the degree of freedom for governments to utilize it (at least in critical circumstances) to influence public sector pay policies for anti-inflationary purposes, with more or less direct effects on the entire economy (France and Germany are clear examples in point).[2] On the other hand, where collective bargaining is allowed, the coverage is typically very high (if not always 100 percent), since in all countries formal or informal *erga omnes* clauses are at work in the public sector (with few exceptions) quite differently from the private sector (Traxler, 1994).

As is well known, a move toward the recognition of collective bargaining rights for increasingly larger groups of public employees (civil servants included), to the detriment of unilateral regulation, has taken place in almost all European countries (and elsewhere) since the beginning or middle of the 1960s, partly as a consequence of the huge growth of welfare state activities (Treu, 1987; Andersen et al., 1997). However, while some occupations or services are almost everywhere excluded from collective bargaining (that is the armed forces, judges, and a few other minor groups), other significant differences still persist across countries.

The most notable case is perhaps that of Germany, where public sector employees are, so to speak, divided vertically into two main groups: that of *Beamte*, who do not have the right to strike or to collective bargaining, and that of *Angestellte* and *Arbeiter*, who have those rights. Such a distinction occurs in other countries too, as in Denmark (Andersen et al., 1999) and in Spain (Jódar et al., 1999). But what is peculiar in the German case is that the area of *Beamte* does not only cover central government civil service (or part of it), but includes a wide variety of other functions and public employees, up to about 40 percent of total public employment, and even higher until recently (Blenk, 1987; Keller, 1999:60). For example, this means that almost all teachers and medical doctors are *Beamte*, and until the recent process of "privatization" so were almost all (state) railways and postal services employees. This area is now slightly decreasing, not only because of the processes of privatization but also because of a more restrictive government policy to offer the status of *Beamte* to new entrants. Thus the legal distinction between the two groups has partly weakened over time and its practical consequences on the pay movements have usually been limited in recent times (Keller, 1999). A distinction still remains, however, which in emergency conditions – by reversing the usual sequence of pay determination between *Beamte* and the other groups of public employees – gives the government the possibility to influence wage increases in the entire public sector and, indirectly, even in the private sector.[3] The distinction also impacts on other labor relations issues, especially on the control of conflict – see for instance the sharp contrast with the Italian case in the transport sector, especially the railways, or also in the school and health sectors (Bordogna, 1993).

France is perhaps the second main exception. Here the point is not so much that of a demarcation within public employees between those with and without collective bargaining rights (as in Germany), but rather that of the very uncertain status of such a right for all the *fonctionaries*. Or, more precisely, of a legal status of collective bargaining which does not rule out the ultimate power of the government to unilaterally determine the pay and working conditions of the *fonctionaries titulaires* (indeed, the great majority of the 4.4 million public employees, armed forces excluded), who are still regulated by administrative law (Bazex, 1987; Guilhamon, 1989; Lyon Caen, 1993; Mossé and Tchobanian, 1999).

The July 1983 law (n. 634), which was approved after a practice of informal negotiations had started in the late 1960s, offers to public employees and their organizations the right to a *négociation préalable* (usually every year) with the government before it takes decisions over pay increases. However, it does not make the outcomes of these negotiations (called *relevé de conclusions*) legally binding for the government itself. Thus, the government is free to decide whether to start negotiations, whether to reach an agreement and whether or not to observe the agreement even after it has been reached. All these cases have actually occurred at least once after the approval of the law, for instance, in 1984, 1987 and 1990, when negotiations ended with no agreement; or more recently, between 1995 and 1998, when no negotiations took place, due to the government's concerns about satisfying the Maastricht fiscal criteria for eligibility to the European Monetary Union (Ministère de la Fonction Publique, *La Fonction Publique de l'Etat*, several years; Mossé and Tchobanian, 1999:142). In the light of these features, Marsden (1997), analyzing the predominant patterns of public service pay determination in a selected group of countries, classified France as a case of "free collective bargaining, but subject to unilateral veto by the government."

To some extent the situation in Denmark is similar. Amendments to the Civil Servants Act in 1969 formally gave civil servants the right to collectively negotiate and conclude agreements over pay increases and other issues, within a very centralized bargaining structure. But at the same time, the law denied civil servants the right to strike; if negotiations on the renewal of the current collective agreement ended in a deadlock, then pay and working conditions for the ensuing period could be determined by an Act of the *Folketing* (Andersen et al., 1999:218–19). This leaves open the possibility of, for quite a significant group of public sector employees, a "unilateral governance," typical of the past. Although the size of this group is declining because of privatization and the employers' policy of limiting the number of employees with civil servant status, it comprises around 20 percent of total public employees, located both in the state sector and in the regional and local authorities sector, including certain groups in the state railways and in the postal services.

Britain is also a relevant exception to the increasing coverage of collective bargaining as the main method of determining pay and working conditions (especially pay), although this does not imply the preservation of a strong unilateral power on the part of the government. In fact, the determination of pay for 1.3 million public service employees (that is, more than 25 percent of the total) is based currently on the recommendations of independent review bodies rather than by means of collective bargaining (Winchester and Bach, 1999; Elliott and Bender, 1997). Until the 1980s, three review bodies covered a relatively small group of employees whose status more or less precluded conventional collective bargaining: senior state officials (the highest grades in the civil service, military and judiciary); doctors and dentists; and the armed forces. The importance of the review body system was transformed, however, by its extension to a half a million nurses, midwives and other health service professional staff in 1982, and to a similar number of schoolteachers in 1991.

The extension of the review body system to nurses and schoolteachers was preceded by major pay disputes and followed a long history of difficult and inconclusive collective bargaining. Senior civil servants on the employers' side of the negotiating machinery exercised a *de facto* power to limit or block proposed pay settlements. Pay increases were often delayed and frequently settled only by the recommendations of *ad hoc* committees of inquiry or involving independent members. Thus, the extension of the more formal pay review body procedures to nurses and schoolteachers was not such a sharp break with past practice as it may first appear.

The formal exclusion of these groups from the coverage of collective bargaining does not mean that pay determination is simply a matter of unilateral government decision-making. While the government has the nominal power to reject totally the recommendations of the review bodies, in practice this has never happened: indeed, governments have frequently paid a high political price when they have delayed or staged the recommended pay increases in an attempt to reduce the annual wage cost of a settlement. Moreover, given that each review body receives detailed written and oral evidence from trade unions, employers and government ministers, it commissions its own research and publishes its findings and recommendations in detailed reports – the process can be viewed as a form of "arm's length bargaining" and one in which the government rarely wins all of the arguments.

At the same time, the review body system cannot be viewed as the equivalent to collective bargaining, neither in principle nor in formal terms. Aside from the nominal power of the government to reject the recommendations, the means by which unions and employers try to influence the independent review bodies is different from negotiating directly with each other: the dynamics are clearly different and it can be argued that sometimes the pay outcomes have sometimes been different from what might have emerged from direct negotiations.[4]

In other countries the move from government unilateralism towards collective bargaining for most public employees is more clearly detectable. This is the case for Italy after the reforms of 1983 and especially, of 1993. The latter "privatized" the employment relationship, moving it away from the framework of administrative law and fully "contractualized" the terms and conditions of employment of all public employees, with the exception of a few groups (mainly the armed forces, judges and university professors, some 15 percent of total public employees). It also extended the scope of collective bargaining to issues previously reserved to the law (Bordogna et al., 1999).[5] This "contractualization" was accompanied by measures to produce a more "voluntaristic" framework than in the past, and by some "barriers" to prevent the interference of politicians and government ministers in labor relations issues. It also involved tighter financial constraints on collective negotiations, stronger managerial prerogatives in personnel policies and a weakening of other sources of regulation of the employment relationship in general and of pay issues in particular (that is through parliament, administrative law and, at times, the constitutional court).

A similar weakening of unilateral regulation took place in Sweden after the reforms of 1965 and in The Netherlands after the mid 1980s. In the first case, the reforms recognized the right to collective bargaining for central government employees, although until the 1980s all collective agreements had been signed under the condition of government approval (Schager and Andersson, 1996, 1999; Elliott and Bender,

1997). In The Netherlands, public sector pays used to be centrally determined by the minister of the interior – after consultations with trade unions – and on the basis of private sector pay trends. The mid 1980s reforms, implemented over the following decade, legally ended this procedure, as well as a number of special privileges associated with civil service status (in the field of pensions and dismissal protection). The reforms also gave all public employees the right to strike and to collective bargaining for the determination of pay and working conditions (Visser and Hemerjijck, 1997, ch. 5).

Finally, in Spain, despite the continuous delays in the approval of an organic civil service statute, several pieces of legislation since the mid 1980s have determined the passage from a system in which pay and working conditions were regulated unilaterally, by legislative and administrative means, to one in which consultation and negotiations with trade unions have become increasingly important for civil servants, who are still the large majority of public employees.[6] However, until amendments were introduced in 1990 and 1994, the autonomy of the bargaining process was severely constrained, since all agreements had to be ratified away from the negotiating table. At the end of the 1990s, negotiating arrangements still have an ambiguous status compared with those in the private sector and controversy persists concerning the legal status of the *acuerdos* and *pactos* (Jódar et al., 1999:164, 185, 190–2).

Briefly, while since the mid 1960s there has been a general trend away from unilateralism to collective bargaining as the main method to regulate pay and conditions of employment, in some European countries rather large groups of public sector employees are still subject to methods other than free collective bargaining and, in a few cases, (especially France) the right to engage in collective bargaining has an uncertain status for all public employees.

Centralization versus decentralization: the level of bargaining

In industrial relations literature, the level at which collective bargaining takes place is often considered as the most important dimension which influences not only almost all other aspects of collective bargaining structure (for example, depth and scope), but also many features of union behavior and labor relations in general (union density, type of union government and distribution of power, strike behavior, and so on; see Clegg, 1976). In political science and economics literature, it has been often identified as one of the most relevant labor market institutional factors influencing national macroeconomic performance, especially in terms of the so-called "misery index," that is the sum of inflation and unemployment rates (Olson, 1982; Bruno and Sachs, 1985; Calmfors and Driffill, 1988; Soskice, 1990, among others).

In particular, Calmfors and Driffill (1988) have suggested, and partially tested, a hump-shape relationship between the degree of centralization in pay determination and macro-economic performance. According to their hypothesis, the best performers would be countries with very centralized or highly decentralized bargaining systems, since in both cases (although through different ways) the actors, and especially the trade unions, have incentives to internalize the costs of their wage demands in real terms. In a later review of this literature, Calmfors (1993) seems more skeptical about this relationship, and other scholars have stressed that not only the degree of centralization or decentralization but also the amount of coordination among the various levels of bargaining is very important (Soskice, 1990; see also below in this chapter).

In any event, the application of this model to the public sector requires significant qualification. The idea of "responsible" trade union behavior in decentralized systems is based on the assumption that individual employers are financially responsible for their firms and for their capacity to compete with other firms, which gives rise to a more or less direct trade-off between real wage increases and employment levels where bargaining takes place. But this is rarely the case in public services – unless very radical structural reforms in the financing and provision of services have been carried out, making each unit responsible for its own budget. This partly explains why the decentralization of collective bargaining in the public sector has been much less frequent and much more limited than is often suggested. It also explains why governments, anxious to reduce or contain public expenditures, often have found that they could control public sector wage costs more easily through a centralized system (at least in the short and medium term) even if, in principle, tight budget control is not incompatible with decentralized bargaining.

Britain offers an example of a movement towards more decentralized bargaining in the public services, but also of the difficulties which can be encountered in the process. In the private sector, there has been a highly decentralized system of collective bargaining since the 1970s, so it is not surprising that in a long and uninterrupted period in office the Conservative governments of 1979–97 strongly criticized the centralized system of public service pay determination and consistently advocated more decentralized collective bargaining. This objective was gradually accepted by many public service managers, but they remained critical of the inconsistencies in government policies, noting that the treasury believed that it could more easily control pay and expenditure through its influence on a national system than would be possible under a more decentralized one. Over the last fifteen years there has been a movement towards more decentralized collective bargaining, but the changes have been uneven and limited (Winchester and Bach, 1999).

The most decisive shift has been in the civil service. The traditional centralized and bureaucratic pay determination system and the unified salary structure covering almost half a million staff have been dismantled and replaced by "delegated bargaining" in more than a hundred "executive agencies" which are expected to develop their own grading, promotion and performance-related pay schemes. Elsewhere in the public services, the national systems of pay determination have proved to be remarkably resilient. While many allow a greater degree of flexibility and discretion for local managers, the pay of most public service employees is still decisively influenced by national systems. The extension of the pay review bodies to nurses and schoolteachers and the explicit public service pay restraint policies that have operated between 1992 and 1998, have both reduced the incentives for local managers to embark on the process of developing local pay structures.

Local employers have, however, been forced by budget constraints to reduce paybill costs through job losses and the reorganization and intensification of work. Thus, there has been a considerable decentralization of decision making concerning non-pay conditions of employment, such as the pattern of working time, the grading and skill mix of work groups and the use of fixed-term contracts. Managers have exercised the increased discretion offered by more flexible national agreements, sometimes after local agreement or consultation with trade union representatives, but often through unilateral decisions. A somewhat surprising conclusion may be drawn from the British experience: namely, that the radical restructuring of public service organization, tight expenditure controls and the extensive devolution of management authority may have reduced the incentives and perceived benefits of decentralized pay determination while facilitating greater flexibility in the pattern of non-pay terms and conditions of employment.

Public service collective bargaining in Italy, characterized by a higher degree of centralization, teaches a similar lesson. The current structure of collective bargaining is quite similar to that prevailing under the 1983 legal regime. The core of the system comprises national collective negotiations, every four years for normative issues and every two years for pay issues, divided into eight bargaining units corresponding to the main components of the public service (central government, local government, education, health and so on). After the 1993 reforms, managers have a separate bargaining unit in each sub-sector (some may be merged in the near future), so that in all, 16 national collective agreements are signed every two years, covering the 2.9 million "contractualized" public employees. This rather high degree of centralization is reinforced by the fact that all national negotiations are conducted, on the employer side, by an agency, ARAN, created by the 1993 reforms. ARAN is a "technical" or professional organization to which the law has given the role of compulsory representation of all public administrations at national level and, on request, also at the local level. Given the fragmentation of the Italian political system and the presence of large coalition governments, the creation of such an agency was designed to prevent the direct political interference in negotiations that had occurred frequently in the past. Apart from this attempt to de-politicize public sector labor relations, ARAN operates strictly within the guidelines and overall financial constraints set by central government, in accordance with the planned rate of inflation set in the state budget laws, although after a 1997 amendment some greater say has been given also to the associations of regional and local governments.

Collective bargaining is also allowed at local and individual unit levels, where it is supplemented by a dense network of information and consultation rights given to trade unions on some aspects of work organization and personnel matters. On pay issues, however, the 1993 law specifies that local bargaining must be restricted to the financial limits fixed at the national level, with little possibility to negotiate additional resources. Thus, most pay is determined centrally, up to a maximum of 95 percent in the education sector. Only at the end of 1997, did an amendment to the 1993 law provide some greater scope for decentralized (or "integrative") bargaining in individual administrative units, including the possibility to contribute with a certain amount of their own resources, within their budget constraints. But protection has also been included to prevent inflationary effects of decentralization over the total public sector pay bill.

In Italy, pay scales are quite similar over all the functional sub-sectors, with low wage differentials between grades, especially so in education. Given the same length of service and the same level in the job classification scheme, pay is usually rather uniform. The collective agreements since the 1993 reforms have tried to change this situation. They have frozen pay linked to the length of service, have encouraged more selective incentives for "collective productivity," and for the first time have allowed managers to partially differentiate the wages and salaries of their employees on an individual basis, through a rather modest system of merit pay (according to criteria agreed upon with trade unions). Despite these changes, at the end of the first four years' bargaining round after the reform, the amount of differentiation and individualization of pay seems very limited (Dell'Aringa, 1997b), while the merit pay system met several difficulties in implementation. There have been greater changes in national collective agreements for managers, however, agreements at local level linking pay more closely to performance have not always been implemented in an innovative way.

France and Germany have moved away to a much lesser degree from their traditional bargaining structure. France has perhaps the most centralized pay determination system in Europe. Since the 1983 reforms, annual negotiations over pay increases have taken place at a national level, between the government (the Ministry of Public Service) and the representative trade union confederations, covering simultaneously all three sub-sectors of the *Fonction Publique* (central government, local authorities and public hospitals). Thus, a single decision, taken at the central level, concerning the *points d'indice*, is applied to the common pay scales and job classification system, directly regulating the pay increases of 4.5 million public employees and indirectly affecting a million others. The recent pressures towards greater pay flexibility, individualization and performance-related pay, found in most other countries, have been very limited in France, although some attempts have occurred after the 1990 "Durafour agreement" to allow greater diversity in the wage and job classification system (Mossé and Tchobanian, 1999:142–4, 156).

The German bargaining system is perhaps a little less centralized, if only because of the separation between *Beamte* and other public employees, as well as because of the federalist constitutional structure of the state which gives the three levels of government autonomous rights in different policy areas. This potentially greater fragmentation, however, is not only compensated for by the tight coordination between and within the bargaining parties – highlighted in the next section (see below) – but also by the pivotal role which in the whole system of determination of pay and working conditions is played by the Minister of the Interior. At the federal level, since 1960 the minister has been responsible for safeguarding the public interest and must formally approve collective agreements. He not only leads the employers' bargaining committee in collective negotiations for wage earners and salaried employees, but also prepares legislation on remuneration and working conditions for *Beamte*, thus being in a focal position in the negotiation and determination of income for all public employees (Keller, 1999:71). As for the *Angestellte* and *Arbeiter*, moreover, on the workers' side the OTV (the largest German public sector union with its 1.6 million membership, affiliated to the main German confederation DGB) is the pattern setter for the whole public sector, so that wages and working conditions are settled in one annual round of negotiations for all public employees at the national, federal state and local levels (Keller, 1999:79). Finally, as in Italy and France, this high degree of centralization of the bargaining structure and of the regulation of employment relations is associated with a rather inflexible pay system, based on a purely collective and uniform character that leaves little or no room for links with individual performance.

The case of central government employees in Sweden has been quite different. Since the late 1980s, within central framework agreements between the government agency for negotiations (AgV) and trade unions which identify the scope for pay increases, the concrete determination of pay has been significantly decentralized to individual administrative units, and forms of individualization and performance related pay have been introduced, replacing the previous system which was based on very centralized pay and grading schemes. These changes have been accompanied by a structural reform in the financing of services, which establishes the principle of cash limits. Accordingly, more than 250 central government agencies receive "frame grants" for their total administrative costs, with no restrictions on how to use the grant for various items. Thus, a centralized control of the running costs of the agencies is pursued along with a devolution of managerial responsibilities in personnel matters (Schager and Andersson, 1996, 1999; Elliott and Bender, 1997).

The coordination of collective bargaining

It was noted earlier that the literature on collective bargaining sometimes conflates the concept of centralization with that of coordination.

If coordination is defined as the organizational capacity of trade unions and employers to aggregate and represent their members' interests and as the degree of consensus between the collective bargaining parties, then it will often be associated with centralization, but not necessarily so. In the private sector, "centralized" bargaining may be weakly coordinated, for example, where wage drift undermines the objectives of national negotiators; and, conversely, the outcomes of "decentralized" bargaining may be strongly coordinated where dominant employers and unions choose to cooperate (OECD, 1997:74). How can the concept of collective bargaining coordination be applied in a comparative analysis of the public services?

First, it is clear that countries with highly centralized levels of collective bargaining have less need for specific institutional or informal mechanisms of coordination than those with more decentralized systems. In France, for example, and also partly in Italy, the pay determination system is "essentially based upon the decisions taken by the political authority at the national level" (Dell'Aringa, 1997b:17; Dell'Aringa and Lanfranchi, 1999; and above). None the less, even in these countries (especially in Italy), the capacity of unions and employers to coordinate and represent their interests *vis-à-vis* central government (and specialized agencies, such as ARAN, in Italy) may have a significant impact on the acceptability of pay outcomes and thus, on the overall stability of the system, or its capacity for change (see above). The importance of coordination, however, can be seen most clearly in those countries that, in some respects, appear to have more decentralized systems of pay determination.

In Germany, the Basic Law of 1949 established a sophisticated division of political power between the federal government, federal states and local authorities, and separate legal systems of employment regulation for *Beamte* and salaried employees and wage-earners. Despite these sources of potential fragmentation, public sector pay determination is viewed almost universally as a centralized system because of the high degree of coordination of policies by both employers and trade unions. As Keller (1999) argues, intensive lobbying and other informal pressures allow the representatives of *Beamte* to minimize the practical consequences of the absence of a formal right to bargain; indeed, these processes, and the changes in pay and conditions of employment they achieve, often influence the bargaining agenda for the rest of the public services. The importance of coordination in German public service pay determination and the degree of consensus achieved within and between the employers' and unions' organizations, partly reflect the similar "corporatist" characteristics in the private sector, although there have been increasing tensions within both parts of the overall system in recent years.

The structure of collective bargaining in Denmark comprises formally separate bargaining rounds for the state and county/municipal sub-sectors. There is a complex structure of representation of employers' interests and, especially on the trade union side, many separate organizations based on affiliation with the three confederations, sub-sectoral location and occupational status of union members. The process of public sector reform – involving some degree of privatization and the devolution of management authority – has also proceeded further than in many other countries. The potential for fragmented or decentralized collective bargaining, however, has been avoided by the development of a very high degree of coordination amongst and between representatives of the government, employers and trade unions.

The bargaining process in the two sub-sectors is coordinated partly by the powerful role of the Minister of Finance in the state sector negotiations. These negotiations typically reach a potential settlement that acts as a framework for the county/municipal sub-sector. Moreover, all the parties involved in negotiations participate in an elaborate form of coalition bargaining, the purpose of which is to resolve conflicts of interest within the employers' and unions' sides as a prelude to a joint agreement. Similar processes can be found in some other countries – in Denmark they seem to be more elaborately developed and to enjoy a greater degree of legitimacy amongst the parties than elsewhere. While there have been a few challenges to the system of coor-dinated coalition bargaining (for example, the nurses' dispute in 1995), and some decentralization in bargaining over non-pay issues, the parties discourage separatist or fragmented actions by members and strengthen the pressures towards consensus through frequent informal contacts between elected representatives and senior professional staff (Andersen et al., 1999).

Finally, in the earlier discussion of levels of collective bargaining in Britain it was argued that outside the civil service, national systems of pay determination remain very important. Even though managers in individual health service and local authority organizations have the freedom to negotiate organization-specific pay and conditions agreements, very few have done so. The impact of the pay review body system, and the return of public service incomes polices in 1992 – after an absence of 12 years – partly explain the resilience of centralized bargaining, but also indicate the ways in which negotiations are structured and coordinated in Britain. Briefly, the pay increases recommended by the main review bodies – whose annual terms of reference typically require review body members to take account of the government's expenditure plans and anti-inflation target – help to establish a fairly predictable pattern of settlements elsewhere in the public services, especially in the health service and the education sector.

The agreements are not identical and, in the last two years, have become more varied, mainly in response to severe recruitment and retention problems for qualified nurses and schoolteachers. Moreover, the trade unions covered by traditional bargaining arrangements resent their frequent inability to match the review bodies' pay recommendations and the government's annual "incomes policy" aspirations. For most of the 1990s, the latter consisted of a paybill freeze, or a requirement that pay increases had to be offset by efficiency gains or improvements in productivity. In practice, although there were variations in agreements within and between the main sub-sectors, pay increases were around the level of price inflation, and below the level achieved in many parts of the private sector until 1999. This resulted from explicit central government intervention that structured and coordinated the pay determination processes. In comparison with the Danish case, however, there is little consensus within and between the separate bargaining parties. The system is inherently unstable and may generate more overt conflict unless the Labor government's plans to reform the bargaining system and pay principles can be implemented successfully over the next few years.

Concluding remarks

Only the most tentative conclusions can be drawn from this chapter as it reports on only one part of a larger program of research (see the chapters in this book by Keller and Due, and Bach and Della Rocca). The analysis has been limited mainly to a comparative analysis of the coverage, scope, levels and coordination of collective bargaining, although it tries to link these aspects of the structure of bargaining to the more general processes of public service reform in a number of West European countries. These wider issues complicate any attempt to place groups of countries into different categories, because it has to identify the distinctive characteristics of the groups and, at the same time assess the pace and direction of change in each country within the categories. Notwithstanding these difficulties, the following concluding comments can be made.

First, there does not appear to be a general and linear trend towards the decentralization of public service collective bargaining. The empirical evidence suggests that central governments are reluctant to delegate a significant degree of autonomy over pay determination to lower-level administrative units or individual public service employers, but more willing to allow decentralized decision making on other conditions of employment and working conditions. The most obvious explanation for the former is that government ministers believe that the control of overall wage costs (and thus, a large component of current public expenditure) is facilitated by centralized and coordinated collective bargaining, linked closely to centrally planned financial controls. In contrast, more decentralized decisions on other conditions of employment and working conditions may be explained by their potential contribution to the improvement in the efficiency and quality of service delivery – an objective shared by all governments and public service managers and by many trade union representatives, in the countries surveyed.

Second, although each country has a unique system of public service collective bargaining, they may be categorized in three broad groups that share some important common characteristics.

1. In France and Germany, a substantial proportion of public service employees have their pay set by unilateral state regulation, collective bargaining is highly centralized and coordinated (apart from its uncertain status in France), performance-related pay is almost unknown, and employment relations are shaped by a deeply rooted and legally regulated system of public administration – a fairly stable bureaucratic model that constrains proposals for innovation or reform.
2. In Britain and Sweden, very few public service employees have their pay set by unilateral state regulation, collective bargaining has become more decentralized, there has been sustained pressure and some movement towards a partial linking of pay to individual performance, and less deeply rooted traditions of civil service status and public administration have been eroded by fairly radical reorganization and the search for a New Public Management. In both countries these changes have been accompanied by structural reforms in the financing of services.
3. Italy and Denmark can be allocated to an intermediate and less coherent category in relation to 1 and 2. In both countries, few public service employees have their pay set by unilateral state regulation, pay determination is highly centralized and strongly

coordinated, but recent reforms may facilitate a process of "controlled" decentralization, and there have been modest attempts to link pay to measures of performance. In other respects, of course, the two systems are very different.

Finally, what can be said of the impact of the "common pressures" on public service employment relations identified in the introduction to this chapter? There is clearly no strong evidence of "convergence" between the different systems in the countries surveyed here, although some common developments can be detected. This is, of course, scarcely surprising. Most comparative analysis of national systems of industrial relations has found that some forms of convergence – arising from global market forces or the process of European integration – coexist alongside sharp differences and, sometimes, increasing diversity. If this is so for national systems as a whole – often dominated by sectors directly affected by the strategies of multinational companies – then it is even more likely that differentiation and continuing diversity may be found in the public services.

The evidence examined in this chapter offers qualified support for such a conclusion. While policy makers in each country face similar problems and have a greater knowledge of the reforms that have been implemented elsewhere, they are invariably constrained by distinctive features of the political, legal and institutional context in which they are located and by differing fiscal pressures. It seems that parts of the public services – in some, though not all countries – are moving closer to private sector systems of employment relations in some respects. It seems most unlikely, however, that a convergence between public and private sector collective bargaining will proceed very far in most countries, and the prospects for convergence between national systems of public sector collective bargaining are even more remote.

Notes

1. These two cases, of course, are not equivalent, since the last one certainly allows greater scope for pressures on the part of both actors (government and unions) and informal negotiations (see above, the text).
2. In some cases, however – as in Italy in the 1994–97 period (ARAN, 1998: 14–15) – wage increases for the not-contractualized public sector employees have been higher than those in the contractualized area.
3. Keller (1999:77) stresses that, although in most years the bargaining procedure for the salaried employees has fixed the agenda for the rest of public sector, this "is by no means an automatic sequence of events because of the

existence of two legally independent sub-systems of labor relations," and adds that in recent times some results have been different (like the postponement of salary increases for some months or the reintroduction of longer working hours for *Beamte* in some federal states) because it is still easier to introduce different conditions for *Beamte* "unilaterally instead of bargaining with unions whose consent may be difficult to obtain."

4. In Marsden's (1997) scheme, the system based on recommendations of independent pay bodies is classified at the opposite pole of collective bargaining on the axis representing the employees' influence on pay fixing. Perhaps this overestimates to some extent the difference between the two systems and assimilates too much the first one to government unilateral regulation, obscuring the possibility of influence also on the part of the unions.

5. Actually, the 1983 reform reserved to the law several aspects of the employment relationship (but not pay) and required that collective agreements be translated into a decree of the President of the Republic before being effective (see Treu, 1987, 1994).

6. This legislation includes: Ley de Medidas para Reforma del la Función Pública, 1984; Ley Órganica de Libertad Sindical, 1985; Ley de Órganos de Raprestención, Determinación del las Condiciones de Trabajo y Partecipación del Personal al Servicio de las Administraciones Públicas, 1987. Civil servants are still the large majority of all public employees despite the increasing number of people hired with ordinary employment contracts, for whom consultation and negotiation arrangements are governed by the same legislation as in the private sector.

References

Andersen, S. K., Due, J., and Masden, J. S. (1999) 'Denmark. Negotiating the restructuring of public service employment relations,' in Bach, S., Bordogna, L., Della Rocca, G., and Winchester, D. (eds.), *Public Service Employment Relations in Europe: Transformation, Modernization or Inertia?*, London: Routledge.

Andersen, S. K., Due, J., and Masden, J. S. (1997) 'Multi-track approach to public-sector restructuring in Europe: impact on employment relations; role of trade unions,' *Transfer*, III(1).

ARAN (1998) *Rapporto trimestrale sulle retribuzioni dei pubblici dipendenti*, Milano: Angeli.

Bazex, M. (1987) 'France,' in Treu, T. (ed.), *Public Sector Labor Relations: Recent Trends and Future Prospects*, Geneva: ILO.

Bean, R. (1994) *Comparative Industrial Relations*, London: Routledge.

Blenk, W. (1987) 'Germania Federale,' in ISAP (ed.), *Le relazioni fra Amministrazione e sindacati*, Milano: Giuffré.

Bordogna, L. (1993) 'Public sector labor relations between macro-economic constraints and union fragmentation. The Italian experience in a comparative perspective,' in IIRA, *Economic and Political Changes in Europe: Implications for Industrial Relations*, Bari: Cacucci.

Bordogna, L., Dell'Aringa, C., and Della Rocca, G. (1999) 'Italy. A case of coordinated decentralization,' in Bach, S., Bordogna, L., Della Rocca, G., and

Winchester, D. (eds.), *Public Service Employment Relations in Europe: Transformation, Modernization or Inertia?*, London: Routledge.
Bruno, M. and Sachs, J. (1985) *The Economics of Worldwide Stagflation*, Oxford: Blackwell.
Calmfors, L. (1993) 'Centralization of wage bargaining and macro-economic performance: a survey,' OECD, *Economic Studies*, (21).
Calmfors, L. and Driffill, J. (1988) 'Bargaining structure, corporatism and macroeconomic performance,' *Economic Policy*, (6).
Clegg, H. (1976) *Trade Unions under Collective Bargaining*, Oxford: Blackwell.
Dell'Aringa, C. (1997a) 'Pay determination in the Public Service: An International Comparison,' *Quaderni dell'Istituto di Economia dell'Impresa e del Lavoro*, (16), Milano: Università Cattolica.
Dell'Aringa, C. (ed.) (1997b) *Rapporto ARAN sulle retribuzioni, 1996*, Milano: Angeli.
Dell'Aringa, C. and Lanfranchi, N. (1999) 'Pay determination in the public service: an international comparison,' in Elliott, R., Lucifora, C., and Meurs, D. (eds.), *Public Sector Pay Determination in the European Union*, London: Macmillan – now Palgrave.
Elliott, R. and Bender, K. (1997) 'Decentralization and Pay Reform in Central Government: a Study of Three Countries,' *British Journal of Industrial Relations*, XXXV(3).
Guilhamon, J. (1989) 'La négociation des salaires dans les services publics,' *Droit Social*, (12).
Jódar, P., Jordana, J., and Alós, R. (1999) 'Spain. Public service employment relations since the transition to democracy,' in Bach, S., Bordogna, L., Della Rocca, G., and Winchester, D. (eds.), *Public Service Employment Relations in Europe: Transformation, Modernization or Inertia?*, London: Routledge.
Keller, B. (1999) 'Germany. Negotiated change, modernization and the challenge of unification,' in Bach, S., Bordogna, L., Della Rocca, G., and Winchester, D. (eds.), *Public Service Employment Relations in Europe: Transformation, Modernization or Inertia?*, London: Routledge.
Kochan, T. (1974) 'A Theory of Multilateral Bargaining in City Governments,' *Industrial and Labor Relations Review*, XXVII(4).
Lyon Caen, A. (ed.) (1993) *European Employment and Industrial Relations Glossary: France*, Dublin: European Foundation for the Improvement of Living and Working Conditions.
Marsden, D. (1997) 'Public service pay reforms in European countries,' *Transfer*, III(1).
Mossé, Ph. and Tchobanian, R. (1999) 'France. The restructuring of employment relations in the public services,' in Bach, S., Bordogna, L., Della Rocca, G., and Winchester, D. (eds.), *Public Service Employment Relations in Europe: Transformation, Modernization or Inertia?*, London: Routledge.
OECD (1993) *Pay flexibility in the Public Sector*, Paris: OECD.
OECD (1995) *Governance in Transition: Public Management Reforms in OECD Countries*, Paris: OECD.
OECD (1997) 'Economic performance and the structure of collective bargaining,' OECD *Employment Outlook*.
Olson, M. (1982) *The Rise and Decline of Nations*, New Haven: Yale University Press.

Schager, N. H. and Andersson, P. (1996) 'Recent Reforms within the Central Government Sector in Sweden with respect to Employment and Pay Policies,' discussion paper at ARAN Conference, Rome. Edited in Italian (1999) 'Recenti riforme del Governo centrale delle politiche del lavoro e delle retribuzioni nell'amministrazione pubblica in Svezia', in Dell'Aringa, C. and Della Rocca, G. (eds.), *Razionalizzazione e Relazioni Industriali nel pubblico impiego in Europa*, Milano: Angeli.

Soskice, D. (1990) 'Wage determination: the changing role of institutions in advanced industrialized countries,' *Oxford Review of Economic Policy*, VI(4).

Traxler, F. (1994) 'Collective bargaining: levels and coverage', OECD *Employment Outlook*.

Treu, T. (1994) 'La contrattazione collettiva nel pubblico impiego: ambiti e struttura,' *Giornale di Diritto del Lavoro e di Relazioni Industriali*, (61).

Treu, T. (ed.) (1987) *Public Sector Labor Relations: Recent Trends and Future Prospects*, Geneva: ILO.

Visser, J. and Hemerijck, A. (1997) *A Dutch Miracle*, Amsterdam: Amsterdam University Press.

Winchester, D. and Bach, S. (1999) 'Britain. The transformation of public service employment relations,' in Bach, S., Bordogna, L., Della Rocca, G., and Winchester, D. (eds.), *Public Service Employment Relations in Europe: Transformation, Modernization or Inertia?*, London: Routledge.

Windmuller, J. P. (1987) *Collective Bargaining in Industrialized Market Economies*, Geneva: ILO.

4
Employer Associations and Unions in the Public Sector

Berndt Keller, Jesper Due, and Søren Kaj Andersen

Introduction

Comparative and international industrial relations have been one of the major growth industries throughout the 1990s (Bamber and Lansbury, 1998; Ferner and Hyman, 1998; Van Ruysseveldt and Visser, 1996; Hyman and Ferner, 1994, among others). One amazing feature of these more recent trends has been the fact that public sector labor or employment relations have not played any major role in this comparative analysis although different kinds of information have been available from national levels and pressures for change and modernization have been increasing in all industrialized countries.

This obvious lack is the basic reason why we will focus, in general, on public sector issues and, in particular, on the present situation of corporate actors and their associations. We will not only include unions, but also management, employers and their associations in our institutionally oriented analysis. Related problems specific to collective bargaining and the most important form of interest representation and intermediation will be dealt with in other chapters. Central to our contribution will be the major changes in organizational policies and strategies and not the traditional and basic institutional characteristics. We will not be giving a detailed description of the well-known country-by-country base (Treu, 1987; Gladstone et al., 1989, Chapter 4; Bach et al., 1999). Our alternative is to deal with a set of common issues in order to analyze recent developments of convergence and divergence as well as some future prospects. For practical reasons we have to limit our study, with few exceptions, to the major Western European countries.

Public sector employers and their associations

Public sector unions, their organizational structures and recent problems have been on the traditional research agenda for quite some time. As in private industry, much less attention has been paid to employers and their representation of heterogeneous interests. There are several more or less convincing reasons why public sector employers and their associations have only rarely been dealt with and analyzed, at least in a comparative perspective.

First, compared with the private sector it is fairly complicated to identify exactly who is the public employer. The public sector is typically characterized by a complex diffusion of management responsibility which is very often closely related to constitutional or political divisions of public tasks and publicly provided goods and services. Within this sophisticated framework of division of power, the nature of the public employer is affected by different variables: political versus non-political decision-making, local versus central control, as well as the multiple funding sources of many public sector organizations (Beaumont, 1992; Ponak and Thompson, 1989).

Second, industrial relations theory has traditionally focused on three important and separate corporate actors: the state, employers (and their associations) and employees (including trade unions) (Dunlop, 1958). Looking at the public sector, the state (for example the treasury or ministry for internal affairs) is quite often the direct opponent and counterpart of trade unions in different fields of interest representation. In other words, the state undertakes what can be termed as a dual role: the state is both the actual employer of a still fairly high, although decreasing, number of public employees, as well as the key actor within the institutional and legal environment. Systems of collective bargaining and/or other, more unilateral, forms of interest representation operate under these specific conditions – and can be more or less drastically changed, not to say completely deregulated, by legal intervention. Another aspect of this dual role is that basic interests of political parties can exert a major influence on the way the state acts and fulfills its role as employer. This facet is most obvious when the counterpart of trade unions is a minister of the present government – for example the minister for internal affairs or the treasury. On the other hand, there is, as we shall see later, a rather clear distinction between the political system and the representation of public employers' interests in some countries. Altogether, this structure – at least not inside the scope of "traditional" industrial relations theory – creates a complex analytical frame of reference.

Third, it can be argued that in fairly decentralized systems (for example in the US, the UK or New Zealand) tasks and functions of associations seem to be fairly limited. In these cases individual employers and/or "their" management have traditionally been far more important for the establishment and governance of employment relations; encompassing organizations of employers are either overtly weak or do not exist at all. On the other hand, in more or less centralized systems (as in the majority of continental European countries) associations do not only exist but exert powerful influence in different forms of "multi-employer bargaining." Furthermore, there can be more or less significant differences between specific sub-sectors (for example, health, education, local and municipal government, central state) being reflected at the institutional level in the presence of different public employers, who do not necessarily coordinate their activities very well.

In private industry there are, at least in some continental European countries, voluntary business (or trade) associations as well as employers' associations for the representation of different, more general versus more specific, interests (Windmuller and Gladstone, 1984). They can be, at least in legal terms, completely independent of each other but cooperate closely at an informal level. This fundamental and peculiar structure, that favors a certain internal division of labor, does not, almost by definition, exist in the public sector. Here, on the other hand, the task of representation of economic interests in the "political marketplace" might be different from collective bargaining in the narrower sense. Because of differences in the sheer numbers of employers, there are greater needs for launching organizations at the local or municipal than at the federal or, if it exists at all, at the regional or intermediary level. Usually, these associations are, at least from a purely legal point of view but not necessarily in their day-to-day activities, completely independent of private sector employers associations and their confederations. In reality, however, at least some informal relationships are likely to exist.

The constitutional structure of nation states (centralization in France versus federalism in Germany or Spain, among others) and the political system with its separation of powers also exert a major impact on the formation of employers associations at different levels. The existence of a high degree of autonomy at the local and/or regional levels (as in Canada or Germany) favors the formation and existence of independent associations. This structure can be seen as an important element in explaining why the role of associations in France, for example, the association representing the municipalities, is quite weak in spite of the centralized industrial relations system.

The pure size of the country also seems to be a determinant of the organizational structure: larger countries (like Australia or Germany) seem to have a more differentiated structure consisting of three (local, regional, central) instead of two levels. Last but not least: in quite a few countries either some or even the major part of public employees have a special status (like *Beamte* in Germany or titular in France or a similar construction in Spain). These legal differences might also lead to organizational consequences for interest representation on the employers' side.

Centralized control versus decentralized flexibility

If we have a closer look at public sector employers' representation, we generally find that different associations exist according either to vertical and/or horizontal divisions of power. Associations organize either at different levels of administration (local, regional or federal state, and federal) or according to different tasks (like health, education, local and central administration and so on). The degree of autonomy from political interference from outside also varies between countries, levels of administration and overtime. Despite voluntary membership in the vast majority of countries, density ratios are very high and surpass those of the private industry to a considerable degree. For these voluntary associations a decrease in membership rates is a very rare event, in contrast to the union situation. Peak associations or confederations (of local and regional employers) which aggregate and mediate individual members' interests do exist.

In the northern part of Europe, for example in Germany, Denmark and the UK, these organizations have mandates and bargain collectively on behalf of their individual members (Germany with its traditional, basically unchanged system of nation-wide collective bargaining seems to be the prototypical case in that regard). The degree of formal and, probably even more importantly, informal coordination on the same, as well as between different levels and tasks varies and has changed over time. In the southern part of Europe, for example in France and Italy, the right to bargain on the employer side is centralized at national state level. This specific allocation of rights means that the peak associations representing local and regional employers are not directly involved in the processes of collective bargaining.

Centralization seems to be positively correlated with coordination. The "scope of bargaining" can also be more or less limited according to different levels of administration or functions and tasks. All in all, the degrees of centralization on both sides of the bargaining table are not independent from each other. Centralization on the union side favors and stimulates similar developments and structures of employers (and improves the opportunities of all kinds of corporatist arrangements). Negotiated agreements are binding for members on both sides of "industry."

One could, of course, argue that the overall picture of decentralized versus centralized systems of public employer representation is more blurred than we have suggested so far. It is still reasonable to argue that the patterns of public employer interests are more fragmented in the UK than in, for example, Germany and Denmark. On the other hand, we have recently observed different mergers and amalgamations in Australia, New Zealand and the UK. In the UK, three different associations representing local government employers formed the Local Government Association (LGA) in the spring of 1997.[1] In the UK the representation of employers' interests in the health service has been problematic. The split between purchasers and providers of service, which used to be one of the basic reform ideas of the Conservative government throughout the 1980s and in the beginning of the 1990s, caused the development of rival employers' organizations (Winchester and Bach, 1999). However, also in this case a merger took place at the beginning of 1997 and the National Health Service Confederation was formed.

Furthermore, we should mention that the decentralization of employment relations in the UK initiated by different Conservative governments from 1979 to 1997 did not, in contrast to widespread expectations, cause an overall fragmentation of the process of pay determination in the public sector. On the contrary, the "national salary structures, grading and employment practices have survived the pressures towards devolution and fragmentation" (Winchester and Bach, 1999). At least, parts of the industrial relations system in the UK public sector seem to be surprisingly stable.

On the other hand, there is evidence for the suggestion that some of the national industrial relations systems, which have often been referred to as centralized systems, have introduced different versions and forms of decentralization in regulating at least some parts of their employment relations. These ongoing processes of decentralization are closely related to a devolution of responsibility taking place in the public sectors in several countries. The reshaping of organizations and management has been most evident in the UK. An important element in this process has been the devolution of management authority

(Winchester and Bach, 1999). The same trends can be identified in continental European countries although their scale and content differ. In the cases of Sweden, Denmark and Italy it can be argued that devolution of management authority has been followed partly by the decentralization of employment relations.

In Sweden, the most popular example, collective agreements covering central government are framework agreements. Agreements concluded at the central level do not stipulate increases in pay rates but pay kitties which then have to be negotiated at the decentralized level. Looking at terms and conditions, one example of decentralization is an agreement from 1995 that delegates the responsibility of regulating the volume of working time to the agency level. Again certain standards have been agreed upon at the national level, but more specific problems must be dealt with at the decentralized level (Schager and Andersson, 1996, 1999).

Denmark has experienced the development of a similar pattern. The most radical step towards decentralization was taken in the spring of 1997 when the social partners agreed to launch a process to reform the public sector pay system. Although there are some differences of opinion, it seems likely that 15–25 percent of the total wage sum will be negotiated at the decentralized level in a not so distant future. Certain questions concerning job function (responsibility), qualifications and performance will be key questions in bargaining processes at the decentralized levels. The reform can be perceived as a show-down – as a determination to dismantle the automatic, seniority-based pay increment system (Andersen et al., 1999).

To a certain degree collective agreements settled at national level in Italy can be characterized as framework agreements too. The consequence is that within the framework (of budgetary constraints and other limits set by the national agreement) bargaining can take place at the local level. Those topics that are negotiated at the decentralized level will typically cover internal and external mobility measures, vocational training and, most importantly, the definition and management of systems designed to encourage and increase collective and individual productivity. This includes the definition of merit pay (Bordogna et al., 1999).

These recent processes in Sweden, Denmark and Italy cannot, however, be interpreted as a unilinear development towards fragmentation of industrial relations systems, or in line with this the fragmentation of employers' interests. Rather, we have witnessed processes of "organized decentralization" (Traxler, 1995) or "centralized decentralization"

(Due et al., 1994). The basic idea behind both concepts is as follows. The necessity to introduce more "flexibility" at the decentralized level has initiated processes that are, at least to a certain extent, under the control of the national level. This development puts new emphasis on "enterprise bargaining" and, thus, on public employers at the decentralized levels. They have to meet new demands concerning management, including the ability to be part of bargaining processes at the decentralized level.

In spite of these recent trends towards decentralization it seems obvious that centralized structures of public employer representation tend to prevail. The need for a certain degree of control at the national level could be the driving force behind maintaining a pattern of, or even a new tendency towards, centralization of employers' interests. A rather high degree of overall fiscal discipline is easier to maintain within continued centralization. These signs of centralization typically develop along two different paths: either by the organization of employer interests at the central government level (for example, in the ministry of interior or of finance or in a specific ministry for public services) or by creating government-related agencies which represent the employer interests of the state, at an "arms-length" distance from the political system. In the first case, central government clearly plays a dual role as the prominent public sector employer as well as (part of) the body being in charge of the overall policy making.

Countries following the first path are, among others, France, Germany, Spain and Denmark. The two agencies for government employers, Agenzia per la Rappresentanza Negoziale delle Pubbliche Amministrazioni (ARAN) in Italy and Arbetsgivar Verket (AgV) in Sweden, are examples of countries following the second path. The aim of this centralization of employer interests is obviously to control the wage bill of the entire public sector (Andersen et al., 1997).

One of the major problems first of all, but not only, in more centralized systems is the effects of recent processes of decentralization on associations and their policies. How do these associations manage to coordinate widely differing interests under changed economic and political circumstances? Do they play the major role in these processes of restructuring and modernization of different parts of the public sector, or are they more or less separated and isolated from these changes? Is there a certain loss of power and/or a shift in influence on one or both sides? Significant differences have to be expected because, in an empirical perspective, trends of decentralization can take various forms in both sectors. Problems common to different countries, such as increases in efficiency, cost effectiveness or introduction of HRM and personnel policies, might have different results and answers because of legal and institutional preconditions.

Initiating change and modernization

It can be taken for granted that public employers and not trade unions have become the "prime mover" also in the public sector. The most important reasons are deteriorating economic and financial conditions, increased by the requirements of the European Monetary Union, and the need to modernize most parts of the national public sectors and to achieve greater efficiency. The broad post-World War II political consensus on the welfare state and the necessity and usefulness of a certain size of its public sector have been challenged for economic as well as ideological reasons in almost all countries. With the exception of New Zealand, the UK is again the most prominent example (Winchester and Bach, 1995). Nowadays, public employers act more like their counterparts in the private industry than in the "golden age" of the 1960s and 1970s when they were considered as "model employers" setting positive examples not only for their own organizational domain but also for different parts of private industry. They were even referred to as the ideal of the state, the "employer of last resort." Among their more recent strategies we find privatization and marketization in their different forms. Quite general trends in the Anglo-Saxon world are attempts to introduce "the market" or elements of it into the public services. A radical solution in this sense is to privatize not only nationalized industries but different parts of the public services. Throughout Western Europe, telecommunications, postal services, railroads as well as different services provided at the regional or local level (such as rubbish collection, cleaning or public transport) are among the most prominent examples. Scopes and forms of privatization differ significantly from country to country (from preserving some sort of public control to selling shares to individuals). Again, the UK has definitely taken the lead, especially in contrast to the Scandinavian countries which have been much more hesitant and reluctant.

Strategies of marketization differ between countries and may include instruments such as contracting out and market testing, the introduction of internal markets, user surveys, competitive tendering and so on. More recently, alternative modes of regulation (like public–private partnerships, "make or buy decisions") have been discussed as alternatives of strict privatization.[2] There is a major gap between rhetoric and implementation of measures and steps. Empirical results on the consequences and results of privatization are somewhat mixed and do not prove the overall, ultimate advantage of the neo-conservative and neo-liberal blueprint. Unions that are directly challenged by these strategies have more or less strictly opposed these approaches of selling the "family silver."

The introduction of different New Public Management strategies especially (but not only) at the local and municipal level has constituted another characteristic feature. These tentative attempts to introduce private-sector like principles and instruments entail processes of trial and error with uncertain, uncontrollable ends and results. Interestingly enough, these forms of "new managerialism" have often been initiated by individual employers or their management with next to no coordination by their associations. From an industrial relations perspective, their consequences are not at all clear. On the one hand, one could convincingly argue that we have experienced a decentralization of organizational structures as well as a devolution of management authority and responsibility, but not necessarily of collective bargaining structures. Individualized employee relations are supposed to supplement, in some countries (such as New Zealand) even substitute, collective labor relations – at least for major groups of public employees. On the other hand, some tendencies toward centralization can also be observed (that is, during the implementation of performance-related pay). The crucial issue is that not all employment conditions must necessarily be determined at the level at which collective bargaining takes place. Furthermore, "new managers" are not employers, but employed by public employers. Various demands for more "flexibility" have been put forward not only by private but also by public employers in almost all countries. The systems of collective labor relations are considered to be highly inflexible, bureaucratic, rigid and resistant to all kinds of change and modernization, and so on. "Flexibility" is a very loose concept that consists, of course, of different dimensions and includes functional (change of tasks, organization of work, quantity and quality of training) as well as numerical (smaller number of employees) and financial (stagnating or lower wages and salaries) components. The exact targets of such encompassing political demands are not always clear.

Recent debates on flexibility have also included civil servants and their special employment status. Public employers have repeatedly argued that the specific rights civil servants enjoy – although there are differences in employment conditions between, for example, *Beamte* in

Germany, *fonctionaire* in France and *tjenestemænd* in Denmark – have become barriers to more far-reaching flexibility within the workplace. In Italy the civil servant status was more or less abolished in 1993 and replaced by a contractualization of employment conditions; this step has often been referred to as the "privatization" of employment relations (Bordogna et al., 1999). In Denmark the number of public employees with civil servant status has been reduced over the last decade. Public sector employer policy has been to limit the number of employees with civil servant status, with the aim of establishing agreement-based employment as the norm. This plan only excludes some groups employed, for example, in the police force and the armed forces (Andersen et al., 1999). In contrast to these trends the number of *Beamte* in Germany and *fonctionaire* in France respectively are, despite opposing political rhetoric, fairly stable or even slowly increasing (Keller, 1999; Mossé and Tchobanian, 1999). Spain, however, seems to be the major exception to the general rule (Jódar et al., 1999).

There have been political plans and some initiatives have been taken in order to deregulate either specific sub-sectors (health, railroads or the postal service) or major areas of employment relations (employment security or even life-long employment), different strategies of qualitative as well as quantitative forms of flexibilization including, among others, more use of part time, usually covering a higher percentage of employees than in the private industry, and different forms of atypical or even precarious employment such as limited contracts or temporary work. The more recent introduction of private-sector like HRM/NPM strategies points in the same direction – apart from the British experience; however, the scope of these initiatives remains uncertain. It seems as if political rhetoric is more far-reaching than everyday practice. All in all, deregulation and flexibilization contribute to a certain degree of decentralization. However, the effective implementation of all these changes will take much longer than expected.

At the same time it is obvious that the scope and pace of change differ between sub-sectors; there might even be some trans-national patterns in these differences. There has been, and still is, a lot of focus on the health sector, and especially hospitals, in Western European countries. Because of medical and technical developments more and more people can be treated for still even more illnesses. The health sector is a labor-intensive sector and the introduction of new technology does not result in reductions in the number of staff. Financial problems and constraints must be seen as important motives for the employer to introduce changes in the organizational structures, organization of work, and so on. The creation of "internal markets" in the NHS in UK, the *"aziendalizzazione"* (hospitals operating like companies) in Italy and the *"contractualization"* of the financial relations between the single hospital and the regional health authorities in France are all typical examples of attempts to introduce competition as well as market-like conditions in the health sector. There is also evidence that these initiatives influence working conditions in certain ways (Winchester and Bach, 1999; Bordogna et al., 1999; Mossé and Tchobanian, 1999).

The outcome of these reforms suggests a much more complex picture of who is actually the "employer" in the hospital sector. This is due to the devolution of managerial responsibility where the policy outcome seems to be the strengthening of both regional authorities and of the management at the hospital level, whereas politicians at the national level are still very much in control of budgets and overall priorities in the health sector. It appears to be an inevitable result of this development that many actors operating at different levels are taking part in the role of being the "employer" in the hospital sector.

In the school sectors throughout Western Europe, however, changes are fewer. In Italy a law from 1997 gives the school unit much more financial and administrative autonomy and also seeks to strengthen the managerial role of the school principal. However, the actual outcomes of the reform are still to be seen. In various countries different initiatives have been introduced such as establishing user boards (in Denmark), an increase in the competency of the user boards/governing bodies (in the UK) and decentralization of the responsibility in school buildings for maintenance and technical facilities (in France). However, the impact of these initiatives on teachers' working conditions seems to be limited – except, perhaps, for developments in the UK (Andersen et al., 1999; Department for Education 1993; Mossé and Tchobanian, 1999).

Even though the general pace of change might not be dramatic, developments over the last couple of decades appear to have opened the doors for different kinds of consultancies in the process of modernizing or restructuring, for example administrative units inside the public sector. This phenomenon might not be completely new. There is evidence, however, for the assumption that different kinds of external consultancies in cooperation with public employers today play a key role in initiating and implementing processes of modernization and restructuring. It seems that these consultancies are in a position to become even more influential actors in defining employment conditions in the broadest sense at the workplace level.

Consultancies involved are organizations directly linked to public employers or private, independent firms. One example of a consultancy linked to public employers is the Kommunale GemeinSchaftstelle für Verwaltungsvereinfachung (KGSt, 1993), a joint establishment of German municipalities and cities, that focuses on the modernization of local government administration. KGSt has developed new, so-called steering concepts (*Neue Steuerungsmodelle* – NSM), which include the devolution of responsibility for resources, budgeting, product definition, external competition, internal comparisons, and so on (Keller, 1999). The content of NSM links this concept of modernization to the patterns of New Public Management (Reichard, 1997). Although KGSt is a fairly old organization, established in 1949, it has experienced rapid development in the 1990s – especially developing consultancy services. Like KGSt in Germany, the Local Government Management Board (LGMB) in the UK is connected to the local government employers, although its services are somewhat different. In Denmark the local government employers (KL) have developed their own consultancy unit throughout the 1990s. Apart from these consultancies related to public employers it seems clear that, in many European countries, we have been witnessing a blooming industry of private consultancies selling their services to public sector authorities.[3]

Regarding social dialogue, the intervention of consultants in public sector workplaces can follow at least two different tracks. Either agreements on the process of modernization will be concluded between management and employees (that is their interest representation) or changes will be implemented unilaterally by the management in more or less close cooperation with their consultants. The development evidently moves along both tracks in Western European countries. It is part of the overall picture that there are collective agreements and/or legislation in certain countries (for example Denmark and Germany) which will force management to inform about and discuss certain initiatives on modernization in joint committees.

Considering these tendencies toward both decentralization and centralization a somewhat conflicting picture emerges. Initiatives to modernize or restructure are very much linked to processes of decentralization or devolution of managerial responsibility (OECD, 1995, 1996). Increased efficiency, better quality of services, ability to meet new customer needs, and so on, are all relatively new elements that should be met by management at the decentralized level. These initiatives could generate the introduction of new management strategies and new ways of work organization, offering vocational training and different sorts of further training for public employees and the use of newly introduced enumeration methods (that is, performance related pay) as part of personnel policies.

At the same time, however, decentralization does not constitute a universal or unilateral trend. It is obviously possible to decentralize certain layers (such as management authority) leaving others (the structure of collective bargaining) basically untouched. Furthermore, decentralization is also quite different from complete fragmentation that could emerge and take on different degrees. A more or less complete fragmentation of so-called "bargaining units" has hardly taken place (probably except for New Zealand and, to a certain degree, Australia); more or less cautious attempts to decentralize have been more frequent. Individual employment contracts that are a part of individualized employee relations are still the rare exception in the majority of countries.

How do individual employers and their associations handle this rather ambivalent situation? Is it possible to restructure (at least some parts of) the public sector and, at the same time, meet financial constraints and restrictions? The immediate answer seems to be "no": Retrenchment measures create unfavorable preconditions for employment relations and dominate, at least for the time being, processes of reform and modernization. The basic problem is that steps of modernization are difficult to achieve under conditions of frozen or even shrinking public budgets.

Trade unions

We have argued above that the characteristics of the public employer differ in many aspects from their private sector counterparts. On the other hand, the patterns of trade union structure in the public sectors tend to mirror the organizational pattern found in the private sectors of the individual countries. As we will show later, there are some important exceptions.

Apart from the questions of organizational structure there are some distinct features for public sector trade unions.

In comparison with the private industry it is significant that a higher proportion of women are employed in the public sector throughout the industrialized countries. In general, half of the employees are women ("feminization of the labor force"). In some specific subsectors, for example hospitals and schools, among others, a vast majority of employees are women (Bach et al., 1999). Another characteristic feature is that a majority of public sector staff are employed in white-collar and professional occupations. It is part of their history that, at least in some countries (the UK or New Zealand), many of the organizations nowadays representing these groups grew out of professional associations. Traditionally they had privileged professional concerns about status, service quality and the ability to influence state policy rather than giving priority to the improvement of terms and conditions of employment. Still, professional concerns remain prominent in many public service unions representing teachers, nurses, postal workers, police officers and fire service personnel (Ozaki, 1990). Consequently, teachers in Western Europe are frequently organized into separate trade unions. Prominent examples are GEW in Germany, SNALS in Italy, and FEN and FSU in France. In general, organization on the basis of occupation has remained a more durable characteristic in the public rather than in the private sector (Bach, 1999).

In a broader perspective on trade unions, there are some well-known differences in the organizational patterns which embrace both the public and the private sector: trade union structures and principles of organization differ widely between, as well as within, countries along industrial, occupational or craft, ideological or political, and sub-sectoral lines. These differences lead to various, centralized versus decentralized union policies. Quite different principles can coexist within the same country and organizational fragmentation can reach a considerable degree in relation to the private industry; competition or rivalry for members occurs to a certain extent in quite a few countries, just as the existence of different confederations and/or independent organizations (Italy, France or Spain) is likely. There are unions which organize exclusively in the public sector and unions with overlapping memberships between both sectors.

As already mentioned above, in the vast majority of countries the general organizational pattern of the private industry is, at least to a certain and frequently high degree, mirrored in the public sector. However, it is not the sheer number of organizations that is of importance for the overall performance but the form and shape of their explicit and implicit cooperation or conflict within a highly fragmented structure. Generally speaking, principles and formal structures of organization should not be overestimated because actual relationships between associations can differ to a large degree.

Different levels of public administration (local and municipal, regional or federal state, in some cases only federal or central administration) and/or sub-sectors (education, health, local and central government) can also be of major importance for the organizational structure of trade unions. If this is the case, formal and even informal coordination of intra-union activities will be necessary but more difficult to achieve. Internal fragmentation is, for obvious quantitative reasons, usually higher at the local than at the regional and federal state or central level. The question of principle of representation (single or exclusive versus multiple or plural) is of crucial importance – and has found different answers between, as well as within, countries.

Legal and actual forms of interest representation, that is collective bargaining (as in private industry) versus more unilateral decision-making by management, individual employers and employers' associations, vary from country to country as well as over time. They create certain, more or less rigid, restrictions for different union activities. Quite frequently there is special legislation governing labor relations and creating legal differences in the status of either all public employees or of selected groups (like civil servants), who quite frequently (as in Germany) can organize into separate interest associations. They do not always have the status of unions in the strict sense of the term, for example they are not allowed to bargain collectively (or at least not about the entire agenda) or to go on strike. Instead of bilateral decision making they have to rely on lobbying politicians and the public. Therefore, and interestingly, dividing lines of bilateral versus unilateral decision-making are more common within the public sector than between the public and the private sector.

Limitations on the right to strike and other forms of industrial action exist in almost all countries, either according to specific core functions (for example police officers, military personnel, fire fighters or doctors and nurses, among others) or to special collective status (like *Beamte*). The justification for this "undemocratic" restriction of individual rights has always been the same in different countries, that is the urgent necessity to provide, without interruption, certain indispensable goods and services to the general public (Ozaki, 1990). The limiting impact of union strategies and opportunities of action is fairly obvious. With few occasional exceptions (Australia or New Zealand in the 1990s) the public sector has traditionally been less strike prone than private industry. If strikes happen at all they are more likely to take place at the municipal or local than at the federal or regional level.

In contrast to a growing number of branches within private industry, unions do exist in all major parts of national public sectors (for example education, health, police, general and local administration, and so on). There are no "union-free" zones in the public sector; the principle of "freedom of association" in both, the positive and the negative sense, does not only exist but also is widely recognized and respected by management and employers. Density ratios, which can vary between sub-sectors, usually are as high or, in the vast majority of countries, even significantly higher than in the private sector (Visser, 1990). They have, in the turbulent times of the 1980s and 1990s with declining overall density ratios and privatization of different parts of the public sector, been more stable than those in private industry (the US and New Zealand are not unexpectedly, prototypical examples). There is evidence from EU member states that the huge gap between public and private sector density ratios widened in the first half of the 1990s (EIRR, 1998).

At first glance, these impressive ratios, being higher than those in private industry, are remarkable for different reasons: the percentage of female and part-time employees has significantly increased. To a certain degree public employers make use of the opportunities of different forms of atypical employment or contingent work, such as fixed-term contracts. All these groups are, according to our general wisdom and knowledge, rather difficult to organize. Among the various factors favoring unionization in the public sector are:

- less resistance from individual public employers than from their counterparts in major branches of private industry, partly explained by the fact that public sector managers are themselves unionized
- therefore, fewer disadvantages to be expected because of union membership (lower opportunity costs)
- active participation of unions in different processes of hiring, promotion, organization of work, and so on probably providing individual advantages of membership
- the fact that many public sector employees are employed in individual large-sized undertakings

In contrast to the private industry in some countries, problems of recognition and/or decertification or repeal of union registration provisions hardly exist. Coverage rates, which should not be confused with density ratios, are fairly high and higher than in the private industry in all countries studied in this context (Traxler, 1996). In the public sector, unions have been widely recognized not only as equal partners for traditional collective bargaining but also for other, more or less formalized forms of cooperation and participation with government agencies at the workplace level.

Specific channels of employee participation in workplace decision-making exist in some countries, especially in those with so-called dual systems of interest representation (Germany). Different rights of participation at the workplace level, ranging from informal information and consultation to strict co-determination, challenge and limit the otherwise existing "managerial prerogatives" on quite different issues. Furthermore, joint or consultative committees (staff councils) can be established on a binding-legal or voluntary-contractual base and can be formally independent from existing trade union and collective bargaining structures at the upper level. A clear division of responsibilities and duties between both levels has to be established.

In Western Europe unions have been integrated partners of rather stable and, at least in the majority of countries (as in the Scandinavian countries and Germany), fairly cooperative systems of labor relations for many years. Even though systems of collective bargaining or consultation differ significantly throughout Western Europe, mutual recognition and trust prevail. The established balance of power is apparently stable, ideological warfare (as can be seen in the UK and France) is the exception. Various systems of dispute settlement are fairly sophisticated. Different forms of conciliation and mediation, including combinations of both, are more frequent than interest arbitration (Norway seems to be the major exception; Keller, 1997).

Coping with change

Some national unions have managed to coordinate their demands implicitly or explicitly in order to overcome a certain degree of fragmentation. External conditions of interest representation and its success or failure have significantly changed since the 1980s. Wages and salaries have, to some extent, been replaced as the main subjects of collective bargaining by management-introduced issues such as privatization, modernization and flexibilization. As in the private industry, these changes have contributed to the relative deterioration of the conditions of employment. In different countries major reasons have been, among others:

- tighter public budgets on all levels, but especially at the local and municipal level, and increasing public debts
- growing unemployment in general creating indirect pressure also on public sector employment relations

88 Strategic Choices in Reforming Public Service Employment

- not only zero growth rates, but even more or less severe retrenchment in different parts of public sector employment, formally being considered as a "good" employer providing fair wages and a considerable degree of job security for its employees as well as "the employer of last resort"
- more or less strictly organized and implemented privatization measures for parts of the former public sector.

How have the unions tried to cope with these new conditions and changed circumstances? Have they rejected plans to reform and modernize? Have they, one way or another, tried to participate in the decision-making processes about modernization and restructuring of their parts of the public sector or even tried to take the lead? Have they changed not only their strategies but also their organizational structures in order to adapt to the patterns of change?

Significant differences between countries are obvious. Looking at initiatives in order to restructure employment relations in the public sector, trade unions have played various roles. We draw a somewhat rough picture, mentioning only examples of trade union positions and responses, which cluster into three different trends.

First, over the last decade trade unions in the Scandinavian countries have taken part in reforms of the public sector in different ways. Martin (1996) characterizes the responses of Scandinavian trade unions as a "twin-track-approach." On the one hand, they seek to preserve workplaces and to promote reasonable development in pay and working conditions, while, on the other hand, they concede that reforms are necessary. Thus, they are prepared to launch dialogues on related issues. One example of the readiness to reform employment relations was the Danish 1997 agreement that included a reform of the public sector pay system. Public sector trade unions agreed to replace the automatic, seniority-based pay increments by a system in which pay more accurately reflects qualifications and performance of each employee, or group of employees. At the same time, this system includes bargaining at decentralized levels. The overall aim is to create a more flexible pay system, which in turn can be regarded as a necessary prerequisite to modernize the public sector (Andersen et al., 1999).

However, not only in the Scandinavian countries are unions prepared to conclude far-reaching agreements aimed at reforming employment relations. In Italy, in 1993, trade unions took active part in and supported major reforms of the collective bargaining structure, the change of employment status (the so called "privatization", for example, contractualization of public employment), the strengthening of the management prerogative, and so on (Bordogna et al., 1999). Several reforms supplement this pattern of change in public sector employment relations. An agreement signed in 1998 redefines the job classification system and introduces a system of pay incentives for employees of local public bodies. Likewise, pay incentives are part of an agreement from 1999 covering teachers. Both agreements include steps towards decentralized bargaining.

Focusing not only on the public sector, but also on trade union policies in general, several unions in Europe, for example in The Netherlands and Italy, have become still more involved in economic and social policy decisions. In The Netherlands there has been a renaissance of the so-called "consultation economy" (Van den Toren, 1998), and in Italy the social partners agreed upon "social pacts" both in 1993 and in 1998 (EIRO, 1999).

Second, in countries like Germany and partly France, trade unions have cautiously argued in favor of the need to modernize (Keller, 1999; Mossé and Tchobanian, 1999). However, major reforms of public sector employment relations have not been achieved in recent years. In Germany, OTV has been arguing for the need to modernize the public sector since the late 1980s. A campaign called "shaping the future through public services" (*"Zukunft durch öffentliche Dienste"*) was enshrined in the idea to unify the interests of public service users, staff and unions. Effects of the campaign have been rather limited both due to problems in integrating this triangle of differing, sometimes even opposing, interests and to the sudden process of unification. In spite of these unexpected problems the campaign was relaunched in 1995, but in a more decentralized version (Keller, 1999). The introduction and step-by-step implementation of new steering models by KGSt is one of the more prominent examples of modernization in Germany. After hestitating for a period the dominant public sector trade union, OTV, has started dialogues with KGSt about the implementation of these new steering models. Among other things, the dialogue has led to joint seminars and different publications.

In France certain unions expressed their willingness to discuss and negotiate modernization plans, while others basically rejected the idea of entering these discussions. Confédération française du travail (CFDT) and the union of teachers, Fédération de l'éducation nationale (FEN), are examples of unions prepared to negotiate on the need for modernization. However, at the same time the issue of modernization gave rise to severe internal conflicts, and consequently led to splits.

The new and more "radical" organizations, Solidaires, Unitaires et Démocratique (SUD) and Fédération syndicale unitaire (FSU), broke from CFDT and FEN respectively. The overall outcome is that major reforms of employment relations have not been initiated in France in recent years (Mossé and Tchobanian, 1999).

From one point of view, developments in Spain can be linked to the situation in Germany and France, although Spain has been going through a particular development since the reintroduction of democracy in the post-Franco years. One result is that the regulation of public sector employment relations has been transferred from a system almost entirely based on legislative and administrative means to one shaped by consultation or negotiation procedures. Policies of reform or modernization of public administration have been focused on the quality and costs of public services. Achievements have only partially been studied (Jódar et al., 1999). Still, trade unions have kept arguing that "modernization" to a large extent has meant that power has been concentrated in the hands of a "managing élite", whereas problems caused by "archaic" organizational systems and procedures and lack of efficiency have not been addressed in a proper way (Martin, 1996).

Third, throughout the 1980s and the first half of the 1990s, conservative governments introduced major reforms in the UK public services. The unions, however, took no part at all in planning or implementing these reforms. On the contrary, in that period it was an integral part of government policies to reduce and curtail the influence and power of trade unions. After Labor won the general election in the spring of 1997 there have been signs that the pattern of development will be different in the future. However, reforms have not been reversed by the Labor government. On the contrary, it seems that a policy of incremental change has been adopted. As a consequence of the development over the last couple of decades trade unions have generally been absent in the processes of reforming public sector employment relations. One of the few exceptions has been the reform of the bargaining structure in local government. In 1997 trade unions and the local government employers' association (LGA) concluded the so-called single-status agreement that established a single national bargaining council, unified the national terms and conditions manual and established a single national pay structure for 1.5 million manual and non-manual employees (Winchester and Bach, 1999).

Taken together, these selected examples of trade union positions and responses suggest that their roles in reforming and modernizing Western Europe's public sectors have developed along rather different lines – from one of direct involvement to a role where the unions "seek involvement" or "push initiatives" to a position of direct conflict and marginalization of unions. The reasons for these differences are varied and complex. Some of the answers can be found in the structural characteristics mentioned above. However, deeply rooted traditions of either cooperation and consensus or of conflict and antagonism between employers and employees as well as patterns of rivalry or unity inside and between national unions also play an important role in the overall picture.

As mentioned above, strategies of so-called union avoidance rarely exist in the public sector, while, at the same time, different forms of participation seem to gain in importance. It should be noted that entering discussions on public sector reforms also means that trade unions take part in the overall discussion on the future of the welfare state. Consequently, the traditional trade union issues, pay and working conditions, become part of a much broader agenda of political action. This strategy of development tends to have major impacts on the whole structure of trade unions: they need professionalized secretariats, including research units, that enable them to participate in these discussions in a well-informed and professional manner. Furthermore, they need to be prepared to give priority to welfare issues, leaving aside the more specific interests of their members.

The adoption of such strategies has serious implications for trade unions. On the one hand, it can be held that this is a necessary development for the unions if they are to avoid marginalization. On the other hand, such involvement will strike some observers as the adoption of employer-led strategies by trade unions – a move which many union members could find difficult to digest. Experience from the Scandinavian countries as well as from Italy and France (see above) shows that trade unions which take part in the formulation and implementation of modernization plans often are faced with heated internal debates on policy strategies.

Outlook

It seems as if formerly existing major differences between private and public sector employment relations have been fading over the last one to two decades. Furthermore, management and individual employers have become the dominant actors or "prime movers" in the vast majority of countries we analyzed. They have launched and vigorously supported processes of modernization and restructuring of different parts of the public sector. Multilayered techniques of New Public Management have, without a doubt, gained in importance. In most countries, however, the change of corporate actors has been of an incremental nature. Interestingly enough, associations of public employers have become much less the focus of political debates and administrative processes, if they exist at all. Within the ongoing processes of decentralization of employment relations they seem to have lost some of their power.

We know that initiatives to modernize or restructure often are linked to processes of decentralization or devolution of managerial responsibility. Still, decentralization does not constitute a universal trend. We have been arguing that empirical data suggests that it is possible to decentralize certain layers of management authority while leaving the structure of collective bargaining basically untouched. Added to this, these processes of decentralization differ substantially from complete fragmentation of collective bargaining systems. What we generally found were cautious attempts to decentralize systems of employment relations and consequently, individual employment contracts are still the rare exception in the majority of countries.

If we are to point to a uniform tendency among public sector unions in the 1990s it could be changes in the structural character of the unions. Mergers of unions have been observed in several countries. Among others, UNISON – the dominant public service union in the UK – was the outcome of a merger of three unions in 1993, in Italy smaller unions have merged, in Germany a major reorganization is underway (*vereinte Dienstleistungsgewerkschaft – ver.di*), and, in Denmark, cartel-like groupings of unions are still growing, for example in the health area. These developments contribute to a certain degree of centralization of trade union activities. There are several driving forces behind this development, an important one being a decline in membership and, subsequently, financial resources. These elements force unions to pool their limited resources in order to be able to cope with future challenges. The devolution of managerial responsibility fosters one of the challenges, meaning that trade unions must be capable of entering negotiations at decentralized levels. One way of doing this is to unite their resources not only at the central – that is national – level but also at local levels.

There is one additional challenge for the public sectors of those countries which participate in the Economic and Monetary Union (EMU) (definitely excluding the UK and, at least in its first stage, Denmark and Sweden). The generally unfavorable public budget conditions of the 1990s have deteriorated further from the necessity to fulfill the criteria for participation, especially the criteria for short-term (no more than 3 percent of the GDP) and long-term deficits (no more than 60 percent of the GDP). Nowadays it is quite obvious that the convergence criteria have a significant impact on all public budgets, not only at the federal state but also at the intermediary and local level. It is of course true that there has been, quite independent from all EMU related aspects, a long-term need to reduce the rising public deficits in order to increase overtly ended public investments and employment opportunities. However, because of the tight EMU schedule defined in the Treaty of the European Union, pressures of fiscal discipline exerted on all public budgets have become more urgent. At least they can be used as an excuse for unpopular retrenchments. Therefore, a key question for the near future is: will budget constraints, more or less dictated from the central level because of growing public debts and increased by the necessity to fulfill the convergence criteria of (EMU), limit the possibilities or even paralyze initiatives of modernization at the decentralized level?

Considering the relatively high percentage of labor costs within public budgets, forthcoming cuts and retrenchments will almost by definition have to include the level of employment, for example, layoffs and/or wages and salaries of public employees. It is most likely that public sector unions and their members will be more seriously affected than their private sector counterparts. Therefore, a future stagnation (or even more or less careful retrenchment in some areas) of employment would be no surprise at all. In the majority of Western European countries real wages will most likely also continue to stagnate (even without official wage freezes) or may even decline. It seems as if public sector unions throughout Western Europe (France is probably the best known exception) finally accepted these changed circumstances for collective bargaining and new constraints on their collective action. Last but not least, the majority of them have, more or less reluctantly, decided to support modernization strategies.

Notes

1. The three former associations were the Association of Metropolitan Authorities, the Association of County Councils and the Association of District Councils.
2. General remarks on public enterprises are difficult because their number and significance for national economies differ to a considerable degree.

3. We have to note, however, that it is difficult to estimate the exact proportions and character of these activities. Consultancies are operating at the decentralized level where it is difficult to get precise information about the scope of activities.

References

Andersen, S. K., Due, J., and Masden, J. S. (1997), 'Multi-track approach to public-sector restructuring in Europe,' *Transfer*, III(1).
Andersen, S. K., Due, J., and Masden, J. S. (1999) 'Denmark. Negotiating the restructuring of public service employment relations,' in Bach, S., Bordogna, L., Della Rocca, G., and Winchester, D. (eds.), *Public Service Employment Relations in Europe: Transformation, Modernization or Inertia?*, London: Routledge.
Bach, S. (1999) 'Europe. Changing public service employment relations,' in Bach, S., Bordogna, L., Della Rocca, G., and Winchester, D. (eds.), *Public Service Employment Relations in Europe: Transformation, Modernization or Inertia?*, London: Routledge.
Bach, S., Bordogna, L., Della Rocca, G., and Winchester, D. (eds.) (1999) *Public Service Employment Relations in Europe: Transformation, Modernization or Inertia?*, London: Routledge.
Bamber, G. J. and Lansbury, R. D. (eds.) (1998 3rd edn.) *International and Comparative Employment Relations*, London: Sage.
Beaumont, P. B. (1992) *Public sector industrial relations*, London: Routledge.
Bordogna, L., Dell'Aringa, C., and Della Rocca, G. (1999) 'Italy. A Case of Coordinated Decentralization,' in Bach, S., Bordogna, L., Della Rocca, G., and Winchester, D. (eds.), *Public Service Employment Relations in Europe: Transformation, Modernization or Inertia?*, London: Routledge.
Department of Education (1993) *School Governors – a guide to the law*, London: Department of Education.
Due, J., Masden, J. S., Jensen, C. S., and Petersen, L. K. (1994) *The Survival of the Danish Model. A historical sociological analysis of the Danish system of collective bargaining*, Copenhagen: DJØF.
Dunlop, J. T. (1958) *Industrial Relations Systems*, New York: Henry Holt & C.
EIRO (1999) 'National "social pact" for development and employment signed', *Eironline* , (January).
EIRR (1998) 'Trends in public sector union membership,' *European Industrial Relations Review*, (293).
Ferner, A. and Hyman, R. (eds.) (1998) *Changing industrial relations in Europe*, 2nd edn., Oxford: Blackwell.
Gladstone, A., Lansbury, R. D., Steiber, J., Treu, T., and Weiss, M. (eds.) (1989) *Current Issues in Labor Relations. An International Perspective*, Berlin: de Gruyter.
Hyman, R. and Ferner, A. (eds.) (1994) *New frontiers in European industrial relations*, Oxford: Blackwell.
Jódar, P., Jordana, J., and Alós, R. (1999) 'Spain. Public service employment relations since the transition to democracy,' in Bach, S., Bordogna, L., Della Rocca, G., and Winchester, D. (eds.), *Public Service Employment Relations in Europe: Transformation, Modernization or Inertia?*, London: Routledge.

Keller, B. (1997) 'Public sector labor markets and labor relations in Norway.' The exception from the European rule,' in Dolvik, J. E. and Steen, A. H. (eds.), *Making solidarity work?* The Norwegian labor market model in transition, Oslo: Scandinavian University Press.
Keller, B. (1999) 'Germany: Negotiated change, modernization and the challenge of unification,' in Bach, S., Bordogna, L., Della Rocca, G., and Winchester, D. (eds.), *Public Service Employment Relations in Europe: Transformation, Modernization or Inertia?*, London: Routledge.
KGSt (1993) *Das neue Steuerungsmodell. Begründungen, Konturen, Umsetzungen*, Köln: KGSt.
Martin, B. (1996) *European Integration and modernization of local public services*, Bruxelles: EPSU.
Mossé, Ph. and Tchobanian, R. (1999) 'France. The restructuring of employment relations in public services,' in Bach, S., Bordogna, L., Della Rocca, G., and Winchester, D. (eds.), *Public Service Employment Relations in Europe: Transformation, Modernization or Inertia?*, London: Routledge.
OECD (1995) *Governance in Transition: Public Management Reforms in OECD Countries*, Paris: OECD.
OECD (1996) *Integrating People Management into Public Service Reform*, Paris: OECD.
Ozaki, M. (1990 4th and revised edn.) 'Labor relations in the public sector,' in Blanpain, R. (ed.), *Comparative labor law and industrial relations in industrialized market economies*, Deventer: Kluwer.
Ponak, A. and Thompson, M. (1989) 'Public sector collective bargaining,' in Anderson, J. C., Gunderson, M., and Ponak, A. (eds.), *Union – Management Relations in Canada*, Ontario: Addison-Wesley.
Reichard, C. (1997) 'Neues Steuerungsmodell: Local reform in Germany,' in Kickert, W. J. M. (ed.), *Public Management and Administrative Reform in Western Europe*, Northampton: Elgar.
Schager, N. H. and Andersson, P. (1996), 'Recent reforms within the central government sector in Sweden with respect to employment and pay policies,' discussion paper at ARAN Conference, Rome. Edited in Italian, 'Recenti riforme del Governo centrale delle Politiche del Lavoro e delle Retribuzioni nell'Amministrazione Pubblica in Svezia', in Dell'Aringa, C. and Della Rocca, G. (eds.) (1999) *Razionalizzazione e Relazioni Industriali nel Pubblico Impiego in Europa*, Milano: Angeli.
Traxler, F. (1995) 'Farewell to Labor Market Associations? Organized versus Disorganised Decentralization as a Map for Industrial Relations,' in Crouch, C. and Traxler, F. (eds.), *Organized Industrial Relation in Europe: What Future?*, Avebury: Aldershot.
Traxler, F. (1996) 'Collective bargaining and industrial change: A case of disorganisation? A comparative analysis of eighteen OECD countries,' *European Sociological Review*, XII(3).
Treu, T. (ed.) (1987) *Public Service Labor Relations: Recent Trends and Future Prospects*, Geneva: ILO.
Van den Toren, J. P. (1998) 'Netherlands', in Fajertag, G. (ed.), *Collective Bargaining in Western Europe, 1997–1998*. Brussels: ETUI.
Van Ruysseveldt, J. and Visser, J. (eds.) (1996) *Industrial Relations in Europe, Traditions and Transitions*, London: Sage.

Visser, J. (1990) *In Search of Inclusive Unionism*, Deventer: Kluwer.
Winchester, D. and Bach, S. (1995) 'The state: the public sector,' in Edwards, P. (ed.), *Industrial Relations. Theory and Practice in Britain*, Oxford: Blackwell.
Winchester, D. and Bach, S. (1999) 'Britain. The transformation of public service employment relations,' in Bach, S., Bordogna, L., Della Rocca, G., and Winchester, D. (eds.), *Public Service Employment Relations in Europe: Transformation, Modernization or Inertia?*, London: Routledge.
Windmuller, J. P. and Gladstone, A. (1984) *Employers Associations and Industrial Relations. A Comparative Study*, Oxford: Clarendon Press.

5
United States Public Sector Employment*

Jonathan Brock

Overview of public sector employment

Employment

The public sector employs 20.2 million people in the US, approximately 14.5 percent of the workforce. Public sector employment is generally divided into three categories: federal, state and local government. The largest division of US public sector employment is local government, comprising 63.5 percent of public sector employment. State government makes up approximately 23.2 percent and federal non-postal workers 8.8 percent (US Bureau of Labor Statistics, 1999a). The services provided by public employees have remained relatively constant over the last few decades. State and local public employees are concentrated in education (52 percent); health, housing and welfare (14 percent); and public safety (12 percent). Other services provided by state and local employees include transportation, utilities and environmental services.[1] Federal employees may be found in the US Postal Service (USPS) (31 percent), followed closely by defense and

---

*Much of the information in this chapter benefits from a nation-wide study undertaken from 1994–96 at the request of the US Secretary of Labor and published in *Working Together for Public Service*, US Department of Labor, June 1996, and from supporting information. The author was the executive director of the Secretary of Labor's Task Force, which oversaw the study. The author gratefully acknowledges the US Department of Labor and of the Ford Foundation for support that assisted in the development of this chapter, and the exacting research and editorial assistance of Alice M. Ostdiek, a candidate for degrees in the School of Law and the Daniel J. Evans School of Public Affairs at the University of Washington. The editorial pen of Ina Chang has contributed immeasurably to the quality of this chapter.

international relations (27 percent); other areas of significant federal involvement include: health, housing and public welfare (14 percent); and the environment (8 percent).[2]

Since 1983, the growth of combined state and local public employment has matched or outpaced the growth of total US employment (US Bureau of Labor Statistics, 1997). Among the three public sector divisions, local government has seen the strongest growth, followed by state government and finally federal government, which has actually seen a negative growth rate.[3] Reductions in federal public sector employment during the mid 1990s reflect the "end of big government" movement that eliminated or reduced the federal role in many areas.

Employment growth in the combined state and local sector has been fairly steady over the last decade, hovering around 2 percent per year. The Bureau of Labor Statistics projects that this growth will continue at a slightly lower rate but will remain ahead of population gain projections of just < .8 percent (US Bureau of Labor Statistics, 1997). By 2008, education, provided by local government, is expected to grow by nearly 1.2 million jobs, ranking fifth among industries (public and private) with the largest wage and salary employment growth (US Bureau of Labor Statistics, 1999b). Local government revenues have been strong in recent years, reflecting a strong US economy. However, because state and local governments rely heavily on highly sensitive revenue sources such as property and sales taxes, these employment projections are susceptible to fluctuations in the economy.

The demographic composition of the public sector workforce is often similar to that in the private sector, but there are a few significant differences. In contrast to the private sector, the public sector employs more women than men. Government employees (combined federal, state and local) were 55.8 percent women in 1998,[4] while the private sector workforce was 46.9 percent women. The trend toward a strongly female workforce in state and local government represents a shift from the early 1980s, when women made up barely half of the state and local government workforce.[5] The federal workforce is 29.7 percent racial or ethnic minority (US Office of Personnel Management, 1999). African–American workers made up 16.7 percent of federal employees while the total US workforce is 11.7 percent African–American. Hispanic workers, however, are less well represented in the public sector. Federal employees are 6.4 percent Hispanic while they are 10.5 percent of the workforce overall (US Office of Personnel Management, 1999).

Educational attainment level, job tenure and average age differ between the public and private sectors. Public employees are typically well trained and well educated despite negative stereotypes about their abilities. The average length of service for federal full-time permanent employees in 1998 was 16.6 years, in contrast to reports of job tenure just under four years in the private sector (US Office of Personnel Management, 1999). Compared to the public sector, the private sector employs nearly double the percentage of workers under age 24 and a smaller percentage of workers age 25–54. Workers age 55 and over account for about 13 percent of the state and local workforce as compared to about 10 percent of the private workforce.

Recent policies

Anti-tax and anti-"big government" sentiment in the 1980s and 1990s has had a large influence on federal employment. Coupled with public pressure to provide better, more cost-effective services these sentiments have resulted in the smallest federal workforce in nearly three decades.[6] State and local governments have also been subject to these pressures. In some areas, privatization has been a politically popular response. However, large-scale privatization has not been as widespread as the level of discussion may make it may appear (Mildred and Hebdon, 1999). Reflecting the experience elsewhere in the country, a recent survey in New York State showed that inter-municipal cooperation was far more popular than privatization.[7] The more promising changes in service quality have come from "quality improvement" or "reinvention" initiatives and cooperative activities between employees and managers. The resultant cooperative relationships have in turn often led to changes in civil service systems and collective bargaining practices.

Applications of information technology in private sector services have placed pressure on the public sector to provide better and faster services. This promises to continue as both a pressure and an opportunity for government. Many government functions, including some types of claims processing and inquiry, are using the Internet and other sophisticated communication and digital technology to speed transactions and remove the need for walk-in and other person-to-person interaction. Changes in jobs and skills requirements are leading to workforce redeployment, retraining and reclassification, but are not directly correlated with a net decrease in employment, at least in state and local government. Labor market demand and recruitment, retention and wage pressures are beginning to emerge around the need for personnel skilled in developing, applying and carrying out technology-based services.

Organizational structure

Federal government

About 2.6 million of the 20.2 million public employees in the United States work for the federal government.[8] A few federal agencies provide direct services to citizens (for example, the National Park Service, the Internal Revenue Service and Federal Law Enforcement Agencies). However, because many federal agencies act only in a regulatory, oversight, or "pass-through" capacity, the states or localities frequently provide actual delivery of federally required government services. Some "traditional" functions of national government such as health care, postal service and transportation that are actually delivered in the private sector or through "public enterprises" at the border of governmental and private activity that receive federal support. Among the two most prominent examples of the latter are the US Postal Service (USPS) and Amtrak, the national passenger rail system. The USPS began as a federal function and has moved toward increasing independence; Amtrak represents the federal takeover of a previously private service. Both seem to be moving toward a modified private sector model.

Most health care in the United States is provided by the private for-profit and not-for-profit sectors. Government involvement in health care is largely limited to programs that subsidize private services for individual consumers, but the federal government does provide direct health care to veterans of military service. Public sector health care delivery is strongest in the area of mental health, which is usually part of the state or local government's public welfare infrastructure. Even in mental health, however, government entities often contract for service delivery with private (often non-profit) care providers. The federal government conducts research and sets or implements policy through the Public Health Service (PHS) and the Centers for Disease Control (CDC). Both of these agencies work closely with state, county and city health departments to respond to health emergencies and anticipate public health issues; this federal-state-local cooperation represents a high level of professionalism and is among the most effective among government services. State and local health departments are concerned largely with public health and sanitation, enforcement of water quality standards, food safety, disease and medical epidemics and health care for undeserved populations, particularly in rural areas or among some urban populations.

Outside of the federal sector, public sector health workers are usually covered under the general personnel arrangements of their jurisdiction.

Employees of private health care providers that contract with the government to provide health services are covered by the private entity's personnel system. While private personnel systems are not subject to civil service classification systems, they are subject to national employment standards, health and safety and non-discrimination provisions, among others. They are also subject to the National Labor Relations Act, the main private sector labor relations statute, which treats health care workers with some special provisions, including limitations on the right to strike. The Federal Public Health Service operates under a separate employment system within the federal government.

State and local government

Although state and local government are frequently measured together, each presents important differences in function and structure. In the aggregate, state governments employ about one-third the number of workers employed by local governments.[9] State workers tend to handle key aspects of public welfare including provision of social services; vehicle and professional licensing and regulation; some environmental protection and consumer protection functions; and may also administer some federal employment-related programs.

State and local employees are responsible for different aspects of education and public safety services. Public elementary and secondary schools (kindergarten through grade 12, or K–12) are operated by local school districts that have varying financial dependencies on the state government. Public universities and colleges, including two-year "community colleges" are usually operated at the state level. Education is by far the largest single category of public sector employment, accounting for approximately half of all workers at the state and local levels.[10] A state police agency and prison system typically exist alongside county and city police forces and jail systems; cooperation between state and local public safety agencies is usually very high. Personnel systems in education and public safety normally have strong civil service and/or collective bargaining protections. States that limit collective bargaining rights for other public employees frequently grant bargaining rights to teachers and public safety officers.[11]

Employment and labor relations models in general local government closely resemble state models, featuring a civil service system that is specific to the city or county and is specified by local charter or ordinance. State law determines the amount of control a local government has over its personnel system. In states that authorize collective bargaining, state law usually governs bargaining for all government employees throughout the state. These state-level statutes differ in coverage and may make distinctions among occupations or levels of government. For example, in Washington State, local government employees have comprehensive bargaining rights, while state employees currently can bargain only over conditions of employment but not for wages. Currently, nine states permit collective bargaining only for certain occupations, often education and public safety.[12] Others grant "meet and confer" rights which do not require bargaining. Public employee bargaining rights rarely include the right to strike.[13] Thus, the mechanisms for reaching contract closure in bargaining vary widely, and no single mechanism has gained preference. Virtually all state collective bargaining statutes create state Public Employee Relations Boards or Commissions (PERBs or PERCs) to administer the bargaining law. The boards generally provide dispute resolution services, most commonly mediation for contract disputes, but also unit determination, election oversight and, in some instances, training.

Qualitative employment and wages

Internal labor market

Classification and hiring

Personnel systems are similar in basic structure across government sectors. In general, a personnel office generates a list of qualified applicants, usually based on standardized testing, from which agencies hire employees. The personnel office also performs classification studies to provide for standardization and appropriate comparability. Experts have long agreed that the US public sector has generally relied too heavily on standardized testing and centralized control and, until recently, has given insufficient weight to individual agency needs or the qualitative requirements of a particular profession or job category.

Most recent shifts have increased the individual agency's flexibility in responding to changing service goals, and reduced the degree of centralized controls. At the federal level, the Federal Civil Service Reform Act of 1978 decentralized the overly bureaucratic federal personnel system. The late 1990s have seen state and local reforms that have increased flexibility and improved service quality through changes in classification, recruitment, screening and appointment. For example, many have moved from a highly centralized and process-oriented personnel office to more autonomous agency-level personnel offices, with the central offices providing more streamlined services where they retained functions, and keeping at least some level of oversight to ensure compliance and uniformity of general practices. However, the overall quality of recruiting and testing still varies widely among agencies and jurisdictions, with some quite advanced, and others still very bureaucratic and favoring process over effective recruitment and selection.

Managers and supervisory personnel

Traditionally, managers and supervisors in the public sector have been promoted from within the agency or the larger personnel system serving the jurisdiction. Candidates come up through the ranks and advance largely according to informal considerations of seniority and based on technical abilities. Lateral entry for mid-level managers has been discouraged by recruitment and examination protocols, but is more common at the higher managerial levels, particularly for positions that are exempt from civil service. Recently, public agencies have begun to weigh leadership abilities more heavily in selecting supervisors and mid-level managers.

The Federal Civil Service Reform Act created the Senior Executive Service (SES) to increase opportunities and mobility for senior-level career employees through training and development and to promote flexibility in assigning executives. Many states followed suit with their own SES-style senior cadres that have more flexible employment policies and training programs. The SES was initially designed to provide inducements such as bonus pay, but due to budget constraints this feature has not been fully realized. Executive services, at any level of government, have rarely succeeded in addressing the problem of wage or salary compression and are variable in quality, but they are generally considered beneficial to management deployment and professional development.

Performance and removal

Civil service systems were introduced in the United States during the late 1800s and early 1900s in response to concerns about politicization of public employment and excessive use of patronage. While largely successful in limiting patronage, and focused on merit appointments, these reforms produced a process-heavy system that resulted in a perception of guaranteed employment except in the case of gross misbehavior or incompetence. The Civil Service Reform Act, and parallel reforms at the state and local level in the intervening years, have made removal for cause less constrained by excessive process requirements, but anecdotal evidence suggests that formal separations are still rare. However, the separation statistics may be misleading because some methods of agreed-upon and forced separation, such as mutual settlements, offers of early retirement and other packages have never appeared in the statistics. Adding to the pressure on effective job performance, customer service demands have led to a focus on greater accountability. This trend, together with higher performance standards and improved employee development programs, seems to have lessened the resistance to using job separation when warranted, and procedures for removal, though still complex, have been somewhat simplified at all levels. Although these trends may feed employees' fears of diminishing job security, there is no evidence that such measures have been used inappropriately or for political ends, and public employment continues to be a stable percentage of the workforce (US Bureau of Labor Statistics, 1999a).

The Federal Civil Service Reform Act and subsequent attempts at reform at the federal and at the state level have required performance measurement and evaluation systems of one form or another. Agency-wide implementation of these systems, however, has proven difficult at all levels of government, especially when tied to pay increases. Although some jurisdictions or agencies have been able to make good use of performance evaluation, individual performance measures have not become a generally useful or acceptable tool despite requirements to use such systems. They are often implemented in a pro-forma fashion without real impact on how work gets done. The best results appear when the system is separated from pay considerations, tied closely to agency goals and management systems, and is accompanied by training in the use of the system. Performance evaluation has been less controversial and somewhat more likely to succeed in special districts that resemble the private sector in terms of flexibility, in single-mission agencies, and in other settings with a long tradition of investment in career development. It is also more likely to succeed or be accepted, though it is not regularly successful, at senior managerial levels than lower in the organization.

Pay for performance and team incentive programs

Pay-for-performance systems are promoted as a way to improve service quality and employee development. Such systems are similar to performance evaluation, but directly tie some element of pay increases or bonuses to periodic measured results. For most of the reasons mentioned above, pay-for-performance systems have had mixed results; they are difficult to structure and implement, and over time most such systems suffer from misuse or disuse. Fearing favoritism, organized employee groups usually oppose pay-for-performance systems.

More promising are systems that tie a portion of each employee's compensation or supplemental pay to the achievement of a team or relevant work group. This involves evaluating the performance of the team against measurable goals relevant to the agency's mission, including cost reductions or service quality measures. To be effective, protocols for measuring results and distributing pay must be carefully developed with the involvement and support of the employer and the affected employees and their representatives. One increasingly popular such approach is "gainsharing" which uses a formula to share cost savings between workers and the agency budget. In Indianapolis, Indiana, workers in one unit recently received around $1,700 each in annual bonuses in addition to negotiated wage increases, and the city's costs in this area (city maintenance garage) were reduced by nearly 20 percent over several years (US Department of Labor, 1996).

Team incentive programs are not widespread, but they have impressed management and are increasingly popular with employees and union leadership. They can encourage employees at different levels, and in different job categories, to work together and pool skills to solve complex problems. Most promisingly, team incentive programs have the potential to create a confluence of goals among the agency, individual employees and unions.

Skill-based pay incentives are another less common program under which individual workers receive pay adjustments for acquiring skills that contribute to their performance. This is a departure from the job classification schemes that have long determined pay rates in civil service systems in that the basis of one's pay is the level of skill actually possessed by the employee, rather than that required by the job classification. Units that have been successful at this seem to have invested substantially in the developing the measurement system in the context of a broader reform of service improvement, teamwork, and individual development. Much of the positive evidence thus far appears to come from smaller jurisdictions or circumscribed units (US Department of Labor, 1996).

The largest and most promising set of activities – including gainsharing and team incentives as well as others – for improving employee performance has arisen in recent years out of cooperative, service-oriented workplace partnerships and related quality improvement initiatives. These can take many forms, but are based on expanding the commitment by front-line workers to service quality and cost savings by substantially involving them (through structured consultation, and sometimes through delegated or shared authority) in joint teams for planning and resolving service delivery questions.

Temporary employment and contracting out

Contingent workers are hired for a short period of time, often a day or a few weeks or on a limited contract basis, and typically receive no employer-provided benefits such as health insurance or retirement plans (US Department of Labor, 1994). The constructive use of contingent workers allows truly temporary or short-term functions to be performed without increasing long-term payroll commitments. The use of temporary and contingent workers in the private sector has grown dramatically even for non-temporary tasks, but apparently to keep payroll flexibility and often to avoid benefit and other obligations. The use of such workers in the public sector seems to be far less pervasive (US Department of Labor, 1994), but there have been instances of shifting work to consultants in an effort to reduce employment rolls and obligations, and also instances of inappropriate use of temporary appointment authorities to keep people working for an extended period, but without the usual benefits or security provided a regular employee.

Temporary, contingent and contract employment is believed to be growing in public employment as well, but no reliable or comprehensive national figures or analysis are currently available, nor is it possible to tell how much is attributable to actual temporary work versus avoidance of employment requirements or strictures. The use of contractors and consultants in the public sector has come under heavy scrutiny from unions and others, and promises to be controversial. Despite the higher level of interest by employers, contingent worker arrangements in the public sector tend to be circumscribed at least to some important extent by most civil service and related statutes.

Contracting has been highly controversial in recent years. Government has traditionally contracted with private entities to provide some public services, including trash collection, maintenance and construction tasks, food services, and many social services, among others. During the 1990s interest in contracting by government became quite active, and a large part of the political debate, but the degree of actual increase appears to be far less than is commonly believed.

In this context contracting has been much talked about recently in areas such as transportation services, administration of prisons, janitorial services and sewage treatment. None the less, the number of instances of continuous new contracting outside of the traditional and expected areas appears to have been relatively modest, despite a lot of debate and discussion. Sewage treatment appears to be one of the areas that has received the most effective attention for reasons that have not been fully analyzed. Even newly incorporated cities, which often contract for services at first often bring some or all of those services in house later on in order to have greater (unpublished testimony before the US Department of Labor, 1996).

Although there has been substantial pressure to contract government services to the private sector, federal, state, and local governments are frequently prohibited by statute or judicial decision from contracting for work that has traditionally been performed by government employees. This effectively prohibits the government in many jurisdictions from privatizing without first negotiating with the relevant union representatives. Some states and local governments do require competitive bidding for certain types of public works, such as the construction of large buildings or maintenance projects.

Instances of privatization have been limited and their record has been mixed. The published and anecdotal record of government service reform efforts over the last decade or so suggests that most service improvements and cost savings have come from quality improvement programs and related initiatives, often within an infrastructure of labor–management cooperation, and not primarily from contracting. (See also US Department of Labor, 1996).

Wages and salary

Most wage and salary increases in the public sector arise out of collective bargaining agreements or from legislative action affecting employees of the jurisdiction across the board. Setting wages and salaries through collective bargaining is most common among public safety employees and teachers and also takes place in other occupations where the local law permits bargaining. Where collective bargaining is not permitted, periodic pay increases are part of the executive and legislative budgeting process, and tend to reflect the political climate and attitudes toward government workers, the financial state of the government unit, and the national rate of inflation. Many states, some local governments and the federal government also perform salary surveys that compare major government occupations with relevant or nearby private sector labor marks, or make other pay comparisons to relevant or nearby public employers. These surveys, however, are rarely tied to automatic pay increases, but are used as indicators for the local pay-setting process. If an agency or jurisdiction has brought to their attention, or identifies major inequities internally or relative to the job market, it can conduct a special classification study and adjust the relevant classifications. Also, such studies can be part of a collective bargaining process or a budgetary process. For example, in the mid 1980s such studies were commonly done in response to the Equal Pay Act to redress gender-based pay inequities. More recent studies have focused on information technology experts because of difficulties recruiting and retaining skilled employees. No matter what the context, special classification studies are frequently controversial and can be methodologically imprecise.

The comparison of relative pay in the public and private sectors is an ongoing controversy. Some say that job security and strong benefit packages make total compensation in government equivalent to private sector compensation, even though the wages may be greater. Others noting the improvement in private benefits and the increasing lag of public sector wages to inflation in most jurisdictions observe the opposite. However, a review of the studies and arguments, and looking at differences among jurisdictions, makes it clear that generalizations are not objectively helpful in supporting adjustments and relevant and supportable comparisons can only be made by looking at specific occupations, pay systems, and local markets.

In addition to other cross-sectoral or cross-jurisdictional comparisons, many senior managers and supervisors in the public sector also face growing salary compression. Salaries for senior managers are occasionally not much higher than those of senior line employees. Because pay decisions for senior managers can be politically symbolic their salaries are often suppressed despite the responsibilities and pressures of those jobs. Particularly where wages are the subject of collective bargaining, political considerations will usually have less impact on the outcome of rank-and-file wage and benefit decisions, contributing to the compression, but also keeping front line wages out of the more political process to which manager's wages are subject. In some places, these pressures have increased unionization and organizing activity among pubic agency managers in the top several (non-political) layers. When managers are included in the bargaining unit, their wages and salaries would seem to have a better chance to keep pace with rank-and-file pay.

Civil service systems and employer associations

Public sector employment is subject to a number of overlapping legal frameworks. Federal laws covering employment discrimination, workplace safety, minimum labor standards and the like apply, with minor exception, to all state and local workplaces, public and private. The federal civil service system covers federal employees, while each state and each local jurisdiction has its own system covering its employees. In the past, the federal government exercised informal leadership by setting examples and framing the debate. The most significant recent push at the federal level is the National Performance Review (NPR), which in 1998 became the National Partnership for Reinventing Government led by Vice-President Gore; the program has produced valuable improvements and innovations in many parts of the federal government. For a variety of reasons, however, standards and examples are today more likely to be set by innovative states and local governments. As described earlier, most of the recent activity in civil service system change has centered on eliminating barriers to service improvement.

Federal civil service

The federal civil service system extends only to the federal non-military and non-postal workforce. In 1978, the Office of Personnel Management (OPM) replaced the old Civil Service Commission (CSC) as the administrator of the federal civil service system. As the OPM's name suggests, the agency now emphasizes "managing" the system rather than following the CSC scheme of centralized regulation. The OPM now delegates more authority to the agencies to manage their own personnel matters and sets standards and requirements that allow considerable flexibility. Allegations of abuse or misapplication of the civil service system are addressed by the Office of Special Counsel of the Merit Systems Protection Board (MSPB). The MSPB is the final level of administrative appeal for such claims. Members of the MSPB are appointed by the president and approved by Congress.

State and local civil service

Each state or local jurisdiction has its own civil service system. State laws may provide testing and eligibility standards for state and sometimes, local employees in select areas such as public safety and sometimes education. In general, local employees are covered by local ordinances that mimic the state's system to varying degrees, but over which the state has no operational or policy jurisdiction. State and local governments have followed the federal trend of delegating more autonomy to the agencies. Many have also made the grievance and appeals boards separate from the personnel department. In most state and local jurisdictions, the chief executive (governor or mayor) of the jurisdiction appoints the director of the personnel department. State personnel directors have tended to be personnel or human resources professionals, but an increasing number are entering from other fields through political appointment process, with mixed degrees of success. Innovative and valuable policies have emerged under directors of both backgrounds, however. At the local level, most personnel directors have a background in public sector personnel management. Most personnel directors are attentive to local politics, but political interference in development of policy or in specific cases is very rare. Political wrangling is usually restricted to funding issues, particularly training programs and innovations. In a few jurisdictions, legislative bodies have a detailed level of oversight and even become involved in the minutiae of hiring or establishing classifications, but legislatures generally control only the number and types of positions through the budgetary process and rely on executive branch recommendations.

Employer and professional associations

Public employers maintain a professional dialogue with one another through several national professional associations, but these associations have no official policy-making role and rarely interact with each other or with labor unions. Such groups can help spread information and successful innovations; they have been useful in facilitating reform trends across jurisdictions particularly in the absence of federal leadership. Professional associations of governors, county executives, mayors, city managers, police chiefs, fire chiefs, legislators and other government officials occasionally examine emerging practices or new legal requirements in public employment. However, these groups pay remarkably little attention to personnel and labor issues. The size and immediacy of their agendas, and diversity of membership from large and small jurisdictions, from areas with and without collective bargaining, and with other significant variation also precludes attention or concerted action on policy or other reform in personnel or labor relations issues. The few professional associations of employers that do focus primarily on public personnel issues are those specifically for directors of personnel systems and chief labor negotiators. These associations have no official policy-making power and primarily focus on sharing ideas, training and policy advocacy. As largely volunteer associations, they are rarely well financed (with a few notable exceptions) and are not in a position to perform substantial research or assess policies or innovations.

Unions

Union membership

Unionization among public sector employees has increased substantially over the last two decades and is most prevalent in jurisdictions where collective bargaining is permitted by statute.[14] In 1998, nearly 43 percent of US public sector employees were represented by unions, in contrast to private sector union representation, which fell to just 10.3 percent of the private workforce (US Bureau of Labor Statistics, 1999e). All employees in the unit are bound by the result of the collective bargaining process and are thus represented by the union, and often are subject to dues check off. Elections and bargaining unit determinations are overseen by the PERC or PERB (state level) or by the FLRA (federal level).

About 8.2 million workers, or 43 percent of the public sector workforce, are covered under collective bargaining contracts. Of those, about 7 million, or 37.5 percent of all public employees are union members. In contrast, only about 9.5 percent of private sector workers are union members. Throughout the 1960s and 1970s, as individual states granted collective bargaining rights to state or local employees, union membership grew substantially.[15] A 1994 study of representation elections showed that 84.9 percent of public employees choose union representation, regardless of profession or occupational level. In similar studies of the private sector, only 48 percent of workers choose union representation (US Department of Labor, 1994).

Union membership is substantially affected by the existence of collective bargaining laws, although there are unions in states and cities that do not have formal collective bargaining.

Major public sector unions and bargaining arrangements

Although there are some important independent local unions, the prominent national unions represent a substantial proportion of public employees through their local affiliates (locals). The national unions are fairly decentralized in terms of member services and role in local bargaining, partly because many locals sought national affiliation only after a history of independent development, and partly because of a philosophical commitment to local control and union democracy. For purposes of sharing information, training, learning about national priorities, trends and needs, and for assistance when needed, locals are usually confederated into a "district" or similar unit, which is a state-level organization or part of a state-level organization. There is no national contract for local employees, but local trends are discussed at the regular national and regional meetings of local union leaders.

Federal

Federal employees were first granted collective bargaining rights in 1963 by Presidential Executive Order. Then, as now, federal employees may bargain over working conditions, but not wages. Federal employees do not have the right to strike or to engage in other job actions. In addition to the representation of postal workers by several major unions, the majority of federal employees are represented by the American Federation of Government Employees, the National Treasury Employees Union, National Federation of Federal Employees, and the National Association of Government Employees. Depending upon occupation, history and other factors, some of the unions described below related to local government workers may represent some other federal employees.

Since the 1978 civil service reforms, federal labor relations have been handled separately from the administration of civil service laws, and now are governed by the independent Federal Labor Relations Authority (FLRA). The FLRA, a three-member board appointed by the president to staggered terms, hears appeals and otherwise oversees labor relations, much in the way that state boards administer state statutes for collective bargaining. However, since wages are not a subject of bargaining at the federal level, the scope of the FLRA's activities is narrower than that of a typical state PERC or PERB.

State and local

Each state, the District of Columbia, and the US territories may grant collective bargaining rights to its employees under its own laws. The available subjects of bargaining are listed in the statute or may be defined by decision of the PERC or PERB or by the state court system. If a state does not provide for state employee collective bargaining, local government employees may still have collective bargaining rights under statutes passed in the local jurisdiction. The occupations with collective bargaining rights can also vary among states and localities. Currently, state and local government employees have full or partial collective bargaining rights in 36 states and the District of Columbia.[16] Only around two dozen grant comprehensive bargaining rights to all public employees in the state, however.

The list of mandatory, permissive, or prohibited subjects of bargaining varies somewhat by state law. If a topic is mandatory, the employer cannot make decisions affecting represented employees in this area, except through bargaining. Permissive subjects may be bargained if the parties agree in their contract to do so, and prohibited subjects may not be bargained. In the latter case, parties in individual jurisdictions may decide to discuss in other forums those subjects if they believe it is useful and productive to do so, but such arrangements are very much subject to the nature of the relationship, as well surrounding politics. If a dispute arises over whether a topic is being appropriately discussed, the administrative agency (PERC, PERB or FLRA) normally has jurisdiction to resolve the dispute.

Twenty-seven states and the District of Columbia grant full representation and collective bargaining rights to all local government employees, totaling over 6 million represented workers.[17] Nine other states grant limited representation and bargaining rights to specific occupational groups, such as teachers, law enforcement officers, or fire-fighters.[18] Twenty-eight states extend bargaining rights to *state* employees, totaling about 3 million workers.[19] Where bargaining is permitted, 58 percent of local government employees and 49 percent of state employees are covered by a union contract (Cimini, 1998).

The largest union representing state and local (non-educational) employees is the American Federation of State, County and Municipal Employees (AFSCME), with 1.3 million members. AFSCME represents a broad array of blue- and white-collar workers, including the majority of employees in several states and municipalities. Similarly, the Service Employees International Union (SEIU) represents most non-uniformed employees in significant sectors such as California state government and in the city of San Francisco, as well as workers in its traditional occupational sectors. In recent decades, SEIU has focused on organizing low-wage workers in schools and hospitals and has a substantial presence in sanitation, transportation, and other traditional areas of unionization. SEIU represents both public and private sector workers; it has 585,000 public sector members.

Special sectors

Two large unions represent primary and secondary school employees the National Education Association (NEA), with nearly 3.4 million members, and the American Federation of Teachers (AFT), with over

1 million members (including some non-teaching educational employees). The two unions have been seriously discussing a merger for several years. AFT has a substantial presence among general government workers in some areas of the country.

Multiple local unions without national affiliation represent police. Those with national affiliation include the International Brotherhood of Teamsters, the International Brotherhood of Police and the International Union of Police Associations, AFL-CIO. Prison guards and related professionals are likely to be represented by unions that represent police, by independent local associations or often by AFSCME. The International Association of Fire Fighters (IAFF) represents most unionized fire-fighters in the United States and has influence even in states where bargaining is not permitted. Most blue-collar transit employees are represented by the Amalgamated Transit Workers Union or the Transport Workers Union of America, AFL-CIO (TWU). Depending upon local or occupational history, particularly in areas such as maritime, construction trades and office support, private sector unions may represent substantial shares of state or local government workers.

The merger of public sector unions has been the most significant recent trend affecting the role of unions and union leaders. Unions such as AFSCME and SEIU owe a portion of their growth to the affiliation of previously independent state or local associations. Unions are also increasingly using coalition bargaining, in which units band together for greater leverage. Also gaining prominence in more progressive relationships are coalitions of unions set up to work more cooperatively across union jurisdictions with each other and the employer to improve service cost and quality of work life.

Bargaining and negotiations

Types of relationships

The general framework of public sector labor relations in the United States has been fairly stable since the early 1980s, by which time most of the states that currently grant bargaining rights to public employees had done so. Among the states the quality and maturity of these relationships varies significantly, as does the extent to which the full range of the bargaining relationship and structure is constructively utilized. Bargaining arrangements normally reflect both standard practices and local history and traditions. Bargaining is carried on most often at a department or jurisdiction level, depending upon the bargaining unit structure and other local features and traditions. In different communities, patterns and relationships may be established, but there is no national agreement, and only in rare instances a state-wide agreement or even jurisdiction-wide agreement

The collective bargaining process and labor-management relationship offers many tools for problem solving that are fully exploited in only a limited number of relationships. Although the number of more broadly focused and productive relationships appears to be growing, more often the relationship is focused largely on bargaining, grievances and other formally defined activities that are left substantially in the hands of professional negotiators on each. These relationships are frequently characterized by disputes over whether under the prevailing contract or statute a party has rights to undertake or expect certain actions. Often, these disputes lead to reliance on formal, legalistic methods of conflict resolution. The range of relationships described here may be characterized as "traditional," and can include productive, stable relationships as well as less productive ones. Probably, most bargaining relationships in the public sector are in this broad category. Traditional relationships are likely to use "positional" bargaining practices, wherein each side presents packages of demands or desires in a set pattern of presentation and response in each bargaining round, though some may try variations on "interest-based" approaches to bargaining.

"Conflictual" relationships are those that rely almost entirely on formal interactions, and positional bargaining in both contract and grievance negotiation; constructive problem solving is rare, there is substantial use of agents and third parties, the range of issues discussed is narrow, and mistrust permeates the relationship. This type of relationship is less common, but certainly not rare, and may be found in jurisdictions of any size or alleged sophistication. Difficult management or union politics, or other dimensions of local history or tradition can lead to, or lead back to, this type of relationship.

The more effective relationships are those that use the tools offered by the collective bargaining structure more completely to address issues. Many traditional relationships have developed in a manner that does so. These more productive relationships, however they have evolved, are referred to here as "cooperative, service oriented." Typically, each side remains conscious and in pursuit of their interests but clearly recognizes common interests as well. It is common for these relationships to function through a joint labor–management committee, composed of union officers (often representing a coalition of unions) and senior department heads, that meets regularly through the year and discuss a wide range of issues of concern to either side. Work life, service quality and cost issues usually come before joint committees and joint project groups for exploration and resolution, rather than before management or the bargaining table. The contracts tend to be more flexible and shorter, having stripped away contract language from years of traditional or conflictual negotiations, and emphasize descriptions of the intentions of the relationship, mutual commitments to problem solving, and methods that will be used for resolving problems.

In states that do not formally permit collective bargaining, union leaders and managers sometimes develop a productive working relationship that includes informal "negotiations" that mimic bargaining relationships. These sometimes consist of memos that resemble bargaining agreements but are specifically not enforceable as contracts. In other instances, the nature of the relationship is even less formal, but discussions and problem solving takes place that can resemble a bargaining relationship. In these circumstances, the parties may use available administrative and legislative mechanisms to gain results similar to that achieved through contract negotiation. Though these "simulated" bargaining relationships are not well researched or documented, and do not appear to be the norm in states without bargaining laws, some anecdotal evidence suggests that the practice is more common in public safety and education than among other categories of government employment.

Negotiations

Whatever the type of relationship, collective bargaining negotiations themselves typically focus on wages, benefits and working conditions, although in the cooperative, service-oriented relationships much of the background and detail affecting prospective change in working conditions comes up in other forums connected to the joint committee. Collective bargaining agreements typically have a term of two to three years. Some parties report completion of bargaining in a few months as a normal occurrence; others (usually in the conflictual or traditional relationships) describe negotiations stretching on for more than a few months or more than a year. This may reflect variations in type and quality of the relationship, or the presence of specific difficult issues. It is usual, by laws or convention, for the terms of the previous agreement to remain in force until a new contract is agreed on. The lack of "final closure" mechanisms in most public sector bargaining laws (that is, strikes are almost universally prohibited, and there is not widespread use of any other mechanism that has similar force) means that many of the pressures that force agreement in the private sector are largely absent. Individual states and local government units are responsible for their own negotiation and collective bargaining relationships with organized employees. The employer is usually the mayor or other chief administrative official, who for all practical purposes delegates the negotiation authority to a bargaining team, led by a designated negotiator who is often from the personnel or budget department. Occasionally, a large department within an agency has its own negotiator, while smaller jurisdictions in conflictual or traditional relationships often hire outside attorneys or independent for-hire negotiators. An increasing number of jurisdictions have a negotiation advisory committee or labor policy committee that consists of legislators and the chief administrative official or his or her delegate, which works ahead of and during negotiations to set policy and parameters for financial settlements. In cooperative, service-oriented relationships, an overall joint committee, consisting of senior ranking officials from labor and from management, is likely to provide input or otherwise frame issues for bargaining.

Where cooperative, service-oriented labor management relationships are developing, these relationships heavily involve senior and mid-level managers in conjunction with their labor counterparts and utilize employee involvement and interest-based bargaining strategies. Under cooperative agreements, substantial responsibility for bargaining on the management side shifts from the labor negotiation professionals to program managers, although the final authority to make financial commitments continues to rest with the legislative branch.

Local bargaining units (locals) and their leaders are generally quite independent from their national and international organizations in negotiating collective bargaining agreements. In some cases, the local's officers or senior staff negotiates directly with little or no assistance from the larger organization although assistance is normally available. Where cooperative relationships prevail or interest-based bargaining is used, members and work-site leaders play an increasingly important role in bargaining. This contrasts with more traditional arrangements, in which a staff negotiator or attorney, or only a few union spokespersons dominate the negotiations for the union.

The mechanisms for closure of negotiations in the public sector are an anomalous dimension of the system. Each state defines available closure mechanisms in its public bargaining statute, so there is no uniform practice. There is also no conceptual or philosophical agreement about what represents appropriate final closure in the public sector. Although the issue was much debated in the literature in the late 1960s and 1970s, since then systematic thought, debate, and innovation has not been widespread. Most state and local statutes and traditions are similar in that they encourage mediation in the event of an impasse. The procedures sometimes include a formal fact-finding step but rarely include the right to strike. Thus, the formal authority to close the negotiations lies with the employer, although unions can sometimes use political ties to elected legislators and executives to force closure when more conventional methods fail. Illegal strikes occasionally take place and have the affect of gaining closure, but they can damage the relationship or diminish public support. In some of the more conflictual relationships, the absence of an accepted closure mechanism creates some mistrust and game playing in bargaining. However, finding a common mechanism is not a high priority in public policy making channels, and most management organizations have little incentive to pursue or respond to this issue, and there has been little debate, less research and only rare consideration of improved closure mechanisms.

Mediation, arbitration and strikes

Each state that permits collective bargaining handles conflict resolution through an administrative body, usually called a Public Employee Relations Commission or Board (PERC or PERB). Typically, this body determines bargaining units, supervises union elections and mediates in the event of an impasse. In the federal government, the Federal Labor Relations Authority (FLRA) performs these regulatory functions; mediation, training, and other services are available to the parties through the Office of Personnel Management. For resolution of interest disputes, state PERCs and PERBs may provide mediation services from their own staffs, or they might, where arbitration of interest disputes is on the books, provide a panel of arbitrators, or a list of arbitrators from which the parties can choose. The system for mediation is highly decentralized, and very flexible in format. Depending on the state, the PERC or PERB might have authority or be required to conduct fact-finding hearings, but this seems to be falling into relative disuse. State boards vary in philosophy, approach and skill in problem solving and policy development. In the last decade or so, state board budgets have decreased, which has reduced the boards' capacity to provide full and timely assistance to parties

Interest arbitration takes several forms. Arbitration to resolve impasse in the public sector is largely restricted to public safety employees, though it is widely used in rights disputes to resolve individual employee grievances. Usually, when provided by statute, interest arbitration is mandatory and binding. Some states require the arbitrator to select one of the parties' final offers as is ("final-offer" arbitration), others allow the arbitrator to select issue by issue from the parties' final offers to create a final package, and still others permit the arbitrator even greater flexibility in designing a new package (Brock, 1982). Although many skilled and practiced arbitrators are available, legalistic procedures and considerations tend to dominate interest arbitration. Arbitrators are restricted to a narrow range of issues, which often may not reach the underlying causes of the dispute. Few arbitration requirements in state public employment law consider the impact on service quality, the public welfare, or on the bargaining relationship itself.

Public sector unions generally favor the availability of arbitration; management groups typically oppose it. The efficacy of arbitration can vary, depending on traditions and applications. In the state of Wisconsin, for example, arbitration has contributed to stability in relationships by speeding up closure (US Department of Labor, 1996). In other places, especially where final-offer arbitration is the dominant procedure, management and union representatives may often be found to take extreme positions and leave much of the responsibility to the arbitrator. A drawn-out bargaining and arbitration process can leave the contract and other aspects of the relationship unsettled for a lengthy period of time. In conflictual relationships or where interest arbitration is otherwise a frequent resort, settlement without intervention by an arbitrator can be rare, and the general problem-solving ability of the parties can break down (Brock, 1982; US Department of Labor, 1996).

Until recently, most states prohibited strikes by public employees, and even now there are few exceptions. The argument has been over sovereignty, that is that the state employer, as an extension of the sovereign and provider of vital services, should not face the risk of work stoppages that private employers face. The argument today holds little weight in debates over whether to grant collective bargaining rights,[20] but the right to strike remains rare. Today, ten states specifically grant the right to strike to certain classes of public employees.[21] Federal employees cannot legally strike.

Strikes by public employees still happen, but they have been relatively uncommon in the last two decades. The Reagan administration's break of the air traffic controllers' strike in 1981 is widely credited with putting a damper on public employee strikes. Between 1982 and 1997, there were 116 work stoppages in state and local governments, which idled 627,750 workers and accounted for 5.4 million lost work days. Approximately four-fifths of the strike activity happened at the local level. Education accounted for nearly three-quarters of the work stoppages, followed by general administration (12 stoppages, idling 81,500 workers) and transportation (15 stoppages, idling 53,600 workers) (Cimini, 1998).

Virtually all contracts have multi-step grievance procedures beginning with an informal resolution step, escalating one or two steps through the management hierarchy, and normally ending in arbitration. Increasingly, contracts emphasize a mediation step early in the process. If the parties fail to resolve their disputes using contractually specified mechanisms the employee must exhaust administrative remedies, including arbitration, before taking the dispute to court. The state and federal court systems have approved of most of the major arbitration practices in use, and courts tend to defer to the contract or to administrative agency's decision unless they identify an "arbitrary and capricious" violation of procedural or substantive rights on the part of an arbitrator or administrative agency.

Exhaustion of administrative remedies usually is required before a court will enforce general statutory employment rights. The Occupational Safety and Health Administration (OSHA) and the Equal Employment Opportunity Commission (EEOC) are the two major federal agencies involved in these types of disputes. Each agency has a different enforcement mechanism or administrative structure for adjudicating issues and for voluntary conflict resolution that ultimately allows the employee to appeal a case in court (US Department of Labor, 1994). Their authority supersedes contractual provisions in most instances, although they are increasingly deferring to private dispute resolution engaged in by the parties. In addition, the US Supreme Court has recently resurrected the state sovereignty argument to prevent state employees from accessing the federal court system in certain instances. This may encourage growth of private dispute resolution and mediation services. In response to a growing backlog of administrative cases and the level of conflict in many workplaces, a group of labor, management, and neutral leaders in the public and private sectors recently produced a set of protocols for voluntary mediation and arbitration in many employment law disputes (US Department of Labor, 1994, 1996). The Massachusetts Commission Against Discrimination has adopted these protocols, and the protocols have been endorsed by major employers and employee organizations, in both public and private sectors, as well as prominent civil rights and civil liberties groups. The protocols carefully preserve the statutory and constitutional rights of employees and provide for faster, less expensive resolution of disputes.

Reform efforts

Legislatures have passed some useful but modest reforms of civil service systems over the last two decades. Some reforms have addressed overlapping civil service and collective bargaining laws; most have concentrated on decentralization, creating more flexibility and agency authority in the hiring process, broadening job classifications, and reducing the overall number of job classifications. Other reforms have responded to pressures on service delivery and governmental budgets. The growing focus on service delivery improvement has dramatically lessened the interest group and labor–management disagreements that diluted attempts at system-wide reform in the late 1970s and 1980s. Employee groups and conservative politicians have actually found common ground in improving service quality and efficiency and the quality of work life. However, conflict and rigidity remain, and many civil service systems and collective bargaining processes continue to be plagued by lack of sufficient problem-solving capacity (US Department of Labor, 1996).

The prospects are reasonably good for continued civil service reforms based on response to service and workplace problems because both unions and management see the potential benefits to both quality of service and quality of work life. On the other hand, the prospects for new state laws granting bargaining rights or reforming existing labor laws are complicated by substantial disagreement in the local and national political communities over the terms of public employee bargaining.

In general, there has been little movement toward legal reform of state bargaining laws, nor for extension of such laws where they don't currently exist. Public employee bargaining is a highly controversial political issue and major battle lines form over any suggested legislative change. Thus, the prospect for legislative leadership on reform does not seem promising. The most useful movement by far is the advent of cooperative, service-oriented relationships that can be developed within most existing statutory frameworks by simple agreement of the involved parties without engaging the larger political mechanisms in the debate. While new legislation could encourage and spread cooperative relationships, such changes do not seem to be necessary. The development, major features and results of cooperative relationships are discussed in depth in *Working Together For Public Service*, the report submitted in 1996 to the US Secretary of Labor on the subject of excellence in government through labor–management cooperation.

Another development that has gotten limited recent legislative and academic attention should be mentioned. Some have argued that the public should play a greater role in public sector labor relations, and that the relationship is not just between the parties as in the private sector because the public has a legitimate interest at stake. So far, public involvement has generally been limited to informal input or membership on specific task forces. Non-traditional relationships of this sort have been most common in school districts, where teachers, administrators and parents join teams that deal with policy and operational issues or general problem solving in areas that have often been reserved to collective bargaining. While interesting and productive in reported instances, movement in this direction has not been widespread.

Cooperative relationships have reduced costs, improved service, facilitated conflict resolution, reduced grievances, and improved the quality of work life by increasing job security, improving skills and advancement opportunities and raising wages or bonuses. Workers have a greater voice, managers gain more control over service quality by the involvement of workers in service decisions, and the elected officials see benefit as well in increased public satisfaction with government services. It is not unusual for these relationships to produce savings or productivity improvements in the 20 percent range, reductions of grievances by up to 90 percent, and reduction of time (and frustration) spent in bargaining from many months or years to only a few weeks or months (US Department of Labor, 1996).

The trend toward cooperation is promising and may overcome typical barriers to a more effective public employment bargaining relationship. However, longstanding traditions and suspicions, external and internal political considerations, the decentralized nature of the state-by-state system, and issues of change from the familiar and accepted all present formidable barriers to cooperative relationships. Additionally, local union leaders and many in management generally favor the approach but remain concerned about the ability to trust the other side. This is normally overcome after a few successful cooperative activities, but the success rate is not 100 percent, of course. The capacity for teaching, training, or providing technical assistance to parties interested in this approach is limited but growing, as is awareness of the impact on quality of service, work life and the collective bargaining relationship.

Conclusions

The personnel and labor laws for public employees are developed jurisdiction by jurisdiction. This has limited both the uniformity and availability of bargaining rights nation wide, but civil service systems tend to be uniform in legal and administrative structure. The decentralization of personnel departments and hiring authority is a trend that has appeared in many jurisdictions. Contracting out or privatization have not emerged as a major set of force affecting employment or how work gets done in the public sector, although it remains controversial.

The labor laws and related mechanisms for the public sector are in many ways similar to those governing the private sector, but prominently different in coverage and dispute resolution. While the traditional public sector labor–management relationship has grown up to be somewhat formal and legalistic, informal relationships and supplementary structures are not uncommon. More comprehensive and more consistently productive relationships are emerging that focus on quality of service and which make use of interest-based bargaining. Where cooperative relationships have formed, existing bargaining structures in the jurisdiction are adapting to broader, more complete use of the relationship. Cooperative, service-oriented relationships supplement bargaining with other problem-solving forums and processes, including joint labor–management efforts, use of quality improvement principles and mediation of grievances.

The high degree of interest in service quality reforms has been a major force in recent years, and extends to the accelerating application of information technology to government service. Information technology is becoming an extremely important factor in public sector employment because of its implications for the delivery of services and information to citizens. It has also been a critical factor in defining and altering the roles and responsibilities of both union and management players in many collective bargaining relationships. In general, the main avenues for reform in recent years have not been from academia, the federal government, or other nation-wide influences or authorities, or even from state-level legislative reform. The leaders in reform have been the states or local relationships that have experimented with responses to political and economic pressures. The results of those experiments has spurred others to follow suit and the results and principles are becoming an increasing part of the national dialogue in academia, in labor and management leadership circles, and among the interested professional associations. It is likely that continued sources of change, improvement and reform will come through these multiple, decentralized channels.

Notes

1. In 1998, the breakdown of state and local (combined) services was approximately: education (52 percent); health, housing and public welfare (14 percent); public safety (12 percent); administrative and other (including libraries) (10 percent); transportation (5 percent); utilities (3 percent); and environmental (3 percent) (see US Census Bureau, 1998a).
2. In 1998, the breakdown of federal services was approximately: postal (31 percent); defense and international relations (27 percent); health, housing and public welfare (14 percent); administrative and other (including libraries) (11 percent); environmental (8 percent); public safety (5 percent); transportation (2 percent); legal/judicial (2 percent); space research and technology (>1 percent); and education (>1 percent) (see US Census Bureau, 1998a).
3. Between 1988 and 1998, total employment growth in all sectors was around 1.6 percent, while state and local employment growth was 1.7 percent. Projections to 2008 show total employment growth falling to 1.4 percent and state and local government employment growth falling to 1.1 percent. Over the 1988–98 period, federal employment fell by 1.0 percent, and is expected to rise slightly to negative 0.5 percent by 2008 (US Bureau of Labor Statistics, 1999b).
4. In 1998, the state government workforce was 51.3 percent women, and local government workforce was 60.4 percent women (US Bureau of Labor Statistics, 1999c). Federal government employees, however, were just 44 percent women (US Office of Personnel Management, 1999).
5. Between 1980 and 1983, women were 49.2 percent (1980), 51.2 percent (1981, 1982), and 51.1 percent (1983) of the state and local government workforce. In 1998, the combined state and local government workforce was 57.9 percent women (US Bureau of Labor Statistics, 1999c).
6. The number of federal employees in 1998 fell to 2.6 million, the lowest level since 1973 (US Bureau of Labor Statistics, 1998).
7. According to survey data in New York State, 54 percent of local government restructuring was accomplished through intermunicipal cooperation. Privatization of government services occurred in 28 percent of the cases, but government entrepreneurship and "reverse privatization" occurred in 15 percent of the cases. The other approach represented in the survey was cessation of government services (Mildred and Hebdon, 1999).
8. US Bureau of Labor Statistics, The Employment Situation, Table B-1 (1999a). Of these, 181,077 work in Washington, DC, 1.5 million are scattered throughout the rest of the country, and the remainder work abroad (US Census Bureau, 1998b).
9. 1998 data: 4.6 million state employees; 12.5 million local government employees (US Bureau of Labor Statistics, 1999d).
10. In 1998, state and local governments employed approximately 7.5 million educational employees (elementary, secondary, higher education and other), roughly 52 percent of all state and local government employees (US Census Bureau, 1998c).

11. Consequently, protective services employees and educational employees (which include some private sector workers) have the highest unionization rate of all occupational groups (41.3 percent) (US Bureau of Labor Statistics, 1999e).
12. Georgia, Idaho, Indiana, Kansas, Maryland, North Dakota, Oklahoma, Tennessee, and Wyoming grant collective bargaining rights only to certain classes of employees (see Cimini, 1998).
13. Federal employees are prohibited from striking under 5 U.S.C. §7311. Some state and local employees have limited statutory rights to strike in ten states: Alaska, Hawaii, Illinois, Minnesota, Montana (nurses only), Ohio, Oregon, Pennsylvania, Vermont and Wisconsin. Court decisions in California, Idaho and Montana have held more generally that public employees have a right to strike even in the absence of specific legislation granting that right (see Cimini, 1998).
14. Forty-nine percent of state employees are covered by collective bargaining agreements in the 28 states that allow their state employees collective bargaining rights. This contrasts with a rate of representation at only 15 percent in non collective bargaining states. Similarly in local government, the representation rates in the 36 states (plus DC) that allow collective bargaining is 58 percent, as compared to only 25 percent in the states that do not permit collective bargaining (Cimini, 1998).
15. Public sector union membership in the US in 1987 was 5.2 million; in 1997 it was 6.7 million. Over the same period, union membership remained steady at 37.2 percent of the public sector workforce, though it grew significantly in individual states with newly enacted collective bargaining laws (US Bureau of Labor Statistics, 1999c). For a summary of the discussion of unionization rates and the effects of the passage of state collective bargaining laws, see Hindman and Patton, 1994.
16. The states that allow at least some state or local public employees collective bargaining rights by statute or executive order include: Alaska, California, Connecticut, Delaware, the District of Columbia, Florida, Georgia, Hawaii, Idaho, Illinois, Indiana, Iowa, Kansas, Maine, Maryland, Massachusetts, Michigan, Minnesota, Montana, Nebraska, Nevada, New Hampshire, New Jersey, New Mexico, New York, North Dakota, Ohio, Oklahoma, Oregon, Pennsylvania, Rhode Island, South Dakota, Tennessee, Vermont, Washington, Wisconsin and Wyoming (see Cimini, 1998).
17. The states granting collective bargaining rights to all local government employees include: Alaska, California, Connecticut, Delaware, the District of Columbia, Florida, Hawaii, Illinois, Iowa, Maine, Massachusetts, Michigan, Minnesota, Montana, Nebraska, Nevada, New Hampshire, New Jersey, New Mexico, New York, Ohio, Oregon, Pennsylvania, Rhode Island, South Dakota, Vermont, Washington and Wisconsin (Cimini, 1998).
18. These states include: Georgia, Idaho, Indiana, Kansas, Maryland, North Dakota, Oklahoma, Tennessee and Wyoming. Texas also allows teachers, police and fire-fighters to bargain collectively under local law rather than state law (see Cimini, 1998).
19. The states that grant collective bargaining rights to all local government employees also grant similar rights to state employees, with the exception of Nevada, which does not permit bargaining by state employees. In addition, Indiana, Kansas and Maryland allow state employees to collectively bargain,

although among local employees in these states, only teachers may do so. State employees in each of these three states were granted their rights through executive order rather than through legislative enactment (see Cimini, 1998).
20. However, the Supreme Court has recently resurrected state sovereignty in restricting the ability of state employees to enforce workplace labor standards under the federal Fair Labor Standards Act in the federal court system in the absence of a waiver of sovereign immunity by the state.
21. States with right-to-strike laws include: Alaska, Hawaii, Illinois, Minnesota, Montana, Ohio, Oregon, Pennsylvania, Vermont and Wisconsin. In addition, public employees in California, Idaho and Montana who are not covered by right-to-strike statutes may still have the legal right to strike as determined by the courts in those states (Cimini, 1998).

References

Brock, J. (1982) Bargaining Beyond Impasse, Auburn House.
Cimini, M. (1998) "1982–87 State and Local Government Work Stoppages and Their Legal Background," in US Bureau of Labor Statistics, *Compensation and Working Conditions*, Fall.
Hindman, H. D. and Patton, D. B. (1994) "Unionism in State and Local Governments: Ohio and Illinois, 1982–1987," *Industrial Relations*, XXXIII (1) January.
Mildred, W. and Hebdon, R. (1999) "Local Government Restructuring in New York – Summary of Survey Results," *Restructuring Local Government*, Cornell University Department of City and Regional Planning, July.
US Bureau of Labor Statistics (1997) Employment Projections, November.
US Bureau of Labor Statistics (1998) Historical Empolyment Data.
US Bureau of Labor Statistics (1999a) *The Employment Situation*, November.
US Bureau of Labor Statistics (1999b) "Industry output and employment projections to 2008," *Monthly Labor Review*, November.
US Bureau of Labor Statistics (1999c) "Employment and Earnings," *Historical Establishment Data*, January.
US Bureau of Labor Statistics (1999d) *Historical Establishment Data*, November.
US Bureau of Labor Statistics (1999e) *Union Membership (Annual)*, January.
US Census Bureau (1998a) *Annual Public Employment and Payroll*, March.
US Census Bureau (1998b) *Census of Governments*, March.
US Census Bureau (1998c) *State and Local Government Employment and Payroll Data*, March.
US Department of Labor (1994) The Report of the Commission on the Future of Worker Management Relations, "Dunlop Report," Section 5 May.
US Department of Labor (1996) *Working Together for Public Service*: Report of the US Secretary of Labor's Task Force on Excellence in State and Local government through Labor–management cooperation, May.
US Office of Personnel Management (1999) *The Fact Book: Federal Civilian Workforce Statistics*, September.

6
Canadian Public Sector Employment
Mark Thompson

Introduction

The traditional Canadian view of the state has been challenged by government efforts to control or reduce expenditures, beginning in the late 1980s. Reduction of government deficits became a primary goal of government fiscal policies. A prime minister made reducing the size of the national public service an election issue in 1984. Virtually all governments have restricted spending, from holding increases to the rise in the consumer price index to absolute expenditure reductions. Where population growth dictates increased demand for such services as health and education, per capita spending declined in real terms. Table 6.1 demonstrates the broad impact of these policies.

Policies used to reduce the size of the state have varied. In broad terms, governments had the options of diminishing the scope of state action or reducing payroll costs. Individual governments have followed both policies, although the latter was more frequent.

Government has withdrawn from a few functions completely. The most common examples are the shifting of physical infrastructure, such as telecommunications, railways and airports, to the private sector or to a quasi-governmental agency. Both federal and provincial governments controlled by all three major national parties have privatized public enterprises in these sectors. Contracting out, especially support services, has increased (Thompson, 1995). By 1996, approximately half of Canadian municipalities contracted out solid waste management, for instance (McDavid and Elder, 1997).

The most common initiative has been to attempt to maintain services while reducing payroll costs, either by cutting the number of employees or controlling compensation. Many governments have followed both

Table 6.1 Government final consumption as a percent of GDP, current prices

Year	Government consumption (%)
1980	19.2
1985	20.1
1990	20.3
1995	19.5
1997	20.0

Source: OECD, National Accounts, Volume 1, Paris: OECD, 1997; Quarterly National Accounts Bulletin (1999).

policies. The number of employees has fallen in several branches of government. To address labor costs, wage controls have been imposed.

Despite these changes, however, governments have not abandoned direct responsibility for traditional activities of the Canadian state: public education at all levels, health care, social assistance, public safety, and the like. Examples of dramatic reorganization of public sector agencies are not frequent, but widely publicized (Borins, 1994; Warrian, 1996; OECD, 1995).

The nation's political system is a significant factor in determining the shape of change. Canada is a decentralized federal state. The national ("federal") government has a relatively modest role in economic and social affairs. The ten provinces control health, education, commerce and natural resources, and deal with most economic issues. Most police, fire protection, local transit, garbage collection and urban infrastructure fall under the jurisdiction of municipalities or government agencies under local political control. Public education is governed separately, usually through locally elected boards. Federal and provincial governments have created a number of public enterprises (known as "Crown corporations") to perform a variety of functions outside of the scope of the public service.

Canada has a Westminster-style parliamentary system, similar to those of other British Commonwealth nations. The degree of decentralization in Canadian political and social affairs is unusual, however. The constitution dictates the separation of powers between the federal and provincial governments. In addition, national political parties are weak (or occasionally non-existent) provincially. Provinces have distinctive political cultures. The second largest province, Quebec, is predominantly French speaking, although a significant English-speaking minority lives there too. A large portion of the French-speaking population favor independence from Canada. Two referenda on separation have taken place, both ending in narrow victories for the federalists, that is, voters who favor remaining in Canada. Because of this separatist sentiment in Quebec, national unity normally dominates federal politics.

Canada's decentralized political system has produced a complex structure in the public sector. For purposes of this paper, "public sector" includes public administration at the three levels of government: federal, provincial and municipal; primary and secondary education, and health. These functions include most of the public sector in Canada. Principal exclusions are the armed forces and national police force (itself a paramilitary organization) and public enterprises.

Organizational structure, employment and wages

Organization

The authority of federal government is concentrated in monetary and fiscal policies, the regulation of transportation and communications (for example railways, telecommunications), plus national defense and foreign relations. A more important federal function is the transfer of funds to the provinces for health care, social assistance and post-secondary education. Reductions in these payments have a cascade effect on the finances of other levels of government.

While the role of the federal government is limited constitutionally, it has exercised political leadership in public sector industrial relations. In 1967, the federal legislation established collective bargaining, modeled on the private sector, as the preferred method for regulating employment relations in the federal public service. Beginning in 1975, the federal government also led the way on restrictions on public sector industrial relations. In that year, the government implemented a three-year anti-inflation policy directed primarily at public sector workers at all levels of government. The federal government reimposed controls on collective bargaining in 1982 when it extended existing collective agreements for two years, imposed limits on new settlements, and prohibited strikes. Most provinces followed the lead of the federal government, imposing their own versions of the federal program (Panitch and Swartz, 1993).

The locus of power in the Canadian political system is with the provinces, and their role in public sector industrial relations reflects that fact. Constitutionally, each of the ten provinces has the authority to legislate the conduct of both public and private sector industrial relations. The provinces are responsible for regulating most business activity, funding health care and social assistance, protecting the environment, part of law enforcement, funding and overseeing the delivery of public education. Health, education and social assistance (welfare) dominate provincial budgets. In the case of health care and education, provinces have traditionally delegated administrative responsibility to local boards, although a process of centralization is underway, as explained below. Each province has at least one statute governing industrial relations for its own employees, and normally several statutes exist for individual segments of the public sector, in particular health care, law enforcement and education.

The combination of constitutional autonomy and weak national political institutions has produced a high degree of variation in many aspects of provincial policy, including industrial relations. While the examples of federal leadership cited above were important, political forces generally limit the role of the federal government. Provincial political and industrial relations climates differ substantially. The importance of provincial governments in Canadian life has contributed to the politicization of public sector industrial relations, since interest groups have ready access to policy makers.

Municipalities are creatures of provincial governments, but they traditionally have enjoyed considerable autonomy in conducting industrial relations. They provide a few social services, the physical infrastructure of urban life, as well as police and fire protection. Municipal politics are seldom tied closely to provincial organizations. Government operations are funded by a combination of provincial grants and local property taxes, with the latter revenue source being the more important. Private sector labor law has governed municipal industrial relations, except for police and fire services, since modern Canadian labor legislation was first enacted in the 1930s. The political and legal autonomy has given a special flavor to municipal labor relations. Structures are highly decentralized and relatively small, so that labor relations are usually peaceful. Civic employees work and live in close proximity to municipal taxpayers (Graham, 1995). In some settings, especially in winter, municipal employees perform essential services, for example snow removal, a factor that also influences the conduct of industrial relations.

Education traditionally has been the responsibility of locally elected school boards in Canada. Gradually, provincial payments to equalize educational opportunities for children in regions with disparate tax bases grew more important and became the major source of funding for local boards in most provinces. The expansion of provincial funding naturally increased the voice of provincial governments in both financial and educational questions. As part of this movement, the number of local school boards or their autonomy has been reduced. For industrial relations, this movement has produced essentially province-wide bargaining for school staff in seven provinces (Thomason, 1995). Health care is also under the authority of provincial governments. A variety of institutions, public, private and non-profit deliver health care. Most institutions are run by non-profit societies dependent almost exclusively on government funding. A traditionally strong local orientation has been undermined by provincial policies to centralize hospital administration in an effort to reduce overhead and divert funds to direct care of patients. Since provincial governments were responsible for costs, they mandated regional or provincial bargaining structures in the 1970s (Haiven, 1995). As the impact of spending restraints was felt in the health sector, governments created regional bodies to coordinate health care delivery in specific areas. In turn, individual hospitals lost their operational autonomy. Hospitals became "sites," operating under the direction of regional management. This model represents an intermediate form of centralization of authority. However, the model is still evolving, and the effects of regional health boards on province-wide bargaining are still uncertain.

Employment

The relative importance of the five segments of the public sector is shown in Table 6.2.

Table 6.2 Public sector employment, 1980–1995

Year	Level of Government				
	Federal admin	Provincial admin	Local admin	School boards	Hospitals
1980	206,573	439,314	292,632	453,172	N/A
1985	223,173	497,274	317,782	434,172	509,628
1990	216,778	470,508	358,853	499,955	572,962
1995	210,517	473,192	368,927	530,470	546,848

Source: Statistics Canada, Cansim (1996); Public Service Commission of Canada. *Annual Report*, various years; Statistics Canada, *Public Sector Employment and Wages and Salaries*. Ottawa: Minister of Supply and Services, Cat. No. 72-209, various years; Statistics Canada. *Provincial and Territorial Government Employment*. Ottawa: Minister of Supply and Services, Cat. No. 72-007, various years.

Of the three levels of public service, provincial governments have the greatest number of employees, consistent with their power in the Canadian confederation. While employment has declined in the public services, the local government, where services are delivered directly to citizens, has increased employment over the time period considered. Population levels drive many of these services. Some functions (and staff) moved to lower levels of government as senior governments reduced spending. Overall, the proportion of the labor force represented by the public sector considered here has declined slightly, as Table 6.3 indicates.

Canada has embraced the concept of a permanent neutral civil service in most regions, with recruitment and promotions administered at least in part by an apolitical civil service commission (for federal or provincial public services) or a professional management function (for local government, health and education boards). Public sector employers traditionally have offered employees a high degree of job security. When collective bargaining appeared in the 1960s (discussed below), unions attempted to reinforce job security by introducing formal recognition of seniority in personnel decisions, entrenching the principle that employees could only be dismissed for cause and negotiated training programs to facilitate the redeployment of staff (Thompson and Fryer, 2000).

The public sector labor force in Canada is predominantly female, and the proportion of women is growing. A study of public services found that women held over 40 percent of the federal public service and over 50 percent of provincial public services. Women are highly represented in traditional occupations, clerical workers, teachers, and nurses, for example, but the proportion of females in executive and scientific positions in the federal public service has grown steadily and approached

Table 6.3 Public sector employment share of labor force, 1980–1997

	Employment all employees (000)	Public sector employment (000)	Public sector percent of total
1980	9,620	2,458	25.6
1985	10,065	2,591	25.7
1990	11,276	2,672	23.7
1995	11,370	2,659	23.4
1998	11,801	2,598	22.0

Source: Table 2, Statistics Canada. *Historical Labor Force Statistics.* Ottawa: Minister of Supply and Services, Cat. No. 71-201-XPP, 1998.

25 percent by 1997 (Peters, 1999). The two largest occupations in the public service, teachers and nurses, are also dominated numerically by women. An estimated 65 percent of teachers are females, as are over 90 percent of nurses.

In 1996, approximately 9 per cent of all employees in federal and provincial public services were managers. Public sector employers use temporary workers frequently, although comprehensive data are not available. A review of public service data revealed that approximately 18 per cent of all employees were on fixed-term appointments. Overall, that figure did not change in the 1990s, but the experience of individual provinces varied considerably (Peters, 1999). In provinces with strong labor movements or relatively benign governments, the proportion of term employees fell, as they bore the brunt of reductions in staff complements. Elsewhere the number rose as governments cut the size of the permanent civil service. The use of such employees has been a major issue in bargaining between the parties in health and education, as unions resist employer efforts to rely more heavily on non-standard workers.

Wages and salaries

Compensation systems in the Canadian public sector are essentially collective. Pay for a job is based on a position with a grade assigned according to levels of responsibility, qualifications and other job characteristics. The rates for specific positions normally are negotiated in a comprehensive collective agreement, leaving few elements of individual compensation exist. A scale usually exists for each position with provision for virtually automatic progression based on length of service, a common practice in public sector compensation (OECD, 1994). The length of the progression varies with the complexity of the position. Promotions are typically based on a combination of seniority and ability. In federal and provincial civil services, these decisions tend to fall under the jurisdiction of a public service commission. At other levels of the public sector, they are subject to collective agreements. The classification and reclassification of positions is a continuing issue in public sector organizations, where career mobility may be limited by the constraints of an internal labor market and the lack of growth in the absolute number of positions in many employers.

Disparity in pay for traditionally male and traditionally female positions in the public sector has been a significant issue. Some differences arose from conscious discrimination against women or other minorities. A more common factor was reliance on job evaluation and compensation systems favoring the characteristics of male jobs as compared with female-dominated jobs. The Canadian Constitution guarantees equal treatment for all citizens by government. All jurisdictions have human rights legislation prohibiting discrimination on the basis of gender.

The combination of these legal requirements and the political visibility of the public sector have made it a leader in efforts to eliminate the results of past discrimination against women in pay. The most common means of resolving pay equity issues has been through a negotiated settlement between governments or individual public sector employers and their unions. Over 100,000 women in provincial and federal public services have received pay adjustments to redress past discrimination. Thousands more have received similar payments in other elements of the public sector (Weiner, 1995). A collective agreement covering approximately 45,000 British Columbia hospital workers signed in mid 1998 provided for two annual payments of 1 percent of payroll for pay equity.

Public sector pay scales are compressed, that is, the ratio of senior management compensation to pay for entry level positions is much lower than the private sector. In general fringe benefits – pensions, paid time off, or insurance plans – are considered to be more generous in the public sector than in the private sector, and the public sector traditionally has offered greater job security than the private sector (Gunderson, 1995).

Because of the decentralized structure of the Canadian public sector, compensation for specific positions can be adjusted to reflect local market conditions, subject to collective bargaining. The exception to this generalization is the federal public service, which has a strong tradition of standard national rates of pay. Where this policy has created serious difficulties with recruitment or retention of staff, small adjustments have been made (OECD, 1994).

For many years, Canadian public sector employers, especially the federal government, attempted to base compensation on comparisons with the private sector. Comparisons became controversial in the 1970s, after the introduction of collective bargaining in large elements of the public sector. A modest public sector advantage, on the order of 5–10 percent existed, favoring lower-paid workers and females. Since the introduction of wage controls, discussed elsewhere in this chapter, the public sector advantage has diminished if not disappeared (Gunderson, 1995). Fringe benefits are normally superior in the public sector. Virtually all permanent public sector workers are covered by

pension plans, for instance. In the entire labor force, coverage is less than 50 percent.
Pay for performance is limited to senior executive positions. Consultants and critics of the status quo in public administration have advocated increased use of this system (Warrian, 1996), but the practice appears to be relatively rare outside higher management. Similarly, pay systems for non-managerial employees have grown more centralized as part of government efforts to control costs. Individual bonuses or productivity pay systems are rare for non-managerial employees. Despite isolated examples of restructuring of pay groups in individual elements of the public sector, this is not a general trend (Marsden, 1993). Rather than alter the structure of pay systems, Canadian public sector employers have concentrated on pay restraint.

The actors: employers and employer associations

Labor legislation establishes the framework for management's position within the division of powers outlined above. Public service labor relations statutes, both federal and provincial, normally provide for an agency to represent the employer. Labor legislation recognizes municipal governments, school boards (for non-teaching personnel) and hospitals as separate employers, with essentially the same rights and obligations as private sector employers. The role of individual organizations in industrial relations depends on the structure of bargaining, discussed below.

Public sector employers are generally represented by professional managers in labor relations matters. At all levels of government, recruitment and compensation of most managers are consistent with the merit principle of public services.

The authority of management in public sector industrial relations depends on factors beyond their legal rights. In general, the authority of public sector management is more diffuse than in the private sector. Some limits on management authority are deliberate, reflecting assumptions about the value of checks and balances, the tension between political and non-political decisions, and local versus central control.

The degree of political influence on industrial relations decisions varies greatly, but open participation by political leaders is rare. In highly centralized negotiations, such as the public service of Quebec, or public education in Saskatchewan, cabinet ministers responsible for the function, or the minister of finance, inevitably take part in negotiations. Public sector unions lobby politicians and the public, but they are seldom able to exercise decisive influence over significant industrial relations decisions by undermining the authority of management negotiators (Ponak and Thompson, 1995).

The combination of provincial funding and local control produces tensions in bargaining. Provincial governments have increased their intervention in bargaining, despite legal rights of local employers to make industrial relations decisions. In 1993, for instance, the British Columbia provincial government established a "public sector employers council" to coordinate bargaining for the entire public sector in the province. Cabinet ministers are a majority on the council, which issues "wage and benefit guidelines" for all employers. While the council has no legal authority to control the results of bargaining, the power of the provincial government effectively makes the "guidelines" binding on employers. This type of control has increased the number of employer associations, as they facilitate the imposition of restrictions on bargaining within branches of the public sector.

Employer associations traditionally have represented management in hospitals and schools. Less frequently, employer associations represent municipalities, although employer groups do coordinate bargaining in some regions without relying on an association to act as their bargaining agent. Nationally, there are associations specifically to conduct labor relations functions and broad-purpose associations, which represent employers' interests in several areas, including labor issues. The single purpose associations normally act as the bargaining agents for their members, that is, they negotiate collective agreements that are binding on member organizations. Depending on provincial legislation and labor relations board decisions, the associations may bargain a single agreement covering all members or a series of separate agreements (which are normally quite similar) for individual employers. Such associations also may provide advice and direct assistance on the administration of collective agreements.

Broad purpose associations serve as the spokespersons for their industry to government, the public and other interest groups. Often they assist members with administrative functions, such as information technology, purchasing, training, and the like. Thus, labor relations is but one specialized service they provide to their members. Unlike the single-purpose associations, these organizations are less likely to have the right to negotiate binding collective agreements on behalf of their members. Individual members, in particular large or specialized facilities, may retain the right to reject agreements or to insist on separate contracts to reflect their needs or desires. In Alberta, for example, large teaching hospitals have insisted on different terms from smaller facilities in their collective agreements (Wetzel and Gallagher, 1984).

The use of employer associations is most developed in Quebec, where public sector bargaining is highly centralized. Health, education, and local government employers all rely on associations as their bargaining agents in that province. Several other provinces, including Alberta, British Columbia, and Saskatchewan, have long had associations in the health sector (Haiven, 1995). Most provinces have established regional agencies to oversee the provision of all health services. While employer associations in the health sector have long represented large hospitals, their role was much less important for smaller health care providers, such as home nursing services, group homes, and the like. Regional boards now control a wide range of service providers. In the province of Saskatchewan, for instance, with a population under 1 million, 366 autonomous entities were amalgamated into 30 districts (Dorsey, 1997). These regional organizations in turn lend themselves to province-wide bargaining arrangements. Provincial governments have also amalgamated local school boards and established centralized bargaining structures. In British Columbia, the government reduced the number of locally elected school boards by one-third and imposed province-wide bargaining. While no data on the number of public sector employers represented by associations are available, it is clear that the significance of these organizations is growing. Provincial governments have favored centralized bargaining structures as a means of controlling compensation, and employer groups are essential to that strategy.

In the Westminster parliamentary system, political appointments are limited to the most senior levels of government, and Canadian governments generally follow that pattern. Thus, governments rely on permanent civil services that do not turn over substantially after changes in government affiliation. Managers are subject to performance evaluation, and virtually the only examples of pay for performance in the Canadian public sector are used for senior managers. In the 1990s, the public sector generally emphasized measurable outcomes for individual units or agencies, including the logical step of linking compensation to performance within specified salary ranges for levels of responsibility. These systems are far from universal and have not yet had a major impact on the compensation levels of most managers. Government emphasis on spending restraint and unilateral freezes on employee compensation has made efforts to change compensation systems for managers politically difficult. From time to time, inferior pay at senior levels creates staffing shortages in government, but in general the cadre of professional public sector managers is adequate for the tasks assigned. Opportunities for post-government employment as lobbyists are limited and do not form a significant part of the career path of public sector managers.

Collective bargaining legislation excludes most managers from union bargaining units. None the less, the norm is that public sector managers are members of informal associations which consult with senior officials and politicians regarding remuneration, job security, and the like.

The actors: trade unions

Unions in the Canadian public sector normally hold certificates of exclusive representation for a specific work place or employer issued by an administrative tribunal, in keeping with normal practice in Canadian industrial relations. Unions that demonstrate they represent a majority of workers in the specified bargaining unit receive certificates. Public service bargaining units often are established by specified in special bargaining legislation; for other elements in the public sector, the tribunal determines the appropriate bargaining unit. This system produced varied and decentralized bargaining structures in the public sector. Many craft or occupational bargaining units exist, especially in health care and local government. It is not uncommon for a municipal employer to have separate bargaining units for blue, and white-collar workers, police departments, fire departments, and supervisors, for instance. Individual bargaining units may have been certified at different times, and their bargaining agents are reluctant to be subsumed into larger organizations, even within the same parent union.

Governments have attempted to deal with this fragmentation in a variety of ways. Most public services have comprehensive bargaining units established by statute. The government of British Columbia has three units, for example. The federal public service statute established over a hundred craft or occupational bargaining units. The parties, under management pressure, negotiated the consolidation of bargaining structures without formally abolishing the craft units. Elsewhere governments have imposed single bargaining structures for multiple employers, effectively certifying an association to represent employers in a particular element of the public sector who bargain with one or more unions.

Nationally, union representation in the Canadian public sector is relatively fragmented. There are separate unions for each of the three major levels of government. The Public Service Alliance of Canada (PSAC) represents federal employees. The National Union of Provincial and General Employees (NUPGE) is a federation of unions representing provincial public service workers outside of Quebec. The Canadian Union of Public Employees (CUPE) represents employees in municipal governments, school boards and many hospitals. The NUPGE and CUPE in particular also represent private sector workers. Some groups were formerly in the public sector, but others have been organized completely from the private sector. All three large unions began with industrial structures but are evolving toward a general union model in response to changes in their employers.

In addition to the three major unions, there are scores of smaller unions, many of them occupational. Police officers, nurses and teachers do not have national unions, but have independent organizations in each province. Other professional employees also have separate organizations. Table 6.4 contains the membership data for the three major public sector unions, plus the total union membership for teachers and nurses, the largest occupational groups without a national union. In health care and education in particular, multiple unions represent workers. It is normal to have at least one union for blue collar and support workers (CUPE) and a teachers union in a school district, for instance. Most hospitals would have at least two unions, one for nurses and another for non-professional personnel, and many hospitals have additional occupational unions.

Major national unions are all affiliated with the Canadian Labor Congress (CLC), the nation's major labor center. Most Quebec public sector unions, in particular the teachers and the provincial public

Table 6.4 Membership, major public sector unions, 1980–1998

Union	Year				
	1980	1985	1990	1995	1998
PSAC	155,731	182,000	162,700	167,800	167,830
NUPGE	195,754	254,300	301,200	299,800	308,970
CUPE	257,180	304,300	376,900	445,000	451,470
Nurses	97,533	130,352	162,806	169,310	165,590
Teachers	273,339	343,535	389,945	360,899	403,800

Source: Human Resources Development Canada, *Directory of Labor Organizations in Canada*, various years, Ottawa: Minister of Supply and Services.

Table 6.5 Public sector union membership and density, 1980–1992

Year	Public administration		Health and social services		Educational services	
	Members	Density (%)	Members	Density (%)	Members	Density (%)
1980	526,966	67.8	N/A	N/A	N/A	N/A
1985	575,921	70.8	N/A	N/A	N/A	N/A
1990	635,254	80.6	588,520	50.8	636,678	77.0
1995	642,600	82.9	592,600	47.4	675,200	70.0

Source: Statistics Canada, *Annual Report of the Minister of Science and Technology under the Corporations and Labor Unions Returns Act*, Cat. No. 72-202, various years, *Unionization in Canada: A retrospective*, Cat. No. 75-001SPE.

servants, belong to a separate French-language central. Police, nurses, teachers and other professional employee unions are normally independent of any labor central. In response to public sector fiscal pressures, a number of small unions have joined CUPE or the NUPGE.

Reductions in government spending, a political climate hostile to government action, and public service layoffs have diminished the bargaining power of these labor organizations. As Table 6.4 indicates, membership of most unions has continued to grow modestly. Other unions have had a similar experience. Because of the fragmented union structure, it is not possible to measure membership changes for all public sector labor organizations, but Table 6.5 indicates that overall union membership and union density have risen slightly since 1980 (Rose, 1995). Public sector union density is about triple private sector levels.

Traditionally, Canadian public sector unions have been relatively apolitical. Few are affiliated to any political party, although officers normally support the New Democratic Party (NDP), a social democratic party. They have enjoyed greater success in their efforts to defend public services. Labor groups find allies among the clients of individual services and promote the maintenance of government functions or the protection of funding for them. Unions' organizational resources are valuable assets to influential, but largely unorganized, client groups.

Public sector labor relations

Existing public policy, expressed in dozens of separate statutes, is that terms and conditions of employment are normally established through a process of collective bargaining. There often are restrictions on a small number of specific subjects, especially pensions and recruitment policies, but collective bargaining dominates.

In broad terms, public sector industrial relations in Canada reflect many of the features of the private sector. Terms and conditions of employment are determined through collective bargaining, which emphasizes detailed regulation of the work place. The parties' rights are spelled out in legislation. Unions are strongly entrenched in the work site, but weak politically. Collective agreements are administered under a system of private grievance handling and arbitration.

The basic features of this system appeared in the 1960s. Employee organizations and collective representation had been common in the public sector for decades. In municipal government, many unions had been certified in the previous thirty years. However, in the public services, health care workers and teachers had not engaged in collective bargaining. Employee associations often consulted with the employer informally. Final decisions rested with management, and there was confusion about the identity of the employer.

Federal legislation enacted in 1967 clearly marked collective bargaining as the preferred method for determining terms and conditions of employment for its own employees. Two years earlier, Quebec had adopted collective bargaining for its public sector, but it was the federal example that influenced other jurisdictions. Negotiation replaced consultation at all levels of the public sector. Teachers' associations evolved rapidly into unions, as did nurses' organizations. Other non-professional health care workers joined existing unions, CUPE in particular. By 1975, virtually all public employees (outside of management) had the legal right to engage in collective bargaining, including either the right to strike or access to arbitration to settle interest disputes. By the late 1970s, public administration was the most heavily unionized industrial sector in the Canadian economy (Ponak and Thompson, 1995).

Since the federal government and each provincial government regulate public sector industrial relations, the number of variations in bargaining policy is substantial. Often provinces have several laws regulating different groups of employees for instance. These laws have arisen out of conjunctures of political and labor relations events and can be highly idiosyncratic. Out of this array of policies and regulations, three typical policies can be identified.

One model is the private sector. All provinces place local government employees under private sector legislation (including non-teaching education workers), and one province covers its public service with private sector laws. The implications of this model are that unions obtain representation at the level of the work place; the parties can bargain over virtually any subject, and labor has the right to strike after the expiry of a collective agreement. The parties construct private systems for resolving mid-contract disputes, ending in arbitration.

A modified private sector model takes private sector legislation as the starting point and imposes specific limits on the parties. Restrictions are most common on the scope of bargaining and the definition of bargaining units. Pensions and the application of the merit system are frequently excluded from the scope of negotiation. Apart from these subjects, the parties are free to negotiate pay and other conditions of employment. Bargaining units are often determined by legislation. When this occurs, the units tend to be large comprehensive groups. The right to strike exists, but it may be circumscribed to discourage its exercise. For example, employees who provide essential services are often required to continue working during a strike by their union. This model prevails in three provinces (Quebec, Ontario and British Columbia) and generally in the health and education sectors. Strikes by health care workers are often illegal. In those cases, the parties resolve disputes through arbitration.

The third type, including seven provinces and the federal government, is restricted bargaining. This model differs from the second set of policies in that restrictions on the scope of bargaining and the use of strikes are more substantial. Not all statutes impose all restrictions, but technological change, procedures for layoffs and promotions may be outside the scope of bargaining. The right to strike is restricted or does not exist. Four of the provinces prohibit strikes in their public services, and a majority ban strikes by police forces and fire-fighters, although arbitration is available (Thompson, 1989).

Public policy favoring collective bargaining leaves the parties relatively free to determine their own procedures and negotiate collective agreements freely. This principle was followed for the first eight to ten years of wide-scale public sector collective bargaining (1967–75). In 1975, the federal government, facing a high rate of inflation, imposed wage and price controls. The controls lasted three years, and normal bargaining resumed in most jurisdictions. A second round of wage controls, confined to the public sector, began in 1982. Since then, some form of wage controls has existed in most jurisdictions.

A new period of controls began in 1991, when the federal government suspended bargaining rights for all of its employees, initially for two years (Bendel, 1992), requiring them to accept a wage freeze or face severe layoffs. Despite the largest strike by a public sector union in Canadian history, the government prevailed. Ultimately, the suspension of bargaining rights lasted for seven years. Following the federal government's action, all provinces imposed some form of restriction on public service wage increases and benefits. Despite the wage freeze, the number of federal employees dropped, largely through attrition and a generous early retirement plan. As Table 6.2 indicates, the number of federal employees fell by about 3 percent during that period, with further reductions planned.

The provinces followed the federal lead in reducing public sector payroll costs. The basic policies followed were to restrict compensation through centralized bargaining and reduce the number of employees in senior levels of government. Restriction on compensation included the suspension of bargaining rights and in some jurisdictions the imposition of absolute reductions in wages and salaries. In general, centrist or left of center governments relied on encouraging resignations or retirements to reduce public sector payrolls, while conservative governments were more likely to use layoffs to accomplish the same objective. A minority imposed cuts, and one, British Columbia, chose to negotiate restructuring plans (Thompson and Fryer, 1994). The NDP government of Ontario forced the parties to negotiate cost reductions under threat of more severe cuts imposed by legislation (Hebdon and Warrian, 1999).

Apart from suspending bargaining rights, the federal government made the most ambitious efforts to restructure the public service to achieve greater efficiencies and to improve service. Beginning in 1990, it embarked on a "far-reaching exercise of self-renewal" (Swimmer et al., 1994). The goal of this effort was to increase the flexibility of the public service of Canada, develop a greater sense of service to the public and to improve efficiency. A range of specific changes were announced, none dealing with the structures or processes of industrial relations, and few directly linked to employment policies more generally. Despite its lofty goals, the exercise attained small successes, partly because it coincided with the suspension of bargaining rights and reductions in the size of the public service, which precluded union cooperation and reduced morale at all levels of government service. A few changes did occur: departments were given operating budgets rather than allocations of personnel, fifteen "special operating agencies" were established to carry out specific government functions in a somewhat independent fashion, and the number of job classifications was reduced (Swimmer et al., 1994). For purposes of this paper, it is noteworthy that the initiative did not contemplate such changes as the decentralization of bargaining units, either on departmental or regional lines, devolution of industrial relations decisions, abandonment of the concept of a significant public service, or alternate forms of employee representation (Dell'Aringa and Murlis, 1993).

Governments neither sought to replace collective bargaining with a more managerialist system of employment relations nor to engage unions in cooperative programs to reduce the costs of government. A few private sector employers and their unions have taken initiatives to improve efficiency and raise employee morale in Canada. However, data available in 1999 show few cooperative programs in the public sector. The Ontario government established a new location for the registrar of vital statistics in 1987, for example. A number of workplace innovations were implemented, affecting training, the organization of work, hiring and output measures (Verma and Cutcher-Gershenfeld, 1996). The NDP government of Saskatchewan agreed to undertake "mutual gains bargaining" with its largest union in the public service, including a commitment to improving service to the public. Participants reported positive results after the first two years (Thompson and Fryer, in press), although the initiative lapsed in 1998. Similar results occurred in British Columbia under an NDP government.

These scattered examples of innovations in public sector bargaining illustrate the possibilities of greater cooperation. The limited number of these cases demonstrates the barriers to transforming public sector industrial relations. Conservative governments, both federal and provincial, have shown little interest in cooperative efforts. NDP governments have had limited success.

Collective bargaining structure

The structure of bargaining in the Canadian public sector historically has been quite decentralized. Local governments, school districts, and some hospitals bargained individually. Provincial and federal civil services carried out centralized bargaining. The existence of employer associations in health care and education described above indicated a degree of centralized negotiations. The provinces of Quebec and British Columbia were the exceptions to this generalization. Quebec in particular combined most public sector bargaining agents into a small number of groups for essentially a single round of bargaining (Hébert, 1995).

During the 1990s senior levels of government (the provinces and the federal government) imposed greater centralization in bargaining. The federal government legally operated under a system of occupational bargaining units, but combined them into ten units, as discussed above, by agreement of the parties, followed by enabling legislation. Several provinces have imposed centralized bargaining for hospitals and other health care providers as part of the restructuring process outlined above. Ontario in particular has attempted to reduce the number of government bodies, including municipalities, which had the result of placing multiple bargaining units into the same negotiation structure. When centralized bargaining occurs, the parties determine the basic outlines of any settlement, especially the financial terms. Often they allow subsidiary negotiations at the local to address issues specific to individual locations. Subsidiary negotiations are not allowed to exceed the parameters of the basic agreement and seldom address major issues.

Collective agreements are consistent with the Canadian norm – legally binding, detailed, and with provision for private arbitration to resolve disputes during their term. The system allows relatively little opportunity for negotiation of special arrangements outside of the scope of the formal agreement. All agreements must have a minimum term of at least one year. During the 1990s, with declining rates of inflation, the average term of collective agreements grew longer. While no data are available for these provisions, three-year agreements have become common, and agreements with five-year terms are not unknown.

Compensation

Prior to the onset of restraint programs, compensation was a controversial issue in Canadian public sector industrial relations. The era of growth in collective bargaining coincided with a period of inflation and general expansion in the role of the state. One cause of the spread of collective bargaining in the public sector in the 1960s and 1970s was the relatively modest compensation levels that prevailed in many organizations. The combination of these circumstances caused the parties to negotiate generous increases in compensation from the mid 1960s through the mid 1970s (Ponak and Thompson, 1995). These increases in turn provoked concern within government and the business community and enabled the federal government to implement the nation's first wage and price control program in 1975.

During the inflationary period of the 1970s and 1980s, public sector compensation surpassed the private sector, at least for some occupations or groups as discussed above. Public sector wage settlements have lagged the private sector in much of the country during the 1990s.

Table 6.6 Cumulative negotiated wage change, private and public sectors, 1980–1996

	1980 index equals 100	
	Public sector	Private sector
1980	100	100
1985	141	139
1990	176	173
1996	188	196

Source: Human Resources Development Canada, unpublished data.

In fact, a number of large public sector employers, including the governments of Alberta, Ontario and Manitoba, imposed absolute reductions in the compensation of their employees, in the form of cuts in rates of pay or requiring employees to take a number of days off without pay each year, with commensurate reductions in take-home pay. Thus, any public sector advantage eroded during the decade and may have disappeared completely. By 1998, the federal government in particular, was experiencing difficulties in recruitment and retention of employees in a number of high demand occupations. Similar pressures are likely to arise in other jurisdictions if unemployment rates decline as predicted. Over time, public sector and private sector settlements have shown very little difference, however. Public sector wage settlements can be volatile, reflecting adjustments after periods of low increases, but they do reflect most of the same economic variables as the private sector (Gunderson and Hyatt, 1996).

Overall, since 1990 negotiated wage increases in the public sector have lagged the private sector slightly, as Table 6.6 indicates. For the previous decade, the public sector led the private sector by a modest margin. The prevalence of wage control measures of course has influenced the results of bargaining, leaving open the question of what the long-term trends in public sector compensation would be without government intervention.

Labor conflict and regulation of strikes

Work stoppages or threatened work stoppages have been a controversial issue in Canadian public sector industrial relations. The social impact of stoppages and their political profile certainly contribute to the high degree of attention paid to stoppages or even threatened stoppages.

Despite these controversies, Canadian policy makers have by and large accepted that bargaining with the possibility of a strike is the preferable technique for resolving labor disputes, a change from a preference for interest arbitration in the 1960s. From the early 1970s, Canada generally had a high strike record compared with most other developed nations, so strikes by public sector workers were part of a larger pattern. Having decided to tolerate strikes in principle, however, Canadian society has been forced to deal with these events when they occur or seem likely to occur.

Overall data on the proportion of Canadian public sector workers who enjoy the legal right to strike do not exist, but the information in Table 6.1 provide the basis for a general estimate. Municipal workers, except for police and fire personnel in some provinces, can strike legally. Provincial employees can strike (with certain restrictions) in seven of the ten provinces (including all of the most populous ones) and in the federal government (Fryer, 1995). A similar proportion of the provinces permit strikes by nurses, the largest employee group in hospitals, again with restrictions to be discussed below (Haiven, 1995). Again with some limitations, teachers, the largest group employed by school boards, have the right to strike in eight of the ten provinces. Taken together, these data lead to an estimate that approximately 75 percent of the workers employed in the public sector universe under discussion have the right to strike. They comprise approximately 40 percent of all union members in Canada.

Against this background, it is clear that public sector workers have a lower propensity to strike and to stay on strike than the private sector. Between 1976 and 1991, the entire public sector (including public enterprises) accounted for an average of 24 percent of all time lost due to strikes and lockouts. The strike rate, that is, strikes as a proportion of bargaining incidents, was 4 percent for the public sector during that time, compared with 14 percent in the private sector (Gunderson and Reid, 1995). However, strike activity declined in Canada, beginning in the mid 1980s, a trend that affected the private sector more than the public sector. Thus, the proportion of time lost in public sector strikes rose relative to the private sector somewhat.

Strike data in the public sector should also be viewed in the context of alternate dispute settlement mechanisms that are not normally available in the private sector. While the strike rate was 4 percent between 1978 and 1991, 9.6 percent of all disputes were subject to interest arbitration, a process not used in the private sector. Another 11 percent of public sector disputes ended with back to work legislation, an event that is more common in the public sector. Thus, approximately 25 percent of all public sector disputes ended in impasse, to be resolved either through a strike or some form of binding third-party intervention.

Within the public sector, the highest strike rates are in local administration, followed by provincial administrations and education/health/welfare. The lowest incidents of strikes have been in the federal administration, where most employees have the right to strike (Gunderson and Reid, 1995).

Despite a general acceptance of public sector strikes, Canadian policy makers have developed a number of mechanisms for avoiding or settling stoppages. Interest arbitration and back to work legislation are common dispute settlement techniques in many countries. Canadian experience with public sector interest arbitration is that the settlement rate declines, to an average of 65 to 75 percent of bargaining incidents. However, strikes are virtually unknown when mandatory interest arbitration exists (Ponak and Thompson, 1995).

A more unusual method is the designation of essential service workers in the public sector, which produces a "controlled strike." In the federal public service, British Columbia and Quebec, there are legislative provisions for the designation of employees who must continue to provide essential services during a work stoppage. Nurses who are in a legal strike position frequently arrange to maintain essential services without a legislative requirement.

The pattern of public sector work stoppages has followed the private sector in many respects. After 1967 until the early 1980s, the most serious labor disputes concerned wages and fringe benefits. After 1983, the number of strikes declined and usually has focused on job security and the preservation of existing terms and conditions of employment.

Beginning in 1998, several large strikes occurred when public sector unions sought to regain some of the economic losses their members had suffered earlier in the decade. When large groups of workers were involved, governments passed (or threaten to pass) legislation ordering the workers to end their strike. Historically, Canadian union members have respected such legislation. Despite public statements attacking federal legislation in 1998, members of the PSAC returned to work after the law was passed. In two provinces, however, nurses' unions openly defied back to work legislation. Both disputes concerned compensation, and the union enjoyed broad public support, a relatively rare circumstance for public sector unions. The nurses forced their employers to revise previous bargaining positions and escaped any penalties for their defiance of the law.

Strike incidence rose nationally in Canada in 1998. Most disputes were over economic issues, in contrast to previous years when job security was the major cause of conflict. The public sector may reflect broader trends in the Canadian economy, but events in the public sector also may be indicators of future unrest in both the public and private sectors.

Where the right to strike is formally absent, interest arbitration is used to resolve disputes. Typically, the parties choose an interest arbitrator. In some systems, the government or an independent agency (a labor relations board) will choose the individual empowered to settle the dispute.

When the right to strike exists, the parties frequently rely on mediation to resolve disputes. The public sector follows the normal Canadian pattern of reliance on professional mediators employed by government. The role of the courts in the daily conduct of Canadian industrial relations is modest. Every jurisdiction has a labor relations board or an equivalent body with the responsibility for the interpretation and administration of labor laws. The common system is that one labor relations board is responsible for private and public sector labor legislation, especially for local government and health care agencies.

Labor management cooperation

Employment relations in many elements of the Canadian public sector began with consultation between employee associations and management representatives. The employee groups were careful to distinguish themselves from unions and generally declared that they were not interested in collective bargaining. This system broke down in the 1960s, when legislation and the desires of public employees combined to promote the emergence of collective bargaining (Ponak and Thompson, 1995).

Because public sector collective agreements regulate workplace behaviors closely, topics often assigned to participatory bodies at the level of the workplace in other national systems are included in the scope of collective bargaining. In civil services, a few institutions for labor–management consultation remained after the arrival of collective bargaining, but their role is marginal. Areas excluded from bargaining often include technological change, retraining and pensions. Consultation on these topics occurs only when the employer agrees. If public sector pensions are outside the scope bargaining, for example, governments may appoint union officials as trustees to the plans. Joint committees on training are not uncommon. However, the legislative restrictions on the subjects of bargaining inhibit more extensive efforts at cooperation. These initiatives frequently involve joint efforts to deal with the effects of technological change, for instance, and employers are unwilling to cede authority over these subjects. For their part, labor unions are reluctant to participate in cooperative programs where their role is restricted.

Conclusions

This review of the Canadian experience demonstrates that, in comparative terms, Canada has experienced evolutionary change in public sector industrial relations. The system certainly has not been static: the results of bargaining have been subject to outside (government) control; bargaining structures have become more centralized; an uncertain volume of contracting out has occurred, public sector employment has declined in many areas. Some of these changes, in particular intervention in collective bargaining, have been substantial. Yet the basic parameters of the system remain intact. Therefore, the system has not been "transformed" as other public sector industrial relations systems have experienced. Rather, change has been incremental. Little significant experimentation has occurred, change has not been especially rapid, and diversity has not increased (Erickson and Kuruvilla, 1998).

Collective bargaining coverage, as measured by union membership and density, has remained stable or increased slightly. The dominance of collective representation through unions remains. Compensation systems have not changed for most public sector employees; especially those represented by unions. Examples of major innovations in industrial relations initiated by the parties are also lacking. Even isolated cases of restructuring of services have taken place within the existing industrial relations system. While governments have restricted the results of negotiations, they have not attacked the principles of collective representation or permanently suppressed collective bargaining. No political party has endorsed the "deregulation" of public sector industrial relations. The focus of government action has been the control of expenditures, not the transformation of the employment relationship.

In light of the conservative political climate in most jurisdictions in Canada and the vigorous protests labor has mounted against government policies, these conclusions may be surprising. They also raise the issue of why public sector industrial relations has not been more affected by the shifts in government policies.

The first explanation for the lack of a direct attack on public sector industrial relations is the lack of a transformation of the public sector itself. There certainly have been suggestions that fundamental changes are needed (Warrian, 1996), and such transformations may still occur. To date, however, the core functions in Canadian public sector have not been subject to major overhaul.

The decentralized structure of the Canadian political system virtually guarantees that change will be incremental, because of local political considerations (Dell'Aringa and Murlis, 1993). Citizens have access to the levels of government that provide social services and they have not shown that they wish drastic changes in the delivery or availability of these services. Public sector unions can form alliances with client groups at that level to defend services. Because of the lack of integration of public functions, no national government, no matter how determined, could bring about major changes in public sector industrial relations without a consensus from at least the most populous provinces. So far, that consensus has existed for intervention in collective bargaining to limit compensation, but not for more fundamental changes, even in the provinces most committed to reducing the size and role of the state.

The performance of public sector industrial relations systems has not provided general arguments for change in either employment relations or the role of the state. The public sector in Canada, for example, has been seen as a "good employer" rather than a "model employer" (Ferner, 1994). This distinction implies that public sector organizations were not chosen instruments to reform employment relations during periods of growth in public spending. Conversely, the performance of the Canadian public sector industrial relations system has not provided general arguments for wholesale change in it. Thus, when the era of rapid growth in public expenditures ended, wholesale reform of the public sector industrial relations was not seen as a major priority by most policy makers.

No crisis in the role of the Canadian state or public sector industrial relations has occurred to crystallize pressures for more substantial change (Erickson and Kuruvilla, 1998). Disruptions in service or political discourse have been local and sporadic. No galvanizing event, such as the British coal miners' strike or the destruction of the American air traffic controllers' union, has occurred. Overall, the Canadian industrial relations system in general has not experienced major structural changes (Thompson, 1998), so the public sector experience is not unusual in the national context.

Historically, the dominant federal Liberal Party has been more favorably inclined toward the public sector and its employees than conservative parties, although these differences have not been substantial and were not uniform across all issues (Blais et al., 1997). The high degree of legal regulation of Canadian public sector industrial relations (reflecting the low degree of integration in the public sector) is also a factor promoting stability. Literally scores of laws regulate various aspects of the employment relationship. Small groups of employees have used litigation to impede changes to which they were not direct parties, giving the parties the opportunity to devise more acceptable means of accomplishing government objectives.

Labor has not been able to stop determined governments from imposing wage freezes or even modest cuts in compensation. It has been more effective in dissuading governments from attacking its basic rights. In either case, labor's political pressures have raised the cost to governments contemplating more substantial changes. In a country as diverse as Canada, public sector industrial relations will certainly adapt to shifts in government spending in different ways. For the foreseeable future, however, incremental reform appears to be the most likely path of change. More dramatic changes in industrial relations are likely to occur as a result of shifts in government ideology rather than any outcomes of the industrial relations system.

References

Bendel, M. (1992) "At the Crossroads: Collective Bargaining and Disputes Resolution in the Federal Public Service," in Kaplan, W., Sach, J., and Gunderson, M. (eds.), *Labor Arbitration Yearbook, 1992*, Toronto: Butterworths-Lancaster House.

Blais, A., Blake, D. E., and Dion, S. (1997) *Parties and Public Sector Employees*, Pittsburgh: University Press.

Borins, S. (1994) *Government in Transition: A New Paradigm in Public Administration*, Toronto: Commonwealth Association for Public Administration and Management 24.

Dell'Aringa, C. and Murlis, H. (1993) "Agenda for the Future Public Sector Pay Policies in the 1990s," in OECD *Public Sector Pay Policies*, Paris: OECD.

Dorsey, J. (1997) *Reorganization of Saskatchewan's Health Labor Relations*, Regina: The Health Labor Relations Reorganization Commission.

Erickson, C. L. and Kuruvilla S. (1998) "Industrial Relations System Transformation," *Industrial and Labor Relations Review*, LII(1).

Ferner, A. (1994) "The State as Employer," in Hyman, R. and Ferner, A. (eds.), *New Frontiers in European Industrial Relations*, Oxford: Blackwell.

Fryer, J. L. (1995) "Provincial Public Sector Labor Relations," in Swimmer, G. and Thompson, M. (eds.), *Public Sector Collective Bargaining in Canada*, Kingston: IRC Press, Queen's University.

Graham, K. A. (1995) "Collective Bargaining in the Municipal Sector," in Swimmer, G. and Thompson, M. (eds.), *Public Sector Collective Bargaining in Canada*, Kingston: IRC Press, Queen's University.

Gunderson, M. (1995) "Public Sector Compensation," in Swimmer, G. and Thompson, M. (eds.), *Public Sector Collective Bargaining in Canada*, Kingston: IRC Press, Queen's University.

Gunderson, M. and Hyatt, D. (1996) "Canadian Public Sector Employment Relations in Transition," in Belman, D., Gunderson, M., and Hyatt, D. (eds.), *Public Sector Employment In a Time of Transition*, Kingston: IRC Press, Queen's University.

Gunderson, M. and Reid, F. (1995) "Public Sector Strikes in Canada," in Swimmer, G. and Thompson, M. (eds.), *Public Sector Collective Bargaining in Canada*, Kingston: IRC Press, Queen's University.

Haiven, L. (1995) "Industrial Relations in Health Care: Regulation, Conflict and Transition to the 'Wellness Model'," in Swimmer, G. and Thompson, M. (eds.), *Public Sector Collective Bargaining in Canada*, Kingston: IRC Press, Queen's University.

Hebdon, R. and Warrian, P. (1999) "Coercive Bargaining: Public Sector Restructuring under the Ontario Social Contract, 1993–1996," *Industrial and Labor Relations Review*, LII(2).

Hébert, G. (1995) "Public Sector Bargaining in Quebec: The Rise and Fall of Centralization," in Swimmer, G. and Thompson, M. (eds.), *Public Sector Collective Bargaining in Canada*, Kingston: IRC Press, Queen's University, 201–35.

Marsden, D. (1993) "Reforming Public Sector Pay," in OECD (ed.), *Pay Flexibility in the Public Sector*, Paris: OECD.

McDavid, J. C. and Elder, K. A. (1997) *The Efficiency of Residential Solid Waste Collection Services in Canada: The National Survey Report*, Victoria, BC: Local Government Institute, School of Public Administration, University of Victoria.

OECD (1994) *Trends in Public Sector Pay: A Study of Nine OECD Countries, 1985–1990* Paris: OECD.

OECD (1995) *Governance in Transition: Public Management Reforms in OECD Countries*, Paris: OECD.

Panitch, L. and Swartz, D. (1993) *The Assault on Trade Union Freedoms: From Wage Controls to Social Contract*, Toronto: Garamond Press.

Peters, J. (1999) *An Era of Change: Government Employment Trends in the 1980s and 1990s*, Ottawa: Canadian Policy Research Network.

Ponak, A. and Thompson, M. (1995 4th ed.) "Public Sector Collective Bargaining," in Gunderson, M., Ponak, A., and Taras, D.G. (eds.), *Union–Management Relations in Canada*, Toronto: Addison-Wesley, 2000.

Rose, J. B. (1995) "The Evolution of Public Sector Unionism", in Swimmer, G. and Thompson, M. (eds.), *Public Sector Collective Bargaining in Canada*, Kingston: IRC Press, Queen's University, Q.

Swimmer, G., Hicks, M., and Milne, T. (1994) "Public Service 2000: Dead or Alive?," in Phillips, S. (ed.), *How Ottawa Spends*, Ottawa: Carleton University Press.

Thomason, T. (1995) "Labor Relations in Primary and Secondary Education," in Swimmer, G. and Thompson, M. (eds.), *Public Sector Collective Bargaining in Canada*, Kingston: IRC Press, Queen's University.

Thompson, M. (1989) "From Compromise to Resistance: Public Sector Industrial Relations in Canada," in Gladstone, A., Lansbury, R. D., Stieber, J., Treu, T., and Weiss, M. (eds.), *Current Issues in Labor Relations: An International Perspective*, Berlin: de Gruyter.

Thompson, M. (1995) "The Industrial Relations Effects of Privatization: Evidence from Canada," in Swimmer, G. and Thompson, M. (eds.), *Public Sector Collective Bargaining in Canada*, Kingston: IRC Press, Queen's University.

Thompson, M. (1998) "Employment Relations in Canada," in Bamber, G. J. and Lansbury, R. D. (eds.), *International and Comparative Employment Relations*, Sydney: Allen & Unwin.

Thompson, M. and Fryer, J. (1994) *Collective Bargaining in Canada"s Public Service*, Kingston: School of Policy Studies, Queen's University.

Thompson, M. and Fryer, J. "Changing Roles for Employers and Unions in the Public Service," in Lindquist, E. (ed.), *Government Restructuring and Career Public Service in Canada*, Toronto: Institute for Public Administration of Canada, 2000.

Verma, A. and Cutcher-Gershenfeld, J. (1996) "Workplace Innovations and Systems Change," in Belman, D., Gunderson, M., and Hyatt, D. (eds.), *Public Sector Employment in a Time of Transition*, Madison, WI: IRRA.

Warrian, P. (1996) *Hard Bargain: Transforming Public Sector Labor–Management Relations*, Toronto: McGilligan Books.

Weiner, N. (1995) "Workplace Equity," in Swimmer, G. and Thompson, M. (eds.), *Public Sector Collective Bargaining in Canada*, Kingston: IRC Press, Queen's University.

Wetzel, K. and Gallagher, D. (1984) "Management structures to accommodate multi-employer hospital bargaining in western Canada," in Thompson, M. and Swimmer, G. (eds.), *Conflict or compromise: The Future of Public Sector Industrial Relations*, Montreal: Institute for Research on Public Policy.

7
Japanese Public Sector Employment
Kazutoshi Koshiro

Introduction

"Public sector" here is defined as national and local government organizations involved in both non-industrial and industrial activities. Non-industrial public employees are covered by specific laws differing from the trade union law covering the private sector and the other two laws concerning public industrial employees. Public employees are theoretically entitled to the basic rights of workers stipulated under Article 28 of the constitution, but are, in fact, deprived of the right to strike. Furthermore, non-industrial public employees are prohibited from undertaking collective bargaining.[1]

The basic framework of current regulations regarding the rights of public employees was reorganized following the privatization of public corporations in 1985 (Nippon Telegraph and Telephone [NTT] and Japan Tobacco [JT]) and in 1987 (Japan Railways [JR]) and is summarized as follows:

	Right to:		
	Organize	Collective bargaining	Strike
Police, firemen and prison officers	No	No	No
National non-industrial public service	Yes	No	No
Employees of four national utilities	Yes	Yes	No
Local non-industrial public employees	Yes	No	No
Employees of local government utilities	Yes	Yes	No

There are some quasi-governmental institutions or agencies such as the Bank of Japan (the Central Bank), NHK (Nihon Broadcasting Corporation), JETRO (Japan External Trade Organization), JIL (Japanese Institute of Labor), and other semi-governmental financial institutions. The employees of these quasi-governmental organizations are classified under the private sector and are covered by trade union law. Furthermore, as defined by Article 28 of the constitution, they are entitled to the above three basic rights of workers.

In 1962 the Japanese government established the Temporary Administrative Research Commission to report the government's recommendations for reducing the number of public employees which had increased over the preceding decade. Following this recommendation the Sato administration decided to set its staff number control under the cabinet decision of December 1967. Between the 1968 and 1998 fiscal years there was a total gross reduction of 301,537 national government personnel with very strict staff number controls being maintained over these three decades. The total reduction of national government employees including industrial civil servants amounted to 31,533.

In 1965, after long-lasting strife with the public employee unions – a continuing conflict since the 1950s – the Japanese government ratified ILO Convention No. 87 concerning the freedom of association and amended the public employee labor relations laws to conform with the convention. In order to set up new industrial relations following these amendments, and to deal with personnel administration of government employees, the Personnel Bureau of the Prime Minister's Office was established. The Management and Coordination Agency of the Prime Minister's Office was placed in charge of staff number control and organizational administration. In addition, the National Personnel Authority (NPA), established as an independent administrative commission in 1948, has been responsible for maintaining the comparative pay of national government employees with the private sector and protecting their basic working conditions.

The Second Temporary Study Committee on Administration, chaired by Toshio Dokoh, former president of Ishikawajima Harima Industries (IHI) and former chairman of Keidanren (Confederation of Economic Organizations) was in operation between March 1981 and March 1983. This was followed by three consecutive Temporary Deliberation Councils on Administrative Reform between July 1983 and October 1993. Thanks to these efforts, privatization of a national public utility and three public corporations took place. In 1983, a small national utility, the Alcohol Monopoly, was privatized. This was followed in 1985 by the privatization of NTT (Nippon Telegraph and Telephone) and JT (Japan Tobacco and Salt Monopoly). Finally, in 1987, JR (Japan National Railways) was privatized and split into seven different companies. Prior to privatization, public corporation and national utility employees had been covered by a special labor relations law (Public Corporation and National Utility Labor Relations Law), but following privatization they were covered only by the trade union law (Koshiro, 1985; Masujima, 1999).

In 1996 the Hashimoto government enforced six reforms (administrative, structural economic, financial systems, social security, public finance and education) – prioritizing administrative reform which had been promised during the election campaign. The government passed the Administrative Reform Program in the cabinet decision of December 1996 and the prime minister, Ryutaro Hashimoto, personally assumed the position of chairman of the Administrative Reform Council established on November 1996. In May 1997 the Public Service Personnel System Council (chairman: Professor Emeritus of Keio University, Kotaro Tsujimura) was established with the aim of conducting a comprehensive review of the current public service personnel system (Institute of Administrative Management, 1998).

Administrative reforms were intensively promoted by the Hashimoto Administration and in June 1998, a new law – the Basic Law to Reform Central Ministries – was enacted.

In 1998 Mr Keizo Obuchi took over, claiming he would carry on Hashimoto's administrative reform programs. On January 26, 1999 the Headquarters for Promoting Administrative Reforms of the Central Ministries and Agencies decided that the "Outline of the Administrative Reforms of the Central Ministries and Agencies" would be implemented from January 1, 2000.

Organizational structure, employment and wages

Employment

The main focus of this chapter concerns non-industrial government employees. Due to the limited basic rights of this category of employees in Japan, industrial relations in this particular sector have not been an issue over the past decades with the exception of a few years immediately after the end of World War II.

In 1995, the total number of public employees accounted for 4.44 million. About a quarter were employed by the central government and the rest by local governments. In 1995 these accounted for 8.5 percent of the total number of employees in Japan (52.25 million),

158 *Strategic Choices in Reforming Public Service Employment*

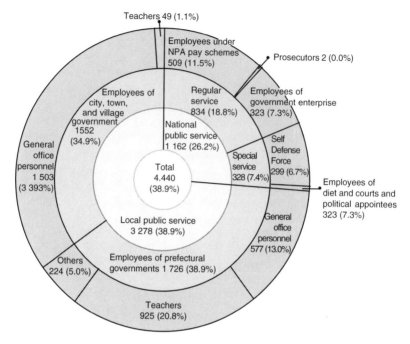

Figure 7.1 Number of public employees (1995)
Source: National Personnel Authority (1997: 4)

compared with 13.9 percent in 1967, the base year for staff number control (Figure 7.1).

Although local government autonomy was introduced by the occupation forces after World War II, the Japanese government has always been highly centralized. The majority of local governments have been forced to rely heavily on financial subsidies from the central government. Education policy has also been highly centralized by the Ministry of Education, although most public school teachers are legally employed by local governments, each local government having its own education commission. Half of a teacher's fixed education salary is subsidized by the central government.

In 1980, prior to privatization of the three public corporations, the central government employed over 2 million individuals while now it employs only about 1.2 million (fixed budgetary number at the end of March 1999, including governmental financial institutions). More than half a million of these are covered by the Remuneration Law administered by the National Personnel Authority (Table 7.1). These are non-industrial public service employees and are the main focus of this paper. Others involve prosecutors and government utility employees (now four: Postal Service, National Forestry, Government Printing Office and the Mint). Moreover, there are only a few full-time laborers and about a quarter of a million temporary employees (Table 7.2). Besides these, there are 330,000 workers classified as special service employees (300 ministers, deputy-ministers and ambassadors; 25,000 judges and court personnel; 4,000 members and employees of both houses and 300,000 defense forces personnel – end of 1997 tax year).

Until recently prefectures and municipal governments had increased their employment numbers, which, by April 1997, amounted to about 3.3 million, of whom more than half were employed by prefectures (Table 7.3). From an industrial relations view point, it should be noted that included in this figure there are 159,000 employed by local government utilities which are specifically regulated by a special labor law (Local Government Utility Labor Relations Law). These local government industrial employees have the right to collective bargaining, but do not have the right to strike. In addition to these, there are about 300,000 local public employees employed by local governments who are engaged

Table 7.1 Budgetary fixed number of national government employees[a]

End of fiscal year	Total	Personnel covered by remuneration law
1970	1,992,793[b]	488,367
1975	1,993,008[b]	500,200
1980	2,002,783[b]	506,506
1985	1,513,925[c]	500,559
1990	1,183,157	497,122
1995	1,173,358	502,467
1996	1,171,322	501,982
1997	1,167,739	533,770
1998	1,159,007	532,735

Note:
[a] Total of (1) employees fixed by a general account, (2) employees fixed by special accounts, and (3) employees of government affiliated agencies including public financial corporations.
[b] Including Japan Tobacco and Salt Public Corporation, Japan National Railways and Nippon Telegraph and Telephone Public Corporation.
[c] Including Japanese National Railways.

Source: Budget Bureau, Ministry of Finance, published by Statistics Bureau, Prime Minister's Office, ed., *Japan Statistical Yearbook*, Tokyo: Japan Statistical Association; 1976, p. 594; do., 1999, pp. 748–49.

Table 7.2 National government employees by employment status

Year and date	Total	Full-time employees			Full-time laborers	Temporary employees
		Employees under remuneration law	Public prosecutors	Employees of national enterprises		
1970	859,791[a]	488,367	2,002	369,422	1,459[c]	242,825[c]
1975	863,723[a]	500,200	2,124	361,399	1,698[c]	259,108[c]
1980	856,405[b]	506,506	2,119	347,700	1,488[c]	254,229[c]
1985	536,204[b]	500,559	2,110	333,535	1,139[c]	236,596[c]
1990	822,600[b]	497,122	2,049	323,429	651[d]	206,817[d]
1995	819,599[b]	502,467	2,120	315,012	459[d]	223,489[d]
1996	817,937[b]	501,982	2,164	313,791	417[d]	224,545[d]
1997	817,123	501,498	2,189	313,436	391[d]	225,975[d]

Note:
[a] Registered number of employees as of July 1 each year excluding "special personnel" (Personnel Bureau, of office of the Prime Minister).
[b] National Personnel Authority, Survey on Recruitment of National Government Employees of General Class. Figures are incumbent number of employees as of the end of each fiscal year, namely March the following year.
[c] Includes those who were employed by public corporations.
[d] Excludes those who were employed by public corporations because of privatization of NTT, JT, and JR.

Source: For 1970 and 1975, Japan Statistical Yearbook, No. 21 (1970) pp. 592–3; No. 26 (1975) pp. 592–3. For 1980–96, Japan Statistical Yearbook, No. 48 (1999) p. 747. For 1997, National Personnel Authority, Survey on Recruitment of National Government Employees of General Class, January 1999, p. 3.

Table 7.3 Local government employees, 1975–1997 (thousands)

As of April 1 year	Total	Prefectures	Cities	Towns and villages	Cooperatives for sectional clerical work
1975	2,937	1,592	936	338	71
1980	3,165	1,706	1,004	365	89
1985	3,219	1,745	1,014	362	98
1990	3,225	1,741	1,019	358	106
1995	3,278	1,726	1,057	376	119
1996	3,274	1,720	1,057	375	122
1997	3,267	1,714	1,057	373	123

Note:
Data is based on the Survey on Wages of Local Government Employees, excluding superintendents of education in each local government and including temporary personnel.
Source: Statistics Bureau, Prime Minister's Office, *Japan Statistical Yearbook*, No. 48 (1999), p. 747.

in local public utilities (but are classified as non-industrial employees without the right to strike and to collective bargaining). Regarding occupational classification, the largest single group is the general administration, followed by teachers and professors, laborers and the police.

Teachers in compulsory public education (six-year primary school and three-year junior high school) are employed by prefecture governments, but half of their salaries are subsidized by the national government. The health sector is basically financed by national health insurance schemes. Most hospitals in Japan are private, although they are also financially supported by national health insurance schemes. A number of public hospitals are owned and managed by local governments. National hospitals offer the best working conditions for nurses.

Out of about half a million national government employees covered by the Remuneration Law in 1998, females accounted for 22.1 percent. Among those covered by the Medical Treatment III Pay Schedule (nurses and midwives), 96.9 percent are female. Besides these permanent employees, as shown in Table 7.2 above, there are also about 226,000 temporary employees. Most of them are part-time workers, paid according to different pay standards. Moreover, a few individuals are reallocated from private companies for a fixed period (usually for two years) across 17 ministries (for example 73 regular employees and 163 temporary employees as of November, 1995) (National Personnel Authority, 1995a).

Since the introduction of staff number controls in the tax year 1968, the total number of cut-backs amounted to 309,558 by TY 1999, while the total number of increases amounted to 255,873, bringing net reduction to 53,685. As a result, by 1995 the number of total government employees per 1,000 individuals had been reduced to 39 in Japan – a figure that is considerably lower than in other advanced countries (Figure 7.2). The largest number of cut-backs took place in the food bureau and agricultural statistics office of the Ministry of Agriculture, Forestries and Fisheries (12,847 personnel, a 45.5 percent reduction). On the other hand, the largest number of increases has been observed in national universities and schools (5,640 employees or 4.4 percent), however, in terms of percentage increases, the largest increase was in Foreign Affairs (46.9 percent, or 1,670 individuals).

In contrast to a decreasing number of national government employees, the number of local government employees increased from 2,276,487 in 1965 to 3,282,492 in 1995, thus showing a 44.2 percent increase; a slight reverse trend – 3,250,000 – only became evident in 1998. The past increase had mostly been due to the increased demand for education, social welfare, fire-fighters, local public utilities workers (water supply, gas, garbage collection, public transportation, and so on), and police. However, there had also been an excessive rise in public expenditure

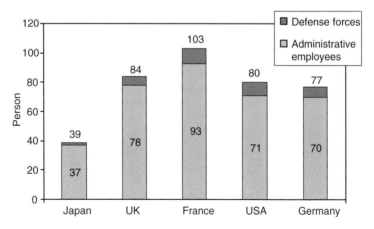

Figure 7.2 An international comparison of the number of government employees per 1,000 population among selected advanced countries in 1995

Note: Administrative employees include national and local government employees as well as personnel of government enterprises.

Source: Management and Coordination Agency, Prime Minister's Office, produced in 1996.

during the bubble economy which contributed to an increase in personnel in the area of public construction. The Ministry of Home Affairs (Ministry of Home Affairs, 1997) does not exercise any uniform budgetary staff number control over local governments. In the second half of the 1990s many local governments suffered from huge financial deficits due to a prolonged depression. They have been forced to cut back on recruitment and contain salaries – this will be discussed later.

Internal labor market

Under the traditional national civil service system prior to and immediately after World War II, recruitment of higher civil service personnel was strictly based on a special selective examination. On the other hand, the lower- and middle-level employees and workers were recruited separately by the local authorities. The pre-war examination system dating from the Meiji period was abolished in December, 1948 when the National Personnel Authority was established in accordance with the democratization of the civil service system under the new constitution of May 1947. After a period the new selective examination system for the higher national government service was reintroduced (November, 1949). The examination system has been revised twice since then, in 1962 and in 1985 (National Personnel Authority, 1998a).

The examination systems for middle- and lower-level government services have also been revised several times and special examinations for specific occupations (for example, foreign services, air-traffic controllers, immigration officers, prison officers, librarians, labor inspectors, and so on) have been introduced. By 1985 the present system of selective examinations was established.

At the moment eight different types of university-level and eight different types of senior high school graduate examinations are held by the NPA for entry into the National Public Service. However, a "university" degree or "senior high school" certificate as such is not required for application. The level merely indicates the level of the examination. Before the United Nations International Women's Year in 1975, the qualifications for several recruitment examinations were limited only to men because of hazardous work requirements, compulsory night shift or merely because of tradition. Between 1976 and 1981 such discriminatory rules were abolished for administrative work B (technical jobs): air-traffic controllers, the air defense force college, the meteorological college, maritime security officers college, tax officers, imperial guards, immigration officers and prison officers. In 1989 Postal Service III B, which required midnight shift work then prohibited to women, was finally opened up to women (National Personnel Authority, 1998a). As a result of these recruitment examinations, 12,162 personnel were taken on (of whom 4,297 were women) in Fiscal Year 1997 (April, 1997), out of 17,465 successful candidates and a total of 206,616 applicants (of whom 73,965 were women) (National Personnel Authority, 1998b).

Each local government undertakes its own recruitment examinations which are similar to those of the national public service. In this case it should be noted that the percentage of women among the applicants and among those who passed the examinations has increased to about 40 percent in recent years. In the case of cities, women candidates made up 50 percent of those who passed in 1997. This seems to reflect the fact that women prefer to work in local governments owing to less discrimination, fewer working hours and more opportunities for childcare, and so on, than in the private sector.

Protecting an official from dismissal and other unjust treatment by external forces, especially political influences, is necessary in order to secure neutrality and stability in public service performance. Therefore, Article 75 of the National Public Service Law guarantees personnel employment status to the effect that an official shall not be demoted, suspended or dismissed unless it is based on reasons as stipulated under the Law or Rules of the NPA. At the same time, an official shall be subject to disciplinary sanctions where unlawful conduct, activities inappropriate to the civil service or inability to perform one's duties satisfactorily may be concerned (Articles 38, 76, and 82). Similarly, Paragraph 2, Article 28 of the Local Public Service Law guarantees job security for local public employees, while Article 28 stipulates disciplinary sanctions.

There are several reasons for job dismissals of public employees, the main ones, being the voluntary resignation of an employee and, secondly, mandatory retirement. Others include death, termination of fixed-term employment contracts, dismissal by status action, disciplinary dismissal, and so on. The average rate of exit in the national public service has remained at around 5 percent among those covered by NPA pay schedules and around 4 percent among employees of the four national utilities. A mandatory public service retirement system was introduced by the government in 1981–85.

Wages and salaries

Following the 1948 democratic reorganization of the civil service system, two basic principles of pay determination for public employees apply: (1) comparability with the private sector; and (2) fair balancing within the public sector. In order to put these principles into practice and protect the basic rights of national public employees the National Personnel Authority has established in compensation an elaborate system for determining pay schedules of national public employees covered by the National Public Service Remuneration Law.

Pay comparability

Paragraph 2, Article 28 of the National Public Service Law stipulates that the NPA must make recommendations to the cabinet and both houses of the Diet if conditions for determining pay (such as cost of living, or wages and salaries of comparable workers in the private sector) change by more than 5 percent. Moreover, Paragraph 2, Article 64 of the Law requires that national public service pay should be determined by taking into account such factors as the cost of living, wages and salaries in the private sector and other conditions that the NPA decides to take into consideration. Therefore, the NPA is expected to maintain public service pay comparable to that in the private sector.

In order to maintain pay comparability with the private sector, the NPA undertakes a comprehensive pay review in the private sector every spring after major company wage negotiations in private companies have been settled.[2] The pay review is based on orthodox statistical sampling methods covering the nation-wide 36,000 of firms employing more than 50/100 persons. In fact, 7,600 sample establishments are selected. Straight-time earnings actually paid in April every year of about half a million employees (wages, salaries, and various allowances) working in these firms and performing 94 comparable jobs (department heads and managers of general administration, guardsmen, university professors, medical doctors, and so on) are directly surveyed by the NPA personnel and compared with those counterparts in the national public service so as to calculate the average pay differentials between the two sectors. Average pay differentials are calculated by using the Laspeyres weighting formula which takes into account such factors as jobs, managerial positions, educational levels and ages (National Personnel Authority, 1998c). Based on this pay review, the three-person Authority Commission (which includes the president) draws up a report and recommendations for the cabinet and both houses of the Diet, before pays are revised in early August every year. The cabinet decides whether it can put into effect the recommendations within the authorized budget or, if not, it must ask for the consent of both houses for appropriations (Article 15, Fiscal Law).

As a result of these improvements as well as annual automatic pay increases, the average pay levels of the national public service have increased, as seen in Table 7.4.

The principle of pay comparability with the private sector seems to have worked effectively to guarantee a reasonable standard of living for those in the national public service who have neither the right to collective bargaining nor that of striking. Moreover, in addition to these monthly payments, they can now receive a 5.25 per month bonus payment which is also linked to that of the average in the private sector. By selecting as a reference group regular employees among private firms employing more than a hundred people, the government has performed as a "good employer" by which the national public employees have been able to maintain if not the best, then a reasonable standard of living. In spite of this, public employees' unions have been insisting that the reference group should be firms employing more than a thousand instead of a hundred; in this way, their pay would be improved even more favorably. However, the NPA judges that national public employees' pay should not be comparable to that of major private companies but rather to the mean level of salaries in the private sector (Koshiro, 1995).

Table 7.4 Average straight-time monthly earnings of the national public service, 1988–1997 (yen)

Year	Basic salary	Family allowance	Regional allowance	Total[a] straight-time	Reference: exchange rate (Y/US$)
1988	257,382	10,469	13,194	281,045	128.27
1989	264,364	10,833	13,561	288,758	142.82
1990	272,657	10,721	14,152	297,530	141.52
1991	284,163	10,582	14,756	309,501	133.31
1992	296,860	11,176	15,626	323,662	124.73
1993	307,279	11,572	16,740	335,591	103.79
1994	315,885	11,871	17,694	345,450	99.33
1995	323,292	12,083	18,266	353,596	96.29
1996	330,077	12,088	18,786	360,951	112.46
1997	337,365	12,145	19,237	368,747	122.59
1998	344,918	12,446	19,904	377,268	115.20[b]

Note:
[a] In addition to the straight-time earnings, extra allowances (housing, commuting, and other allowances) are paid; these additional payments amounted to 21,134 yen in 1998.
[b] As of the end of December 1998. Other rates are the annual average.

Source: NPA, A Guide to Pay of the National Public Service, March 1998, p. 41. *NPA Monthly Journal*, September 1998, p. 43.

Inside fairness

Pay for local government employees is also determined unilaterally by law. The basic framework of pay determination for local government employees is regulated by the Local Public Service Law of 1950. For employees of local government utilities, the Local Government Utility Labor Relations Law of 1952 has been applied. For the former group (non-industrial local public service) wages are regulated by local ordinances based on the recommendations of each local personnel commission. Procedures are similar to those applied to the national non-industrial public service. In fact, pay recommendations of local personnel commissions tend to follow those of the NPA, ignoring pay differentials between private and public sectors in their respective localities. In many metropolitan areas local government employees are better paid than the majority of workers in the private sector.

Salaries of local government employees in metropolitan areas such as Tokyo, Yokohama, Osaka and Nagoya used to be very high compared with those of the national public service. By providing information the Ministry of Home Affairs has been trying to bring their pay level into line with that of the national public service. The ministry developed the pay differential statistics between the national and local public service based on the Laspeyres formula which includes years of experience and education (Ministry of Home Affairs, 1997). In the 1980s and 1990s the ministry succeeded in containing pay differentials within tolerable limits (Figure 7.3).

As for prefectures, the largest pay differentials *vis-à-vis* the national public service were observed in the Tokyo Metropolitan Government: 5.2 percent in April, 1997. Designated metropolitan cities, having more than one million inhabitants, and several satellite cities in the Tokyo and Osaka prefectures pay higher salaries than the national public service level. Osaka City paid 7.4 percent higher, Minoo City in Osaka Prefecture 7.9 percent more, as well as Komae City in Tokyo (Ministry of Home Affairs, 1997). Instead, an increasing number of small cities and villages have begun to pay lower salaries than the national public service levels (Figure 7.4).

Several reasons were the cause for higher pay in large local governments. (1) In local government, non-industrial public service can take advantage of the bargaining power of industrial public service employees such as sanitary workers and garbage collectors – Jichiro (Federation of Unions of Local Government Employees) organizes both kinds of public employees under the same umbrella; (2) special treatment to shorten the required years of service for progression of salary grades

168 Strategic Choices in Reforming Public Service Employment

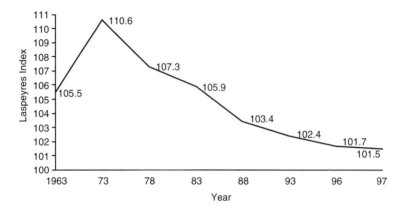

Figure 7.3 Changes in the average pay differentials (Laspeyres Index) between national and local government employees, 1963–97
Source: Ministry of Home Affairs, *Summary of the Local Public Service Pay Research* in 1997 as of April 1, 1997, p. 2.

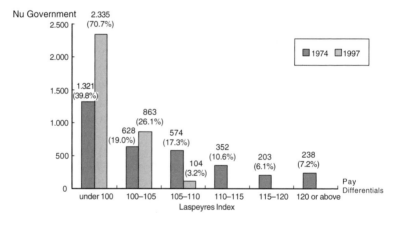

Figure 7.4 Distribution of pay differentials (Laspeyres Index) between the national and local public services in 1974 and 1997
Source: Ministry of Home Affairs, *Summary of the Local Public Service Pay Research* in 1997 as of April 1, 1997, p. 4.

known as "shorten"; (3) excessive automatic progress which disregarded ceilings in each classification called "watari" – in this way a worker with long years of service in a lower classification can exceed other workers in a higher classification with shorter years of service; (4) disguised pay increases through several loopholes or almost illegal agreements between local management and unions – when the bonus payment of national public service was reduced by the 1976 and 1978 NPA recommendations, many local governments followed it by amending local ordinances and some local governments made an agreement with the unions to compensate for the reduced amount by various allowances or fictitious overtime payments; (5) ineffectiveness of local public personnel commissions which were expected to maintain fair pay comparability between local and national public services on the one hand, and the private sector in each locality, on the other. In fact, they tend to merely follow the recommendations of the NPA for the national public service; (6) governors or mayors supported by socialists and communists tend to prefer paying favorably to their own local public employees.

However, these practices by local governments have been diminishing as a result of both continuous guidance and suggestions from the Ministry of Home Affairs (Ministry of Home Affairs, 1997) and because of deteriorating local government finances since the middle of the 1990s.

Among local public services, teachers of compulsory education (six-year primary and three-year junior high school) hold a special position. They are employed by each prefecture government, but half of their salaries are subsidized by the national government in order to preserve its control over the standard curriculum throughout the country. Teachers' unions had been one of the most militant forces in the postwar labor movement, involved in continuous confrontations with the Ministry of Education over government education policy and the merit rating of teachers by headmasters. In order to improve the quality of teachers and pacify tensions with rank-and-file teachers, the government of the Liberal Democratic Party moved to increase teachers' pay by 25 percent between 1974 and 1978. The Japan Teachers' Union also joined Rengo and modified its policy toward the government, seeking a more cooperative approach by the fall of 1995 (Koshiro and Rengo, 1996).

Employers and employer associations

State policies and actions in relation to the public sector regulation

As already mentioned in the introduction, the most recent innovative political strategies are principally directed at the central administration. These are illustrated in the government paper "Outline of the Administrative Reforms of the Central Ministries and Agencies." The government's aim is to reduce the national public service to 25 percent, or 140,000 units within the ten years between 2001 and 2010. In order to achieve these goals, five organizations with 4,700 personnel will be privatized or abolished; ten businesses will be commissioned to the private sector; 84 organizations with 67,000 personnel will be transformed into "agencies" (the idea borrowed from British reforms in the 1980s). Through these measures several governmental organizations such as the postal service, national hospitals, national institutes, national museums, and so on, will be reorganized.

The fundamental purpose of this reform is not fiscal rationalization, but is said to be "the reform of government–bureaucrat relations" (Masujima, 1999). The main thrust is to strengthen the function of the cabinet. The Cabinet Office (*Naikaku Fu*) is to be established as the center of power in which the Advisory Council of Economy and Finance (*Keizai Zaisei Simon Kaigi*) is to be established to deliberate on macro-economic policies, basic management of fiscal policies and budget making and general social infrastructure planning. The major function of the present Economic Planning Agency is to be absorbed within this office. The Ministry of Finance, the center of power for over a century (since the Meiji Restoration), will pass over to the treasury whose major function is to be confined to budget control. Its other function, supervising financial institutions, will be transferred to a separate organization. The Ministry of International Trade and Industry will be reorganized into the Ministry of Economy and Industry. The Ministry of Labor will be merged with the Ministry of Health and Welfare. Only five ministries will remain intact (the Ministry of Justice, the Ministry of Foreign Affairs, the Ministry of Agriculture, Forestries and Fisheries, the National Public Safety Commission and the Defense Agency).

The total number of ministers will be reduced from the present 20 to 15 then 17. Deputy ministers (new positions) and other top officials in each ministry will be appointed by each minister with the consent of the cabinet. The secretariat of the cabinet will be directly appointed by the prime minister, not only from inside the government administration, but also from the private sector. The total number of departments will be reduced from the present 128 to about ninety. The total number of sections will be initially reduced from the present 1,200 to about 1,000, a 15 percent reduction, and ultimately to 900, a reduction of 23 percent (Masujima, 1999).

Public employers

The basic administrative organization of public employers is defined by the State Administrative Organization Law of 1949. The legal status of the national public service is defined and regulated by the National Public Service Law of 1948, whereas that of the local public service by the Local Government Public Service Law of 1950.

The responsibility of the national government as employer concerning basic policies on pay and other conditions of work, and budgetary staff number control is shared by the Prime Minister's Office, the National Personnel Authority and the Ministry of Finance. The personnel offices of each ministry and agency are responsible for daily administration of their own personnel affairs. On the other hand, governors, mayors and heads of municipalities are responsible respectively for the basic policies concerning their personnel while the Ministry of Home Affairs coordinates personnel policies for local governments.

National Personnel Authority

In order to perform the function of administering the public service, the National Personnel Authority has been set up under the jurisdiction of the Cabinet (Article 3, the National Public Service Law). The NPA is responsible for the thorough implementation of the National Public Service Law. The authority is made up of three commissioners, one of whom is appointed as president, and the secretariat as its operating organ. The commissioners are appointed by the Cabinet with the approval of both houses of the Diet (parliament). The secretariat is headed by the secretary-general and is made up of five offices and other organs (Management and Coordinator Agency, 1998).

1. The Bureau of Administrative Service performs research and studies on the Japanese and foreign civil service systems; work pertaining to the position-classification plan; coordination of international activities; and work relating to the training of government employees.
2. The Bureau of Recruitment is made up of the Recruitment Policy Division, the Appraisal Division and six principal examination officers. It is laid down that appointment of personnel shall be made on the basis of the results of competitive examinations, the record of work performance or the evaluation of other demonstrated abilities, and that recruitment examinations shall be open to all persons and be conducted in an impartial manner.
3. The Bureau of Remuneration is responsible for maintaining and improving the remuneration of the national public employees who are denied the right to collective bargaining. To achieve this end, the bureau prepares data to submit reports and recommendations to both houses and the Cabinet about suitable remuneration for

national public employees on the basis of investigating the remuneration in private industry. Pertaining to the implementation of the Remuneration Law prepared on the basis of the above-mentioned recommendations and regarding the results of the implementation of this Law by the ministries and agencies of government, the Bureau of Remuneration conducts the auditing of payrolls of ministries and agencies under their jurisdiction. The Bureau also conducts research and studies on the remuneration systems in the civil service both in Japan and abroad.

4. The Bureau of Equity protects the individual rights of national public employees. On receiving a complaint or request, the Bureau conducts fact-finding investigations on the case, prepares a report on the results of its hearing so as to collate all data necessary for the Authority to reach a decision, or exerts every possible effort to solve the points at issue through mediation or other similar means. Findings of the Authority are final in so far as decision by an administrative agency is concerned and are subject to review only by the Authority, without prejudicing the right of access to the courts on questions of law.

5. The Bureau of Employee Relations is responsible for those activities concerning service discipline, efficiency and accident compensation for employees as well as for those involved in employee organizations. It performs those activities concerned with the maintenance of health and safety of employees. As for employee relations, with a view to contributing to harmonious employee–management relations by insuring the democratic and independent character of employee organizations, the Bureau performs the activities concerning the maintenance of the employee–organization system.

Management and Coordination Agency of the Prime Minister's Office

In the Prime Minister's Office there are a few offices dealing with national public service personnel affairs and industrial relations matters. Of note: the Personnel Office; Administrative Management Bureau; the Pension Bureau (Management and Coordination Agency, 1998).

Ministry of Finance

If one looks at the organizational structure of the Japanese government, the Budget Bureau of the Ministry of Finance does not appear to represent the government as an employer. This office, though, is actually able to control basic personnel administration matters of the national public service through budget controls (Management and Coordination Agency, 1998).

Ministry of Home Affairs

Until the end of World War II and the democratization thereafter, the Ministry of Internal Affairs was the strongest ministry in the government power structure, however it was split into several organizations, one of which was (and still is) the Ministry of Home Affairs. Within this ministry, the Local Administration Bureau is in charge of the administration of the Local Autonomy Law in planning, designing and guiding the systemic formation of local governments and their operations in general. The Bureau presents opinions in national policy making related to, and influential on, local government administration from the standpoint of establishing effective local autonomy. It is also responsible for rationalizing the scale of each local public entity and its management, as well as designing local administrative systems suitable for metropolitan areas, and so on (Management and Coordination Agency, 1998).

The Ministry of Home Affairs also plans and sets out local financial and tax systems and is responsible for affairs related to the local transfer of taxes raised by the central government, and national grant allocations to municipalities where non-taxable government properties are located (Management and Coordination Management, 1998). If a local government suffers from a certain degree of financial deficit, the ministry takes control of its management, by which pay and other personnel matters might be controlled. In the second half of the 1990s several prefectures suffered from huge financial deficits and were obliged to undertake the rationalization of their administrations including cut-backs in personnel as well as pay freezes and reductions in their own bonus payments in order to avoid the direct interference of the ministry.

The Employer Association

As explained above, there is no single organization nor agency responsible for the personnel management of national public employees as a whole. Those managers of personnel affairs of each ministry or agency are recruited and appointed from career personnel (those who were recruited by passing the Recruitment Examination I) of each organization. They are not professionals of personnel administration nor are they human resource management as such but, for a few years, usually perform their duty while remaining working in the position of personnel affairs.

There is no political appointment of those managers nor appointment of experts of personnel management from outside of the national public service. The same is also true in the case of the local public service. There is no such idea as "city manager," as in the United States.

There is no formal employer association to deal with public employee unions. Each ministry or agency is responsible for dealing with their own employee organizations. When the government faced a series of serious troubles in dealing with a union movement promoting the ratification of the ILO Convention No. 87 (Freedom of Association) from the late 1950s up to 1965 and seeking the restoration of the public employees' right to strike (until the privatization of public corporations was completed in the mid 1980s), the government appointed several study committees and councils to deliberate on these problems. The Japanese Federation of Employers' Associations (*Nikkeiren*) does not have any representative from the government organizations as employers.

Trade unions

Legal framework regulating representation

Labor laws in Japan are based on the principle of pluralistic representation owing to the stipulation of Article 28 of the Constitution. The Trade Union Law protects the workers' right to organize, but it does not apply the exclusive representation system such as exists in the United States. This leads to plural representation of workers according to ideological preference or political affiliation.

Therefore, if any group of two or more workers wants to organize a union of their own choosing and wishes to negotiate with the employer on behalf of its own members, the employer is obliged to bargain with it, and even a larger union cannot prevent the organizational rights of rival unions.

There is one marked difference between the private and the public sectors. In the private sector closed-shop agreements are allowed, indeed, most of the larger companies have closed-shop agreements with the most representative employees' unions. They also automatically deduct union dues every month from the wages of employees belonging to the union. On the other hand, in the public sector, closed-shop agreements are legally prohibited because the laws permit not only the right to organize, but also the right of personnel not to organize (Paragraph 3, Article 108-2 of the National Public Service Law; Paragraph 3, Article 52 of the Local Public Service Law).

Japan's system of employee representation is single channeled both in the private and the public sectors. Unlike the German system of works councils (*Betriebsrat*), there is no official system of dual representation.[3] However, there are well-developed joint consultation schemes to promote communication and mutual understanding between labor and management, rather than negotiating through collective bargaining, both in the private and the public sectors. The Postal Service has employed a highly elaborate system of labor–management communication since the middle of the 1970s.

Trade union composition, structure and organization

There are now about 12 million organized workers in Japan, representing 22.6 percent of the total employees in 1997 and 22.4 percent in 1998. Union density once exceeded 50 percent in the late 1940s, but declined to one-third during the period of high economic growth until the first oil crisis in 1973. It started to decline in the middle of the 1970s and continued to decline up to 1998. This was caused by (1) declining employment among large private companies due to rationalization during the past decades; (2) increased employment in small- and medium-sized firms; (3) the increase in part-time employment; and (4) a decrease in employment in the public service including the privatization of public corporations. The changed state of organized labor is exhibited in Table 7.5, showing that only one out of five organized workers now belongs to the public sector.

The largest national labor union center, Rengo, includes about 1,871,000 organized public employees under its umbrella, whereas a rival national federation led by communist forces, Zenroren, organizes about half a million public employees, including 125,000 non-industrial national public service units in most of the national ministries who are affiliated to the Federation of National Public Service (Kokko Roren) and left-wing forces among local government employees and teachers. Leaders of Zenroren unions represent the interests of the lower-level national public service who do not have the opportunities for promotion to the top posts within each ministry. Job classification systems based on separate recruitment examination systems tend to cause a kind of class distinction within the public service which arouses anti-establishment sentiments among those employees.

There is also a third, small, national center named Zenrokyo (Federation of All Trade Unions in Japan) which consists of the once powerful Kokuro (Union of the Japanese National Railways) plus a few small public employee unions. Besides these three umbrella

Table 7.5 Number of organized workers classified by the applicable laws, fiscal year 1953–1997 (Unit: 1000, % in ( ))

Private/Public	Applicable law	1953	1963	1973	1985[a]	1987[b]	1992	1997
Private sector	Trade union law	3,822 (64.5)	6,519 (69.7)	8,841 (73.1)	9,393 (75.6)	9,652 (77.9)	9,919 (79.1)	9,639 (79.2)
Public sector	PCNELR law[a]	861 (14.5)	973 (10.4)	1,014 (8.4)	552 (4.4)	288 (2.3)	273 (2.2)	255 (2.1)
	LPELR Law	73 (1.2)	166 (1.8)	220 (1.8)	222 (1.8)	204 (1.7)	197 (1.6)	223 (1.8)
	National Civil Service law	221 (3.7)	285 (3.0)	284 (2.3)	283 (2.3)	279 (2.3)	271 (2.2)	251 (2.1)
	Local Public Employees law	951 (16.1)	1,415 (15.1)	1,718 (14.4)	1,968 (15.9)	1,939 (15.8)	1,880 (15.0)	1,797 (14.8)
	Sub-total of public sector	2,105 (35.5)	2,838 (30.3)	3,257 (26.9)	3,025 (24.4)	2,710 (22.1)	2,621 (20.9)	2,526 (20.8)
Total organized workers		5,927 (100.0)	9,357 (100.0)	12,098 (100.0)	12,416 (100.0)	12,272 (100.0)	12,541 (100.0)	12,168 (100.0)

Note:
PCNELR Law = Public Corporation an National Enterprise Labor Relations Law LPELR Law = Local Public Enterprise Labor Relations Law
[a] National Enterprises Labor Relations Law after 1987.
[b] NTT and JT were privatized in April 1985.
[c] JR was privatized in April 1987.

Source: Ministry of Labor, Basic survey of Trade Unions, as of June every year.

organizations, there remain some independent unions of the national and local public service. It should be noted that the majority of Rengo union members belong to the private sector, whereas the majority of Zenroren and Zenrokyo belong to the public sector.

Union policies toward reform

The public employee unions affiliated to Rengo agree in principle with the administrative reforms and have been trying to protect their interests through the participation of their representatives. For example, unions of the Postal Service, which hold wide financial resources and political influence, have been trying hard to maintain their employment status as national public servants – even after its reorganization into a public corporation or "agency" (an independent administrative entity, an idea borrowed from 1980s British administrative reforms) in the early twenty-first century.

In Rengo's statement on the Final Report of The Administrative Reform Council, it was stated that "we waited hopefully and watched what kind of reforms would be produced as a result of discussions thereon. – However, we regret that the results ended in the mere reduction of the number of ministries and agencies without any real fruits. – We are afraid that the present reforms would have the danger of bringing about a few behemoth bureaucracies without any real policy goal (Rengo Liaison Council, 1997, 21–22).

On the other hand, Kokko Roren (the Federation of National Public Employee Unions, Zenroren) is strongly opposed to the proposed administrative reforms. It criticizes the proposed reforms for the following reasons: (1) the proposed transformation of 85 governmental organizations with 550,000 national public employees into "agencies" will jeopardize their public service job security; (2) the proposed reforms will force a reduction in the budgeted staff number in offices such as the Social Insurance Office or the Patent Office and so on by 10 percent within the next ten years; (3) evaluation of individual performance as well as achievement of organizational goals to be set annually by the minister in charge of respective agencies will be intensified so as to increase work effort. In order to improve the financial conditions of "agencies," it may become necessary to introduce more part-time workers or fixed-term employment contracts which, in turn, deteriorate the working conditions of regular public employees; and (4) pay of personnel in the proposed "agencies" will be negotiated in each agency based on comparability with national public employees. This may mean a *de facto* unilateral determination by the Ministry of

Finance (or its successor, treasury). Bonus payments will become more flexible according to the performance of each agency (Odagawa, 1999, 4–9).

Public sector labor relations

Structure of labor relations

As explained in the introduction to this paper, national non-industrial public employees do not have rights to collective bargaining or striking. Industrial public employees of both national and local government have the right to collective bargaining, but not that of striking. Because of these legal restrictions, the role of "independent" regulatory commissions such as the National Personnel Authority and the Central Labor Relations Commission, as well as their local government counterparts, is very important.

As explained earlier, the NPA is authorized and obligated to recommend improvements or changes in pay, hours of work, and other national non-industrial public employee conditions to the Diet (both houses) and to the cabinet based on the principle of comparability with the private sector. Besides this, the NPA meets and confers with the unions concerned in order to listen to their opinions. Article 108-5 of the National Public Service Law stipulates the following:

> When a registered employee organization proposes to negotiate in accordance with the law with the proper authorities on employee remuneration, work hours or other conditions of work or, in connection therewith, on matters concerning lawful activities including social and welfare activities, the authorities concerned shall place themselves in the position to respond to such proposals.
>
> Negotiations between the employee organization and proper authorities shall not include the right of collective agreement.
>
> Matters concerning the administration and operation of government business shall not be made the subject of negotiation.
>
> The proper authorities with whom the employee organization may negotiate shall be those who have the legal power to administer the matters to be negotiated or make decisions thereon.
>
> The negotiation shall be conducted between the persons designated by the employee organization from among its officers and the persons designated by the proper authorities, within the number of such representatives as previously agreed upon between the two parties

concerned. In conducting the negotiation, the employee organization and the proper authorities shall agree in advance upon the agenda, time and place of the meeting, and other necessary matters concerning the negotiation.

In the case provided in the preceding paragraph, the employee organization may, if special circumstances exist, designate persons other than its officers, provided that the persons so designated shall be able to prove in writing that they have been duly authorized by the executive organ of the employee organization concerned to negotiate on specific matters that are the subjects of the negotiation in view.

The negotiation may be terminated when it has failed to conform to the provisions of the preceding two paragraphs, obstructed the performance of duties by other employees or hampered the normal operation of government business.

The negotiation, to be conducted lawfully in accordance with the provisions of this Article, may also take place during work hours.

No employee shall be denied the freedom to express dissatisfaction or voice opinions on any of the matters stipulated in paragraph 1 by reason of his/her non-membership in an employee organization. (National Personnel Authority 1994)

The NPA undertakes "negotiation" with the employee organizations concerned very frequently. In recent years, the central and regional offices of the NPA have met and conferred (or "negotiated" if we use the terminology of the law) with employee organizations more than four hundred times a year.

The Central Labor Relations Commission is in charge of mediating or arbitrating labor disputes for national utilities. Formally speaking, national utility unions can bargain collectively with the proper authorities on pay, hours of work and other conditions – but not on matters concerning the administration and management of the business of each utility (Article 8, National Utility <Enterprise> Labor Relations Law). However, since the very beginning of the establishment of public corporations and national utilities, the negotiating powers of the authorities of national utilities have been strictly circumscribed by financial controls from the Ministry of Finance. Therefore, the authorities of each public corporation and national utility have been forced to respond to union demands only within the limits set via the consent of the Ministry of Finance.[4]

As such ineffective collective bargaining has been embedded within the national utilities, unions thereof have had to seek the yearly compulsory mediation and arbitration of the Central Labor Relations Commission, as well as its predecessors, on their disputes concerning wage increases. The established practices therein are to settle wage disputes through the compulsory arbitration awards of the Commission, since the government is obligated to "respect" them (Article 35, the National Utility Labor Relations Law) (Koshiro, 1985; Harari, 1973; ILO, 1966). The arbitration panel of the CLRC has an elaborate system of pay comparability of its own, thanks to improvement through half a century's historical lessons (Koshiro, 1985, 1995).

Public employee unions also "negotiate" with the head of the Prime Minister's Secretariat, the director-general and/or the head of the Personnel Bureau, or the head of the Administrative Management Bureau of the Management and Coordination Agency on many occasions when it is necessary for them to "demand" pay increases and improvements in other work conditions. They also meet LDP leaders and propose their demands concerning administrative reforms.

Labor conflict and the regulation of strikes

For a few years after the end of World War II all workers including public employees – except for police, fire-fighters and prison officers – had the right to organize and strike. Indeed, public employees were the core of a revolutionary labor movement, particularly between the fall of 1946 and the summer of 1948. However, as explained earlier, the national and non-industrial local public services were deprived of their right to strike by Article 38 of the Labor Relations Adjustment Law in October, 1946.

On the other hand, industrial public employees (including teachers) still held the right to strike until July, 1948. Despite the prohibition of industrial action by public employees, first by order of General MacArthur, and then by the amended National Public Service Law, they dared to conduct illegal industrial actions frequently until the end of 1975. Public corporation and postal service unions affiliated to Sohyo were the core of a "spring offensive" every year until the middle of the 1970s. They also organized incessant, energetic campaigns against productivity movements and rationalization during that time. They did not hesitate to repeat illegal industrial action, culminating in an eight-day unsuccessful strike demanding the restoration of their right to strike in November and December 1975. This untimely illegal strike, conducted in the midst of the recession following the oil crisis, created strong criticism against unions of public employees among the public and accelerated the downfall of the labor movement in the public sector.

It should be remembered that for a certain period after the ratification of the ILO Convention No. 87 in 1966, there were strong social tendencies toward liberalizing the rights of public employees to some extent. The Supreme Court decision on the Tokyo Central Post Office case (*Zentei V. Tokyo Central Post Office*, Supreme Court decision on October 26, 1966. Criminal Court Decisions, Vol. 20, No. 8, p. 901) paved the way for relaxing the criminal and administrative punishment of public employees committing illegal industrial action. However, another Supreme Court decision (*Zennorin v. Ministry of Agriculture and Forestries*, Supreme Court Decision on April 25, 1973, Criminal Court Decisions, Vol. 27, No. 4, p. 547) concerning political strikes by national public employees of the Ministry of Agriculture and Forestries against the introduction of the Amended Police Act, overturned the previous decision in 1966. Furthermore, the Supreme Court decided that work stoppages by postal workers would be punished criminally in its decision on the Nagoya Central Post Office Case (*Zentei v. Nagoya Central Post Office*, Supreme Court Decision on the 4th, May 1977, Criminal Court Decisions, Vol. 31, No. 3, p. 182). This new decision by the Supreme Court gave a serious shock to postal workers, so that *Zentei* (Postal Workers, Sohyo) were forced to change their strategy concerning industrial action. Within a few years they had chosen more cooperative ways of dealing with the authorities. In fact, it was the end of large-scale illegal industrial action by postal workers.

The dissolution and privatization of the Japanese National Railways in 1987 was the last time serious disputes occurred between public authorities and public employee unions. Most of the unions in the National Railways changed their strategy toward reorganization and privatization by the middle of the 1980s, but *Kokuro* (National Union of the Japanese National Railways) stuck to resisting privatization and thus failed to maintain its strength among employees (Shimoi, 1998).

Conclusions

It is expected that the government will submit to the Diet a set of bills to implement the administrative reforms for individual organizations in April, 1999. The central ministries and offices will be reduced from the present 22 to 12 ministries and to one office within five years after the implementation of the Basic Law, possibly by January 1, 2001 (Article 5 of the Basic Law to Reform the Central Ministries and Agencies of 1998).

The employment status of personnel to be employed by the "agencies" still remains ambiguous. There will be two kinds of "agency:" one is "quasi civil service type," whose personnel will be covered by the Trade Union Law and the Labor Standards Law, so that they can determine their pay, hours of work and most other conditions of work through collective bargaining (but remain under the mutual benefit society of the national public employees in terms of pension, medical care and other welfare facilities). Another is the "public service type" agency, whose personnel would retain their employment status as national public servants, including tenure, while being able to negotiate pay, hours of work and other conditions of work through collective bargaining. The latter system of industrial relations seems very much like that now applied to national utilities. However, how to regulate their industrial relations under what laws still remains ambiguous (Odagawa, 1999).

Zenroren's Kokko Roren submitted a set of questions on November 6, 1998 to the Headquarters for Promoting Administrative Reforms of the Central Ministries and Agencies, in which they emphasized that most of the personnel of those organizations to be affected by the proposed reforms belonged to their unions. They raised the question of how to interpret an ambiguous stipulation in Article 36 of the Basic Law concerning "independent administrative agencies." They asked the government to clarify the reasons why each individual organization should be transformed into "agencies" – and upon which criteria. They are very wary of such agencies becoming an alien third public service separated from traditional industrial and non-industrial public services without employment security or any guarantee of their basic labor rights. They also fear that those personnel transferred to agencies will not be covered by the NPA pay schedules and will be subjected to excessive rationalization.[5]

Notes

1. It should be recalled that public employee unions were an important part of revolutionary labor movements immediately after World War II. In order to maintain administrative discipline, the government restricted public employees' rights to industrial action between 1946 and 1953. Public employees' unions succeeded in restoring their freedom of association by 1965 through the help of ILO. They also tried to restore their rights to strike,

but the government reacted by privatizing public corporations and national utilities. In fact, after privatization, those employees were restored their right to strike, but have seldom conducted industrial action due to the competitive pressure of the market. For more details, see Koshiro (1985).
2. Usually, most wage negotiations in the private sector finish between late March and the end of April every year. However, wage settlements in a few companies tend to be delayed to May or June. Therefore, NPA undertakes an additional review of delayed wage increases in the private sector, and adds it to the pay differentials found by the pay research mentioned above.
3. However, the Labor Standards Law Amended in 1998 introduced a formal employee representation system with regard to the introduction of "discretionary work" of professional employees. Such employees may be exempted from overtime premiums if the employee committee representing the majority of the employees of a said establishment, or the trade union representing the majority of a said establishment, comes to a unanimous agreement and the principal agrees to it. This does not imply dual representation if there is any union organization representing the majority of eligible employees. However, if there is no majority union, then the management must ask the consent of the said employee committee if it wants to introduce the "discretionary work" arrangement.
4. The Ministry of Finance has the power to set the budgetary total payroll of each ministry and agency. The authorities of each ministry and agency may theoretically have the autonomy to respond more favorably to union demands even within the budgeted limit through reallocation of funds among different accounting items. However, the authorities are afraid of adverse future reactions from the Ministry of Finance if they accept a pay increase higher than that agreed by the Ministry of Finance. Such impotency on the part of the authorities of public corporations and national utilities humiliated them and provoked dissatisfaction among unions and union members of these utilities hampering the industrial relations thereof. For more details, see Koshiro (1985).
5. Kokko Roren, "Questions Concerning the Privatization and Transformation of Government Organizations into Independent Administrative Agencies" submitted to the Headquarters for Promoting Administrative Reforms of the Central Ministries and Agencies, November 6, 1998. Also see the Central Executive Committee of Kokko Roren, "Declaration: Let us do our best to kick out Administrative Reforms", dated January 26, 1999.

References

Harari, E. (1973) *The Politics of Labor Legislation in Japan*, Berkeley: University California Press.
Institute of Administrative Management (1998) *Administrative Management and Administrative Reform in Japan*, Tokyo: Institute of Administrative Management, Summary of the 1997 Annual Report of the Management and Coordination Agency, March.
ILO, Dreyer Commission Report (1996) *The Fact-finding and Conciliation Commission on Freedom of Association Concerning Persons Employed in the Public Sector in Japan*, Geneva: ILO.

Koshiro, K. (1985) "Labor Relations in the Public Service and the Impact of Union Activity on Public Administrations Actual Organization and Functioning," *Economia*, (86), September.

Koshiro, K. (1987) "Labor Problems of Public Utilities," in Ichinose, T., Ohashima, K., and Higo, K. (eds.), *On Public Utilities*, Tokyo: Yuhikaku (in Japanese).

Koshiro, K. (1995) "Wage Flexibility in the Public Sector," in Kurasawa, T., Wakasugi, R. and Asako, K. (eds.), *Structural Changes and the Corporate Behavior*, Tokyo: Nihon Hyoron Sha, 3–37 (in Japanese).

Koshiro, K. (1998) *Trade Unions*, Tokyo: Japan Institute of Labor.

Koshiro, K. and Rengo Soken (eds.) (1996 2nd edn.) *50 Years of Industry, Employment and Labor*, Tokyo: Japan Institute of Labor.

Management and Coordination Agency (1998) Organization of the Government of Japan, Tokyo: Prime Minister's Office.

Masujima, T. (1999) "Characteristics and Problems of Administrative Reforms by the Basic Law To Reform the Central Ministries and Agencies Compared With the Temporary Administrative Reforms," *Leviathan* (24).

Ministry of Home Affairs (1997) *Summary of the Local Public Service Pay Research as of April*, Tokyo: Government of Japan (in Japanese).

National Personnel Authority (1994) *The National Public Service Law*, Tokyo: NPA.

National Personnel Authority (1995a) *Annual Report of Final year*.

National Personnel Authority (1995b) *Handbook for Remuneration System of Public Service Employees in Japan*, Tokyo: NPA.

National Personnel Authority (1997a) *Annual Report of the Fiscal Year 1995*, Tokyo: NPA.

National Personnel Authority (1997b) *The Recruitment Examination for the National Public Service*, Tokyo: NPA.

National Personnel Authority (1998a) *A Guide to Pay of the National Public Service*, Tokyo: NPA, Remuneration Bureau (in Japanese).

National Personnel Authority (1998b) *A Profile of the National Public Service, FY 1998*, Tokyo: NPA Pay Bureau (in Japanese).

National Personnel Authority (1998c) *The Summary Report of the Survey of Top Management Salaries and Remuneration*, Tokyo: NPA, Remuneration Bureau (in Japanese).

National Personnel Authority (1998d) *Fifty Years History of Personnel Administration*, Tokyo: NPA (in Japanese).

Odagawa, Y. (1999) *Chosa Jiho Zenroren*, (433) (January) (in Japanese).

Rengo Liaison Council (1997) Statement of the Liaison Council of the Public Sector in The Protocol of The conference of The 17th Delegates of Liaison Council of the Public Sector (1998, September).

Shimoi, T. (1998) "Some Comments on Unfair Labor Practices Cases Against JR in Hiring Former JNR Workers," *The Monthly Journal of the Japan Institute of Labor*, **XL**(11) (in Japanese).

L # 8
Public Sector Industrial Relations in New Zealand

Pat Walsh, Raymond Harbridge, and Aaron Crawford*

Introduction

During the last decade a highly centralized public sector employment and industrial relations system in New Zealand began to unravel. The unraveling process was an integral consequence of the radical program of state restructuring undertaken in New Zealand since 1984 (Scott et al., 1990; Boston et al., 1996; Schick, 1996). This restructuring program, arguably the most radical in the OECD, resulted in dramatic changes to the size and structure of the state, its role in the society and economy and the objectives of state activity.

Historically, employment relations in the public sector were controlled from the center. Central employing authorities encountered centralized trade unions and between them they resolved most issues of importance with little direct involvement by employees or union members. All staff in the public service were employed by the State Services Commission (SSC), the government's central employing agency which held all personnel authority (although in practice it delegated some of this authority). Public sector employees were members of a unified public service and were eligible for appointment to any position in any department or agency. A single occupational classification system and a uniform performance appraisal system applied to all employees in the core public service. Public sector unions were strong. They enjoyed high levels of membership, in part due to their other role

---

*The research on bargaining outcomes under the Employment Contracts Act is funded by a grant from the Public Good Science Fund (Contract VIC 703) administered by the Foundation for Science, Research and Technology. The authors are grateful to the Alex Harrington, Brigette Hughes, and Ross Nelson for research assistance.

as professional associations. Ministerial recognition of a single union in most branches of the public sector ensured the dominance in each branch of a large occupationally based union. These unions negotiated pay and other employment conditions with central employing authorities according to legislative criteria which required these to be broadly comparable with the private sector. This ensured that most public sector employees received the same pay increase each year and kept other employment conditions broadly similar across the whole public sector. Other rules governing the employment relationship which were not subject to union negotiation were centrally prescribed and laid down in manuals. In this chapter, we trace out how, from 1988 onwards, this highly centralized and uniform system began to unravel.

At a general level the public sector in the New Zealand context includes two separate spheres of government: central and local. This chapter focuses on the structural and industrial relations reforms introduced in the central government sector (including both trading and non-trading sectors). The local government sector will not be considered. The key reason for this is that local government workers did not hold the legal status of state employees, and industrial relations and personnel management in the local government sector had been conducted, by and large, under the same legislative regime that prevailed in the private sector.

Central government itself consists of a number of branches. The public service is responsible for administration, policy, and associated monitoring and enforcement activities. In addition to the public service there are a large number of organizations designated as crown entities. This group includes the public education providers and public hospitals (which will both be dealt with separately) as well as other organizations involved in delivering a diverse range of non-commercial services to government and the public. Commercial operations owned by central government are governed by a specific Act of Parliament, the State Owned Enterprises Act 1986. The SOEs were obvious targets for privatization which began under Labor in 1988. The final branch of central government, which will not be considered further, are the police and defense forces.

Organizational structure, employment and wages

Quantitative composition of employees by sector, gender, job classification and type of employment (1980)

The number of workers directly employed by central government has fallen markedly since restructuring began. The official data in Table 8.1

Table 8.1 Public sector employment, 1980–1998

Year to February	Central government core (000s)	Central government trading (000s)	Total central (000s)	Total local government (000s)	Total public sector (000s)	Total private sector (000s)	Public sector share %
1980	——	——	——	——	334.0	626.5	34.8
1983	——	——	——	——	326.3	614.6	34.7
1987	——	——	——	——	326.5	742.1	30.5
1988	——	——	——	——	315.8	719.7	30.5
1989	186.4	80.4	266.7	41.2	307.9	689.3	30.9
1990	183.7	63.7	247.4	43.4	290.8	695.4	29.5
1991	186.3	40.7	226.9	43.5	270.4	695.7	28.0
1992	183.7	36.4	220.0	39.0	259.0	669.8	27.9
1993	182.6	26.6	209.2	36.4	245.5	679.0	26.6
1994	184.1	21.0	205.1	35.5	240.5	732.2	24.7
1995	179.1	19.6	198.7	34.3	233.0	778.7	23.0
1996	183.3	20.9	204.1	35.8	239.9	803.1	23.0
1997	188.3	18.2	206.5	35.5	241.9	832.3	22.5
1998	187.3	18.4	205.6	33.7	239.4	836.8	22.2

Source: Data for 1987 onwards are calculated from Quarterly Employment Survey. Data are reported as full time equivalents calculated as full-time employees + (part-time employees ÷ 2). Data report total filled jobs excluding working proprietors. Survey excludes businesses employing fewer than three FTE employees, workers employed in agriculture, members of the armed forces, and domestic servants. Data for 1980–1983 are from the Department of Labor's discontinued quarterly employment information survey and are not directly comparable with later data. They are included for indicative purposes.

show that this fall has been both in absolute terms and as a proportion of total employment. The bulk of this fall has been concentrated in the public service and in the state-owned trading enterprises, and in large measure was a deliberate goal of the state sector reforms.

Employment trends in the public service have been affected by two aspects of state sector restructuring. First, the recasting of government's commercial activities saw 14,000 public service employees transferred to the new SOEs and a further 5,200 accept voluntary severance or early retirement (Department of Statistics, 1988). Second, internal restructuring of the public service was guided by the desire for smaller, single-purpose departments (Boston, 1991a). Table 8.2 gives a breakdown of public service organizations by size. The data show the extent to which the restructuring undertaken between 1984 and 1998 has reduced both the size and concentration of the public service.

The decline in employment amongst central government's trading organizations is more dramatic and is a direct result of the corporatization

Table 8.2 Public service organizations by size, 1984 and 1998

Size (no. of employees)	31 March 1984		30 June 1998	
	No.	Total employed	No.	Total employed
Less than 100 employees	3	114	9	352
100–499 employees	4	1,510	14	3,407
500–999 employees	9	6,349	8	5,940
1,000–1,999 employees	4	5,346	2	3,460
2,000–2,999 employees	3	6,775	2	4,522
3,000–3,999 employees	5	17,465	1	3,725
4,000 or more employees	7	48,179	2	10,453
Total	35	85,738	38	31,859

Note: Data are on a headcount basis.
Source: State Services Commission Reports.

Table 8.3 Staffing in selected SOEs, 1987–1991

Organization	Staff numbers (March years)					Change 87–91	% Change
	1987	1988	1989	1990	1991		
Coalcorp	1,861	892	806	715	675	−1,186	−64
Electricorp	5,999	4,424	4,066	3,950	3,974	−2,025	−34
NZ Post	12,000	9,800	9,500	8,500	8,200	−3,800	−32
Telecom	24,500	23,931	19,151	17,131	15,066	−9,434	−39
NZ Rail	14,900	12,500	9,900	8,400	5,900	−9,000	−60
Forestrycorp	7,070	2,652	2,547	2,597	2,587	−4,483	−63
Total (selected)	66,330	54,199	45,970	41,293	36,402	−29,928	−45

Source: Duncan and Bollard (1992). The reduction in staffing levels at New Zealand Rail began prior to corporatization. In 1982 New Zealand Rail employed over 21,500 staff this number had reduced to 15,000 by the time of the State Owned Enterprises Act 1986.

and privatization process. Corporatization established the centrality of commercial goals and ended the practice of using the crown's commercial operations as a means to soak up unemployment (Bassett, 1998; see also Smith, 1997). Moreover, in restructuring the SOEs to meet these commercial goals, substantial numbers of staff were laid off with staffing levels in some SOEs reduced by as much as 65 percent during the first years of corporatization (Lister et al., 1991; Duncan and Bollard, 1992). Table 8.3 reports data on staff numbers for selected SOEs. The subsequent sale of SOEs to private sector interests further reduced direct employment in the state sector.

Table 8.4 Employment in public health and education sectors, 1984–1998

Year	Employment in public Hopitals (FTE)	Teaching staff employed by state schools (FTE)	Teaching staff employed in tertiary institutions (FTE)
March 1984	48,824	34,810	6,317
March 1985	48,313	34,827	6,905
March 1986	48,274	35,544	7,206
March 1987	49,197	35,227	——
March 1988	50,088	35,062	8,413
1989	——	35,441	8,483
1990	——	36,057	——
1991	——	36,085	8,796
1992	——	35,879	9,372
1993	——	35,440	9,669
1994	42,480	35,809	9,783
1995	41,385	36,039	10,073
1996	41,087	37,539	10,198
1997	41,118	38,811	10,356
1998	40,527	39,406	10,409

Source: Data to 1988 from New Zealand Official Yearbook (various years). Data for staff employed directly by public hospitals from 1994 onwards were supplied by the Crown Company Monitoring Advisory Unit (CCMAU) and exclude contract staff.

By comparison, available data show employment in the public health and education sectors has remained relatively stable over the reform period. Notwithstanding this stability, employment in public hospitals has fallen after the 1993 restructuring of the health sector. The greater autonomy extended to senior managers of Crown Health Enterprises allowed, and changes in funding policy justified, cost-saving policies, for example contracting out of non-medical support services, such as cleaning, food preparation, maintenance trades, and so on. Comprehensive data on the employment in public education is not available. Table 8.4 reports employment in public hospitals and teaching staff employed in state primary and secondary schools and in tertiary institutions.

Data on gender show the increasing "feminization" of the public sector labor force. To some extent this can be explained by the structural changes in public sector employment outlined above which have seen male full-time employment in the public sector halve since the early 1980s. The data in Table 8.5 report the gender composition of the full- and part-time labor force in the public sector and compare this against the private sector. The data show that women now make up over half

Table 8.5 Gender breakdown of employment, 1980–1998 (selected years)

March Year	Full-time employees				Part-time employees			
	All public sector			Private sector	All public sector			Private sector
	Male (000)	Female (000)	Female %	Female %	Male (000)	Female (000)	Female %	Female %
1980	194.2	122.5	38.7	31.5	6.1	28.5	82.3	76.6
1983	189.1	118.2	38.5	32.1	5.9	32.0	84.4	77.9
1987	176.6	125.2	41.5	35.6	8.2	40.7	83.2	76.5
1988	166.4	121.1	42.1	35.8	10.2	46.3	82.0	75.9
1989	153.4	128.1	45.5	34.3	8.6	44.1	83.7	70.0
1990	142.6	120.3	45.8	35.8	10.6	44.9	80.9	72.4
1991	125.2	115.3	47.9	36.2	12.1	47.6	79.7	72.4
1992	117.1	113.0	49.1	36.4	11.6	46.1	79.9	71.2
1993	108.7	106.9	49.6	36.5	12.3	47.4	79.4	71.7
1994	102.5	106.3	50.9	36.3	13.7	49.8	78.4	70.6
1995	97.4	106.1	52.1	36.0	13.2	45.9	77.7	70.7
1996	97.7	111.2	53.2	35.9	13.0	48.9	79.0	70.8
1997	94.9	111.7	54.1	36.2	16.6	53.8	76.4	70.9
1998	92.6	111.5	54.6	36.4	16.5	53.9	76.6	70.9

Source: Data after 1987 calculated from QES data. Data for 1980 and 1983 are from the Department of Labor's discontinued quarterly employment information survey and are not directly comparable with later data. They are included, however, for indicative purposes.

of all full-time employees in the public sector, compared with just over one-third of full-time employees in the private sector.

While the extent of restrictions on the employment of workers on other than a full-time basis was limited, employment in the public sector was traditionally full time. The data in Table 8.5 show an increasing number of workers (both absolutely and proportionally) have been employed part time in the public sector since restructuring began. In 1980, 10 percent of state employees were part time; by 1998 this figure had risen to over 25 percent. Full-time employment, however, still remains the predominant form of engagement in the public sector.

Comprehensive data on the duration of engagements are not available. By tradition employment in the public sector was permanent or open ended. What information is available suggests that the public sector has made greater use of the practice of engaging employees, other than senior management, on individual contracts of a fixed duration (Anderson et al., 1996). While this has often been in response to short-term imperatives of restructuring and reorganization within departments, it has helped to further break down the concept of permanent lifetime employment in the public service (Boston et al., 1996). Recent figures show that just under 10 percent of public servants are engaged on fixed term contracts (State Services Commission, 1998a). This figure has remained relatively stable, even declining slightly in recent years, indicating a trend away from fixed-term contracts which may be a result of the somewhat convoluted case law that has built up around their usage (see Kiely, 1997).

Recent data on job classifications of public sector workers are not available. In part the breakdown of traditional occupationally based employment practices and the decentralization of responsibilities for employment matters removed the need for this information in coordinating wage matters. Data on the distribution of earnings give a rough guide to the split between management and non-management employees.

Qualitative characteristics of public sector labor market

Public servants were traditionally employed for life in a unified career service. Once employed, public servants were eligible for appointment to any position in the public service and were protected by the requirement that for any position above the entry grades an outsider had to demonstrate "clearly more merit" than an applicant from anywhere in the service. The dominance of the state in the provision of health and education services also impacted markedly on the structure of the labor markets in these sectors.

The State Services Commission was constituted as the central employing agency for the state service. The Commission had its origins in the Public Service Act 1912 which established a politically independent office to manage personnel matters in the public service (Henderson, 1990). The Commission's role extended to matters of appointment to and promotion within the state service, and to more serious instances of misconduct (which were defined under statute).

After the passage of the State Services Act 1962 the Commission increasingly delegated appointment and promotion functions for lower-level positions to individual departments, maintaining a supervisory role through the operation of appeal procedures (Henderson, 1990). The operation of the delegated personnel authorities, however, remained subject to centrally established bureaucratic guidelines and controls.

Recruitment was controlled centrally through a system of "staff ceilings" under which each department was subject to a limit on maximum staffing numbers. Promotion decisions were also made principally on the basis of merit. In both cases "merit" was defined by the State Services Act 1962 to include work experience, competence, relevant personal attributes and qualifications. By and large the primacy of the merit criteria seems to have been abided by, although Smith (1974) suggests there was a perception by public servants that other factors, including seniority, were important.

An appeals system allowed a current employee to appeal an appointment of a candidate from outside of the public service, or any promotion decision, to the Public Service Appeal Board established under the 1962 Act. These appointment, promotion and appeals procedures were abolished by the State Sector Act 1988. In line with the managerialist thrust of the Act, chief executives were given greater authority over appointments, promotions and dismissals.

The job security of state employees has been one major casualty of the reforms. As outlined above, the reduction in public employment has been widespread, and the use of contingent labor has also increased. Prior to the State Sector Act public servants, consistent with the culture of lifetime employment, were not covered by formal or informal redundancy arrangements. The restructuring of the public sector, which was begun in the mid 1980s with the corporatization of government owned trading enterprises, involved the first substantial public sector redundancies (see Lister et al., 1991). In response the union negotiated a deployment agreement with the State Services Commission which set out a number of options in the event of surplus staffing, with voluntary severance being the last option. Redundancies continued, however, and as part of the 1989 bargaining round the union and State Services Commission negotiated an enforceable redundancy agreement to cover all public servants. By contrast with contemporary private sector agreements, the Union/SSC agreement on restructuring and redundancy provided a specific process of consultation and review and generous compensation in event of an employee accepting redundancy. Notwithstanding this, public service restructuring has continued to give rise to redundancies (State Services Commission, 1998a).

Wages and salaries

As part of the Labor government's tax reforms, changes to the personal taxation regime were introduced to check the growth of untaxed non-wage benefits paid to employees (Dickson, 1989). As a result of these changes labor costs in New Zealand are highly transparent. The wage component (ordinary and overtime payments) constitutes around 80 percent of labor costs in the public sector. The bulk of the non-wage components are in the form of paid annual leave, payments for public holidays and employer contributions to employee superannuation schemes. Common private sector non-wage benefits (medical insurance, motor vehicle, low interest loans, and so on) make up less than half of 1 percent of public sector labor costs (Statistics New Zealand, 1997b).

Data on the use and extent of performance-related payment systems for employees other than those in management roles in the public sector are partial. While the rhetoric of "rewarding performance" is appealing to public sector managers, implementation is more problematic. A number of public service contracts have introduced performance pay pools where a percentage of the departmental salary budget is set aside for bonus payments to staff determined on the basis of assessment of individual performance. The introduction of performance payment systems in other branches of the public sector is often complicated by the nature of the work undertaken (Powell, 1995a). Irregular performance bonuses, however established, typically constitute only a small proportion of total earnings.

More substantial efforts to introduce performance pay have come through changes to payment systems. After the passage of the State Sector Act, departments moved to introduce a payment system based on ranges of rates. "Ranges of rates" were intended as a performance pay system; individuals were placed in the applicable salary band according to their skills, experience, and so on, and subsequent progression within this band was to be dependent upon assessed performance. In practice, payroll systems required that steps within the ranges be introduced, and ceilings or bars existed with the ranges which individuals had to be promoted beyond. Furthermore, the expectation of employees for an annual progression to the next step continued and was largely met (Boston et al., 1996). The operation of the ranges of rates pay system to provide annual increments in conjunction with static general wage movement led to the clustering of large groups of employees at or around the bars in pay ranges, irrespective of individual performance, and with no prospect of further increments without promotion. This situation contributed to the groundswell of industrial action in pursuit of a general wage increase that occurred from late 1995.

The actors: employers and employer associations

State policies and action in relation to the public sector regulation

One of the key aims of state sector reforms was to free public sector managers from traditional bureaucratic controls and give them greater scope to manage the resources allocated to them, including personnel resources. This necessarily had important implications for the organization and conduct of industrial relations.

These reforms were advanced through three separate but interrelated Acts: The State Owned Enterprises Act 1986; The State Sector Act 1988; and the Public Finance Act 1989. The Acts were premised on a theoretical model of government management enthusiastically embraced by key politicians and policy advisors (Boston, 1991b).

Prior to these reforms the government's central personnel agency, the State Services Commission (SSC), was the employing authority for the majority of state employees. The SSC, acting through various tribunals and committees, was largely responsible for negotiating and monitoring employment conditions across the state services. The commission had authority over personnel matters, although as noted earlier, some functions were often delegated to individual departments. The reforms have seen the SSC's control function progressively scaled back.

The State Owned Enterprises Act 1986 radically altered the management framework for government-owned trading organizations. The overriding principle was to establish these organizations as successful businesses, with managers to have powers comparable to their private sector counterparts.

There were important industrial relations implications flowing from changes to the managerial framework of SOEs. Each SOE was made the employer of its staff (a role previously vested with the State Services Commission). While employees of the SOEs were to retain their status as state employees, managers were given much greater flexibility to negotiate employment matters.

The State Sector Act 1988 extended many of the same principles to the management of the non-commercial activities of the public service (Palmer, 1988). The Act replaced tenured permanent departmental heads with chief executives employed on fixed-term contracts of up to five years and renewable for a further period of up to three years. The process for appointing chief executives was radically different to that used to appoint permanent heads. Previously, appointments were made by a five-person panel which included three current permanent heads elected by their peers. Under the State Sector Act the SSC recommends the appointment of chief executives to cabinet which may accept or reject the SSC's nomination. In the latter case, cabinet may request an alternative nominee from the SSC or proceed to make an appointment itself. This possibility raises the specter of political appointments (Boston et al., 1996).

The Act extended to chief executives (and by delegation to lower levels of management) broad autonomy in managing the resources allocated to their departments. With this autonomy came corresponding accountability for departmental performance. It also provided for the establishment of a senior executive service (SES), an inter-departmental pool of senior management immediately below chief executive level. The SES was intended to preserve the sense of a unified public service in an environment of fragmentation emerging under the shift to departmentalism. Chief executives were given the authority to appoint, monitor and remunerate members of the SES. This power is, however, subject to a number of constraints and the State Service Commission retains an important coordinating role with regard to SES pay and conditions.

The State Sector Act also had profound impacts on industrial relations. The Act made chief executives employers of their staff, and replaced service-wide, occupational determinations with departmental agreements as the primary means of pay fixing. While this had the effect of changing the structure of bargaining arrangements, the process of bargaining itself remained highly centralized. The SSC's role as employer party to negotiations over employment conditions continued, despite the ongoing thrust of state sector reforms, and the tension between centralized control and decentralized responsibility was a source of resentment among chief executives and human resource managers of government departments (Boston et al., 1996). Continued centralization was largely intended as an instrument of fiscal discipline (Walsh, 1993). These perceived tensions were exacerbated with the introduction of the Employment Contracts Act with its emphasis on decentralized negotiations. The SSC responded in 1992 by delegating responsibility for negotiating employment contracts to departmental chief executives. The Commission, however, retained an important supervisory role and set constraints on the outcomes which chief executives could negotiate, the most important of which was the "fiscal neutrality" of settlements (discussed below). The State Sector Act also reformed personnel practice, including removing the traditional preference given to job candidates from within the public service, and abolishing centralized promotion and appointment review procedures.

The Public Finance Act 1989 completed Labor's reforms of public sector management (Pallot, 1991a,b). The Act introduced an accrual accounting system and moved the budgetary focus from input controls – voting money for a department's programs – to an output-based system – voting money for specific and agreed outputs. Ministers and chief executives now negotiate a purchasing agreement in which chief executives contract with ministers to deliver agreed outputs and to report on results by way of a statement of service performance. Chief executives are responsible for ensuring the agreed outputs are in fact produced by their staff.

Reforms to the role of management in the public health sector have proceeded in two distinct phases. The Labor government adapted the State Sector Act model to management of public hospitals, focusing on improving both performance and accountability structures. Pressure for these reforms came largely from the increasing burden public health expenditure was claimed to place on government finances (Britton et al., 1992). Organizational reforms saw the consolidation of individual hospital boards into 14 Area Health Boards. AHBs were responsible for the funding and provisions of health services for a specific region and comprised a mixture of ministerial appointees and locally elected representatives. Each board entered into a contractual agreement with the Minister of Health based around an agreed business plan for the delivery of health care services.

The second stage of reforms was initiated by the national government elected in 1990. National government's funding reforms extended the reforms begun by Labor (the full implementation of which had been hindered by opposition from health sector unions). Purchasing and providing functions were split and it was clearly envisaged that private sector providers would compete with government-owned providers for public funding.

The approach to the reform of management structures in the public education sector differed between compulsory (primary and secondary schools) and post-compulsory or tertiary education (universities, polytechnics, and so on).

The Education Act 1989 abolished the ten regional education boards which had acted as the employing agency for primary teachers and replaced these with boards of trustees. Each school is governed by a board of trustees which is comprised of a majority of parent-elected representatives, plus the school principal and a staff representative. Each board is responsible for the management of the school, for developing school policies, and for employing staff, although the latter "responsibility" does not extend to determining the number of teaching staff to be employed, nor to negotiating their conditions of employment. Under the State Sector Act the SSC acts as bargaining agent for all state-owned schools and negotiates separate national agreements for primary and secondary school teachers with the two respective teacher unions. From 1997 the SSC delegated this role to the Ministry of Education.

The principal of each school is responsible for operational management of the school within the framework of the school board's policies and charter and the school's legal obligations to the Minister (Ministry of Education, 1992). Principals are appointed by the board of trustees which is free to determine its own appointment procedures. In 1997 the option of electing to receive bulk funding of salary costs was extended to individual boards of trustees, in line with government policy of increasing the self-management of schools. The bulk funding of teacher salaries has been strongly opposed by national teacher unions who fear the system will be used as a means to reduce funding levels. The number of boards electing bulk funding of salaries has remained relatively low – around 14 percent as at July 1998 – despite significant financial incentives offered to select this option (*Dominion*, July 28, 1998).

Reforms to the management structures of state owned post-compulsory or tertiary education institutions were more limited in their extent due to the nature of existing governance structures. The bulk of reforms to the tertiary sector focused primarily on the basis of funding from central government although, in line with the general thrust of state sector reforms, local management and accountability mechanisms were strengthened.

The SSC was designated as employer party for collective bargaining purposes and negotiated agreements in consultation with the chief executive officers (vice-chancellor or principals). This was intended as a transitional arrangement and §74(b)(2) of the Act established that this role would be transferred to individual CEOs from January 1, 1992, but required them to consult with the SSC before entering negotiations.

Until 1988 conditions of work for senior state sector employees, including senior public servants, university lecturers and medical doctors employed by hospital boards, were set by the Higher Salaries Commission. The commission's determinations were to be guided by the principle of fair relativity with private sector salaries. The State Sector Act all but ended the role of the HSC. The employment conditions of heads of government departments, now chief executives, are negotiated on appointment between the individual and the State Service Commission according to the central pay policy guidelines. New policies were introduced in 1997 to enable a more flexible approach to be taken, and to increase the performance-related component of chief executive salaries. The single chief executive pay line (with pay increasing in direct proportion to job size) was replaced by a series of overlapping bands, giving the SSC greater discretion in negotiating salary packages. The concept of strategic incentive plans (SIPs) was sketched out, establishing performance incentives linked to the achievement of the strategic goals of government policy (State Services Commission, 1998b). By contrast, the majority of university academic staff and medical practitioners employed in public hospitals have continued to have their conditions of work determined through collective negotiations.

In summary, there are a number of common threads to the state sector reforms as they impact on the role of public managers. Ideology has played a key role (Boston, 1991b). Personnel changes have been important in giving effect to the ideological shift. To this end management positions have been removed from collective bargaining coverage and fixed-term contracts have been used to establish employment conditions. The ending of tenured managerial appointments had important implications for the career nature of public sector management, and allowed a greater scope for hiring private sector managers to senior positions in the public sector.

A much vaunted element in New Zealand's state sector reforms has been the increase in autonomy extended to management over operational management of government organizations at the expense of central control agencies (especially the SSC). None the less, important limits on autonomy of management at a strategic level have been maintained (even strengthened) through the use of contractual agreements between ministers and CEOs or boards which specify organizational objectives and around which the measurement of managerial performance is based. More significantly, perhaps, the role of central government as founder of the public sector has meant that very tight centralized control can be maintained through the use of fiscal restraints. The reforms to the public sector management have been one means for central government to shift the responsibility for implementing of austerity measures surrounding public sector pay from ministers to public managers.

The trade unions

Legal framework regulating representation

Prior to 1988 state sector unions had little legal basis for representing their memberships and were largely reliant on tradition of ministerial recognition in securing their bargaining role. The State Sector Act 1988 allowed public sector service organizations (as they were known) to register as trade unions under the Labor Relations Act 1987 for the first time. Registration brought with it a raft of rights and obligations which had guided the development of unions in the private sector since 1894. A registered union enjoyed the exclusive right to represent the group or groups of workers defined in the union's membership rules in negotiations for an award or agreement. The Act also extended to public sector unions the right to negotiate unqualified preference (effectively compulsory membership) provisions for the first time, although only one major union – the union representing primary teachers – exercised this option. The quid pro quo for unions was that they accepted the detailed regulation of their internal affairs, including the level of fee that they could levy on their membership.

The Employment Contracts Act 1991 ended nearly a century of state sponsorship of trade unionism. The ECA abolished the specific regulations that governed trade unions and deemed each registered union to be an incorporated society under the Incorporated Societies Act 1908 (Employment Contracts Act §185(1)) and hence, no different from any other non-trading body corporate. While the abolition of historical privileges associated with registration has had disastrous impacts on many private sector trade unions (see Harbridge and Crawford, 1998a), it essentially returned public sector unions to the situation that had applied prior to the State Sector Act 1988, albeit against the backdrop of a radically different institutional setting.

Under the ECA union membership is voluntary. Part 1 of the Act establishes the freedom of association in both a positive and negative sense – the right to associate and the right not to associate – and prohibits discrimination on the grounds of membership or non-membership of a union. Closed shop arrangements are illegal on the grounds that they breach the freedom of association as defined in the Act. The elaborate legal rules regulating representation in collective bargaining have been abolished altogether. The ECA provides that any employee can authorize a bargaining agent (who or which need not be a trade union) for the purposes of negotiating an individual or collective employment contract. While an employer is required to recognize a worker's agent, there is no concomitant obligation to begin or conclude negotiations with that agent. Without regulation there were no formal mechanisms to protect existing bargaining units, a factor which led many unionists to criticize the instability inherent in the Act's model of bargaining (Douglas, 1993). Moreover, and in keeping with the contractual model introduced by the Act, an employment contract bound only those individuals who were party to its negotiation. While the Act allowed that the parties might agree to extend a contract to cover additional employees (or employers), there was no automatic extension or "blanket coverage" mechanism as had existed under the former award system. Thus, employers were free to exclude existing workers from the coverage of a collective contract (often even when they became union members) and to engage staff, particularly new staff, on individual contracts. These options were exercised widely (Dannin, 1997).

Trade union composition, structure and organization model by sector/occupation

Public sector unions in New Zealand have several distinctive features *vis-à-vis* their private sector counterparts. Historically many public sector unions were established primarily as professional associations with their industrial role a somewhat secondary one. Public sector unions enjoyed high levels of membership without the support of compulsory membership provisions enjoyed by private sector unions under the award system. Moreover, membership of public sector unions traditionally extended to include senior public servants. While the dominant form of private sector union under the award system was small, regional, and craft based, unions in the public sector were typically larger national bodies organized along industrial lines (Keating, 1974; Walsh, 1994). The organizations themselves were centralized and bureaucratic in keeping with the system they operated within.

The Public Service Association (PSA) is the traditional representative of public service employees, although its coverage also extends to include workers employed in the health and education sectors, in current or former SOEs, and in the local government sector after the 1993 merger with two of the three local government officer unions. The diversity of its coverage (the PSA administered over 150 occupational determinations under the old system) and the contestability of union membership introduced by the ECA left the PSA potentially vulnerable to defections by disaffected sections (Boston et al., 1996; Dannin, 1997). Indeed, since the passage of the ECA, several groups have broken from the PSA and formed their own unions or bargaining associations including officers in the Customs Department's northern region and employees of the Department of Social Welfare. Sizable groups of prison officers and staff of the Inland Revenue Department have defected and established their own unions which maintain a workplace presence alongside and in competition with the PSA.

Union representation in the health and education sector is primarily along occupational lines. In the compulsory education sector teaching staff are represented by two national unions: the New Zealand Educational Institute (NZEI) representing primary teachers (and which also covers pre-school teachers) and the Post-Primary Teachers Association (PPTA) as representative of secondary school teachers. The Service & Food Workers Union is the primary representative of support staff in both primary and secondary schools, including cleaners and caretakers, library and administrative staff.

In the post-compulsory education sector the Association of University Staff (AUS) is the main representative of both teaching and support staff in universities. The PSA also retains coverage in some universities, and the Association of Staff in Tertiary Education (ASTE) covers former college of education staff transferred to universities as a result of institutional mergers. Various private sector craft and general unions cover trades staff employed by universities.

National occupational unions predominate in the health sector. The NZ Nurses Organization (NZNO) is the largest of these and primarily represents nurses and nurse aides in both the public and private sectors.[1] Senior and junior doctors are represented by their own unions, the Association of Salaried Medical Specialists and the Resident Doctors Association respectively. The PSA is the primary representative of other professional, technical, administrative and clerical workers employed in public hospitals. In 1992 the National Union of Public Employees was established. The core of the new union comprised health workers in the upper South Island who were upset at the PSA's failure to back calls for a general strike in response to the introduction of the Employment Contracts Bill/Act (Harbridge and Hince, 1994; Dannin, 1997). Like the examples in the public service, NUPE's more militant presence at the workplace is in competition with the PSA. The New Zealand Council of Trade Union (CTU) is a central organization to represent both public and private sector unions. It is the result of the merger of the Combined State Service Organizations (CSSO) and the private sector Federation of Labor (FOL). A rival central organization is the Trade Union Federation (TUF) that was set up in 1993 as a militant alternative of CTU both in the private and public sector.

Overall, recent changes (since 1988) in the patterns of union representation in the public sector have been radical and uneven. These developments have stemmed from two sources: state sector restructuring, and the reforms to industrial relations law.

The structural reorganization of government significantly reduced the number of state sector employees, reducing the pool of potential members for public sector unions. There was also substantial fragmentation of bargaining structures resulting from the end of service wide bargaining (although the prevailing industrial relations framework for the first period of reforms, from 1988 to 1991, granted unions a secure institutionalized presence). Increasing managerialism within the state sector impacted through the removal of public sector managers from collective bargaining coverage (and consequently from union membership). Moreover, a number of the ideological precepts of managerialism were fundamentally hostile to collective bargaining and unionism in the workplace, and these found expression in the conduct of industrial relations (especially after 1991) (Boston et al., 1996; Dannin, 1997).

Radical reforms of employment law were introduced in the Employment Contracts Act. The principles of freedom of association enshrined in the Act raised the potential for competition between unions for the right to represent groups of workers. Union (and worker) responses have been in two contradictory directions. First, unions have attempted to consolidate through mergers and amalgamations (a trend initially set in motion by the requirements of the Labor Relations Act). Increasingly these have been driven by the imperatives of organizational survival rather than a desire to rationalize representation. The unions that have emerged have often had sizable coverage in both public and private sectors. Second, the prevailing environment of decentralized bargaining has seen new unions emerge to challenge existing union coverage leading to further fragmentation of representation at the workplace.

The ECA's implicit preference for individualizing the employment relationship is inimical to union representation. The increasing use of individual contracts of employment in the public sector has reduced the number of employees for whom union membership is relevant. Moreover, where a collective contract was in place, it became common practice for public sector employers to extend the same conditions to non-union employees, exacerbating the free-rider problem inherent in the new system (see Harbridge and Honeybone, 1996).

Unionization: raw figures by sector, occupation, confederation

Official data on union membership by sector is partial at best. With the ECA's abolition of union registration mechanisms (and of the Office of the Registrar of Trade Unions who oversaw these) the official collection of data on trade union membership ended. Since 1991 private surveys have provided the only data on union membership. Available industry data show that while membership has declined across all major industry groupings, the decline has been lower in those industries in which the public sector predominates (Crawford et al., 1998). The results of Brosnan and Walsh's (1997) workplace survey confirm this impression. Over 90 percent of public sector workplaces surveyed were unionized, compared with just 13 percent of private sector workplaces, and 19 percent of the entire sample. Moreover, density of membership in unionized public sector workplaces was much higher than that in unionized private sector workplaces.

A partial picture of trends in public sector union membership can be gleaned from the unofficial surveys. Table 8.6 gives an approximation of the numbers of public sector unionists.

The data show that, with the exception of the education sector, union membership in the various branches of the state sector has fallen markedly since the ECA. With the exception of education, the falls reflect the decline in employment in the public sector outlined above (although this has been less marked since 1990). More significant, perhaps, is the impact of the increased use of individual contracts between employer and employee to set terms and conditions of work. The increase in union membership in the education sector is reflective of both the increase in employment in this sector and the persistence of centralized national bargaining for primary and secondary teachers.

Table 8.6 Public sector union membership, 1990 and 1997

Unions/Sectors	Approximate membership 31/3/90	Approximate membership 31/12/97
PSA	81,250	51,500
Other public service	44,500	12,000
Public health unions	42,250	28,500
Education unions	42,250	55,750

Source: Data calculated from Department of Labor (1990) and unpublished data. The 1990 figure for "other public service" includes the approximately 5,000 members of the Police Association which had not registered under the Labor Relations Act (McGill, 1992). Note the data do not include several predominantly private sector unions with significant (though unquantified) representation in public sector, including the Engineers Union which represents the bulk of staff employed in SOE New Zealand Post. PSA figure for 1988 includes the two local government unions that merged with the PSA in 1993. Figure for membership in health unions in 1990 includes the figures for the Private Sector Nurses Union which merged with the public sector Nurses Association in 1993.

Public sector labor relations

Brief outline of the present situation and main features

The regulation of industrial relations typically comes from three sources: legislation establishing minimum conditions of employment, common law requirements, and voluntary regulation agreed to by way of collective agreements.

The Employment Contracts Act 1991 provides the legal framework for industrial relations in both public and private sectors. The Act marked a radical shift in direction with the abandonment of the historical preference for collective bargaining in favor of a model of labor contracting which, while ostensibly neutral as to the structure of bargaining arrangements, implicitly favored individual negotiations to establish conditions of work (Anderson, 1991; Dannin, 1997).

The ECA does not prescribe either the structure of an employment contract – which may be individual (between a single employer and a single employee) or collective (between two or more employees and one or more employers) – or the content of what is agreed (beyond several general requirements). Parties have almost total freedom to agree on both the structure and content of an employment contract. Protections for workers exist in the form of a safety-net of minimum conditions guaranteed under various statutes and covering such matters as minimum hourly rates, entitlement to paid leave and public holidays, and so on.

In marked contrast to the historical approach of industrial relations legislation, the Act is almost totally reticent on matters of process. There is no requirement that an individual or collective employment contract be an outcome of negotiation, nor any requirement for representation if negotiations in fact take place (under the principle of freedom of association the use of a representative is left to the individual employee, or for that matter employer, to determine).

Collective bargaining structure (with special reference to pay setting institutions)

The new system contrasts sharply with the traditional basis for fixing pay and conditions in the public sector. Prior to 1988, public service wide occupational bargaining prevailed. Pay rates were set according to the principle of fair relativity with the private sector. Two mechanisms were in place to ensure this relativity was maintained. General adjustments applied a uniform increase to all public sector wages determined on the basis of surveys of prevailing increases in rates of pay in the private sector. Separate determinations were employed to address any disparities in rates for specific occupational classifications. The State Services Conditions of Employment Act 1977 specified the conditions of work which could be set by determination of the appropriate tribunal. The system was thus highly centralized, although the size of the "bargaining unit" varied markedly across the 300 established occupational classifications.[2]

The State Sector Act 1988 shifted the bargaining focus in the public service to departmental level. The transition was achieved through the consolidation of the multitude of occupational determinations which formed the basis of new departmental agreements. In the health and education services the new awards remained occupationally based. A major impact of the Employment Contracts Act 1991 has been to reduce the coverage of collective bargaining in New Zealand (Harbridge and Crawford, 1998a). There is no prescription on the level at which bargaining takes place, nor on the structure of the bargaining units in the Act and, as a consequence, a great deal of fragmentation of bargaining units has resulted in both public and private sectors. In the public sector this fragmentation has arisen from several sources:

- the use of individual contracts to set pay and conditions (largely where employees are not union members)
- the emergence of new unions
- internal reorganization and restructuring in the public sector.

Detailed data on coverage of individual contracts are only available for the public service. Data collected by the State Services Commission show that just over 30 percent of public servants are currently employed on individual employment contracts. This figure had risen steadily from 17 percent in 1994. Another group, consistently between 10 and 20 percent, were employed under the terms of an expired collective contract (State Services Commission, 1998a). Prior to the ECA, it was a legal requirement that the terms and conditions of a collectively bargained award or agreement automatically extend to new employees. The ECA removed this requirement, leaving the issue of extension to the parties themselves to determine. Available data show that the automatic extension of contracts to new employees is provided for in around 80 per cent of public sector contracts (Harbridge and Crawford, 1998b). Typically these clauses extend the terms of the contract to new employees who become union members.

As noted above, a number of new unions emerged to challenge the traditional coverage of the Public Service Association within different government departments, with the most notable such cases occurring in the Inland Revenue Department and in the prisons division of the Department of Corrections. These emerging unions caused the further fragmentation of bargaining units along representational lines.

Restructuring and reorganization saw both a continued reduction in staff numbers across the public service and an increase in the number of departmental units. Again, the effect was a reduction in the size of bargaining units.

Arrangements in other branches of the public sector vary. The coverage of collective bargaining in the SOEs has undoubtedly reduced. Industrial relations strategies pursued by SOE management sought to limit the traditionally important influence of public sector unions on personnel and operational matters (Walsh, 1988). The ECA provided even greater scope to pursue and implement such strategies, particularly through promoting individual negotiations with employees (Walsh and Wetzel, 1993).

While collective bargaining in the public health sector has continued to be along occupational lines, the level at which this bargaining has taken place has shifted. Prior to the ECA, workers employed by public hospitals were predominantly covered by a national award. Negotiations under the ECA were undertaken at the level of individual AHBs. Further fragmentation occurred when the 14 AHBs were restructured into 23 Crown Health Enterprises after 1993. The fragmentation of health sector bargaining has had some unforeseen consequences. Medical specialists have had considerable success in achieving large pay increases with the loss of national bargaining coverage weakening the ability of individual employers to resist patterned bargaining claims (Powell, 1995b).

Collective bargaining remains prevalent in the education sector. Teaching staff in state primary and secondary schools are each covered by a national CEC, negotiated between the respective unions and the Ministry of Education as employer party for the over 2,600 state schools. The structure of bargaining arrangements in the post-compulsory education sector differs across institutions. Prior to the ECA, employees of universities, polytechnics and colleges of education were covered by national awards which applied to broad occupational classes in each group of institutions. These have subsequently been replaced by "enterprise" agreements, which have largely retained the traditional occupational groupings as the bargaining unit. Ancillary functions not covered under the general staff CECs typically have their own collective agreement. Academic staff of universities, whose pay and conditions were formerly set by the Higher Salaries Commission, are covered by separate, university specific, CECs.

The picture, then, is one of increased fragmentation of bargaining units in the public sector. This has led inevitably to some fragmentation of outcomes. One obvious effect has been on the term of collective agreements. With the end of coordinated bargaining rounds, parties have been left to determine both the timetable for negotiations and the length of resulting agreements.

Available data show a perceptible trend towards longer contracts, which may partly be the result of increased transaction costs of bargaining. Around 40 percent of collectivized public sector employees are on contracts with a term of two years or more (Harbridge and Crawford, 1998b). The lag period between the expiry and renegotiations of an agreement has varied.

At one extreme, the Professional Fire-fighters' Union has been locked in negotiations to renew the expired collective contract covering the bulk of its members since 1992. While the process of these negotiations has given rise to substantial industrial action and litigation, no new agreement has yet been reached.

There has arguably been less scope for fragmentation in wage outcomes. On the one hand, funding of the public sector has remained under tight, centralized control through the principle of fiscal neutrality. With initial delegations of bargaining authorities to chief executives, the SSC made clear that additional funds would not be made available by central government for wage settlements and that any wage increases would need to be funded out of existing budgets (that is, be fiscally neutral). More pragmatically, the need to recruit and retain staff would tend to limit the scope for pay leadership by any section of the public sector, whilst ensuring some degree of wage conformity.

Relativity with the private sector is another matter. The formal requirement of fair relativity with the private sector ended with the abolition of state pay fixing machinery. Available information suggests that public service departments were experiencing some difficulties in attracting middle- and senior-level applicants to vacancies due, in part, to an inability to meet the salary rates demanded (State Services Commission, 1997a,b).

Recruitment difficulties have not been limited to the public services or to occupations where public and private sectors are in competition for skills. Teacher unions have blamed the shortages of teaching staff in the compulsory education sector on poor salary rates. Official data show that from December 1992 (when the index was begun) until June 1995 changes in labor costs in the non-trading central government sectors lagged behind those in the private sector. Some measure of comparability was achieved after mid 1995 when the pressure for general wage increases grew and central controls over wages were loosened but prior to this time the bulk of the increases in public service wage costs came through non-negotiated increases such as promotions, salary increments, bonus payments, and so on (Boston et al., 1996).

In the most recent period (from December, 1997) the data show wages in the public sector have increased at a higher rate than in the private sector, partly attributable to the large increases agreed in the primary teachers' contract (Table 8.7).

The service wide non-wage conditions of work which were carried over into state sector awards and agreements negotiated in 1988 have largely persisted, despite fragmented bargaining. In the private sector changes to working time arrangements have been one of the major adjustments the Employment Contracts Act has enabled. Many industries, particularly those in the service sector, have seen the wholesale removal of penal rates (premium rates for work undertaken outside of the normal hours of work) and the reduction or removal in the premiums paid for hours worked in excess of ordinary weekly hours (Harbridge and Crawford, 1998b). In contrast, working time arrangements in the public sector have remained relatively little changed under the Employment Contracts Act.

Table 8.7 Labor cost index by sector, 1992–1998 (base: December, 1992 = 1000)

	Central government sector			Private sector		
	Ordinary	Overtime	Non-wage	Ordinary	Overtime	Non-wage
Dec 92	1,000	1,000	1,000	1,000	1,000	1,000
Jun 93	1,002	1,002	985	1,007	997	979
Dec 93	1,004	997	982	1,012	997	988
Jun 94	1,007	998	1,004	1,019	999	1,031
Dec 94	1,013	992	1,003	1,026	1,004	1,038
Jun 95	1,019	994	1,058	1,033	1,010	1,083
Dec 95	1,032	1,004	1,070	1,045	1,014	1,095
Jun 96	1,038	1,019	1,089	1,055	1,020	1,134
Dec 96	1,058	1,039	1,111	1,064	1,031	1,146
Jun 97	1,074	1,046	1,132	1,077	1,041	1,162
Dec 97	1,085	1,052	1,131	1,082	1,047	1,170
Jun 98	1,104	1,055	1,119	1,096	1,048	1,136

Source: Statistics New Zealand.

Industrial disputes

The Employment Contract Act recognizes the worker's right to strike and the countervailing right of the employer to lock out. Part 5 of the Act governs the conduct of strikes or lock-outs. Strikes in the public sector were excluded from official data prior to 1988.[3] The reforms of industrial relations did not immediately lead to widespread outbreaks of industrial conflict amongst state employees, despite measures intended to restrain wages. In 1990, the last full year of bargaining under the Labor Relations Act, work stoppages in the public sector accounted for 31 percent of all stoppages and 42 percent of all workers involved. In 1995 the public sector's share of strikes had risen to 43 percent of all stoppages and 79 percent of workers involved. This meant that in 1995, while the public sector itself employed less than 20 percent of the total paid workforce, nearly four out of every five strikers were public sector employees (Table 8.8).

The data are not desegregated to the degree that would enable more detailed analysis of the branches of the public sector where strikes have been most frequent. The impression, however, is that strike action has been relatively widespread across the state sector (Harbridge, 1997).

The data show the increase in public sector militancy comes at a time when strikes in the private sector have fallen away dramatically. Several possible factors may contribute to this. As noted above, the impact of the ECA on union coverage and collective bargaining has been more dramatic in the private sector than in the public sector. Thus, on average, public sector employees and their unions have greater organizational capacity to undertake industrial action. Further, the impact of the government's tight fiscal policies, and the unfavorable impact of these on

Table 8.8 Work stoppages, involvements and days lost by sectors, 1990–1996

Year ended 31 December	Public sector stoppages	Workers involved (000)	Total days lost (000)	Private sector stoppages	Workers involved (000)	Total days lost (000)
1990	43	21.2	64.2	97	28.8	266.7
1991	31	31.5	54.5	43	20.5	44.5
1992	25	21.9	21.3	30	4.9	92.4
1993	29	18.8	19.2	29	2.5	4.5
1994	23	6.5	10.2	46	9.5	28.1
1995	30	25.2	27.4	39	6.8	26.0
1996	36	7.0	24.3	36	35.2	45.1

Source: Statistics New Zealand. Public sector includes local government.

collective bargaining settlements has provided a trigger for industrial action. In notable cases, (especially in election years) political sensitivity to industrial action may have convinced public sector unions and employees that a more militant position in contract negotiations would be beneficial in expediting favorable settlements.

The pattern of stoppages in the public sector has remained one of relatively short protest strikes, in contrast to the longer stoppages in the private sector. This is perhaps reflective of the persistence of political overtones in public sector industrial relations.

Mediation, conciliation and arbitration

The provision of compulsory conciliation and arbitration was a distinguishing feature of New Zealand's private sector industrial relations system for the best part of a century. In the public sector, pay-fixing was underpinned by arbitration of a service tribunal with the power to issue binding orders. The State Sector Act abolished these tribunals but allowed state sector unions and employers to access the mediation services of the Arbitration Commission, and to proceed to arbitration where both parties agreed.[4] The Act also allowed the opportunity for inclusion in state sector awards and agreements of the provision for compulsory and binding arbitration of unresolved bargaining disputes where the union agreed to forego its right to strike (with the exception of the ASMS representing senior doctors in public hospitals, none did so).

A notable feature of ECA was its abolition of all procedures for resolving disputes of interest, leaving the parties reliant on their own bargaining power to secure a favorable settlement. It has also meant there are no specific means for resolving bargaining impasses (Dannin and Gilson, 1996), a factor which has acted to draw out contract renegotiations in the public sector. Traditional reliance on ministerial intervention is, for the most part, no longer an option as the thrust of the reforms (especially those since 1991) has been to remove ministers from the bargaining arena.

Conclusions

During the 1980s and 1990s much of the legislation and many of the institutions which established and upheld the unique nature of public sector employment in New Zealand have been abolished. Public sector pay-fixing and personnel matters are now largely determined under the same framework of rules as governs their conduct in the private sector.

The tightly bound centralized and uniform system which prevailed for many decades has unraveled over the last 15 years. It has given way to a decentralized system with much greater diversity in structures, operating procedures and outcomes than in the past. Public sector employees are now employed by the chief executive of their organization rather than by a central employing authority. There are no longer any centrally prescribed rules governing the employment relationship. Occupational classifications, job descriptions, performance appraisals, salary scales and other human resource management policies and practices, once centrally laid down, now vary from one organization to the other. Perhaps the most important change has been the shift from complete uniformity to relative or emerging within the bargaining system. A key factor in this has been the move from centralized bargaining to bargaining at the level of the individual department, agency or trading enterprise. Accompanying this has been a shift from a system based almost completely on collective bargaining to one that combines individual and collective employment contracts, including in many cases more than one collective contract in the one organization, and mixes standard permanent employment with fixed-term contracts and other non-standard arrangements, including the use of external contractors and consultants. Participation in the bargaining process has widened to include, on the employer side, the chief executives of public sector organizations rather than just the central employing authorities for each sector, and, on the employee side, the dominance of the traditional unions has been challenged by the emergence of new rival unions. The historical monopoly over bargaining enjoyed by centralized employing authorities and their union counterparts has been broken. None the less, a cautionary note is still warranted. The consequences of this diversity for the employment conditions of public sector employees should not be overstated. Most still enjoy broadly similar conditions of employment, as is to be expected given similar labor-market factors and the continued importance of union-based collective bargaining.

A new social democratic government, the Labor–Alliance coalition, was elected in November 1999 and soon announced its intention to make significant changes to industrial relations law. Although their new legislation had not been introduced at the time of writing this chapter, it was clear that the legislation will encourage the growth of collective bargaining over individual employment contracts and will facilitate the negotiation of multi-employer or sector-wide agreements. It is certain that public sector unions will embrace the first objective but it is less obvious that they will support the second. Unions did not oppose the introduction of bargaining at the level of the individual organization and have organized themselves around it more than a decade now, while for a generation of union members, the centralized system of the past is but a very distant memory. The most likely outcome is that although the decline in collective bargaining will be halted, there will be no return to a highly centralized system. The unraveling of central control in New Zealand's public sector industrial relations will continue.

Notes

1. The NZNO also represents X-ray workers employed in some public hospitals after the Association of X-ray Workers' decision to cease to operate as a bargaining agent during 1996 (Crawford et al., 1998).
2. In 1988 nearly 50 per cent of all public service employees were included in the Executive/Clerical occupational group (26,463 of 59,082 permanent employees), while other groups covered barely a handful of public servants (State Services Commission, 1989).
3. The exceptions being stoppages involving unions registered under the private sector award framework, principally railways and the post office.
4. A 1984 amendment to the Industrial Relations Act 1973 had made recourse to arbitration voluntary in the private sector.

References

Anderson, G. (1991) "The Employment Contracts Act 1991: An Employer's Charter?," *New Zealand Journal of Industrial Relations*, XVI(2).

Anderson, G., Brosnan, P., and Walsh, P. (1996) "The New Public Sector Management and Human Resources Management Policies: Numerical Flexibility in the New Zealand Public Sector," *International Journal of Employment Studies* IV(1).

Bassett, M. (1998) *The State in New Zealand 1840–1984: Socialism Without Doctrines?*, Auckland: Auckland University Press.

Boston, J. (1991a) "Reorganising the Machinery of Government: Objectives and Outcomes," in Boston, J., Martin, J., Pallot, J., and Walsh, P. (eds.), *Reshaping the State: New Zealand's Bureaucratic Revolution*, Auckland: Oxford University Press.

Boston, J. (1991b) "The Theoretical Underpinnings of Public Sector Restructuring in New Zealand," in Boston, J., Martin, J., Pallot, J., and Walsh, P. (eds.), *Reshaping the State: New Zealand's Bureaucratic Revolution*, Auckland: Oxford University Press.

Boston, J., Martin, J., Pallot, J., and Walsh, P. (1996) *Public Management: The New Zealand Model*, Auckland: Oxford University Press.

Britton, S., Le Heron, R., and Pawson, E. (eds.) (1992) *Changing Places in New Zealand: A Geography of Restructuring*, Christchurch: New Zealand Geographical Society.

Brosnan, P. and Walsh, P. (1997) "Why are New Zealand Unions Stronger at the Workplace under the Employment Contracts Act than Australian Unions under the Accord?," in Bramble, T., Harley, B., Hall, H. and Whitehouse, G. (eds.), *Current Research in Industrial Relations*, Brisbane, Queensland: Proceedings of the 11th AIRAANZ Conference.

Crawford, A., Harbridge, R., and Hince, K. (1998), *Unions and Union Membership in New Zealand: Annual Review for 1997*, Wellington: Victoria University, Industrial Relations Center, (1).

Dannin, E. (1997) *Working Free: The Origins and Impact of New Zealand's Employment Contracts Act*, Auckland: Auckland University Press.

Dannin, E. and Gilson, C. (1996) "Getting to Impasse: Negotiations Under the National Labor Relations Act and the Employment Contracts Act," *American University Journal of International Law and Policy*, **XI**(6).

Department of Statistics (1988) *New Zealand Official Yearbook 1987-1988* (Wellington: Department of Statistics.)

Department of Labor (1990) *Handbook of Union Information*, Wellington: Registrar of Unions Office, Industrial Relations Service.

Dickson, I. (1989) "Taxation," in Walker, S. (ed.), *Rogernomics: Reshaping New Zealand's Economy* Auckland: Center for Independent Studies.

Douglas, K. (1993) "Organizing Workers: The Effects of the Act on the Council of Trade Unions and its Membership," in Harbridge, R. (ed.), *Employment Contracts: New Zealand Experiences*, Wellington: Victoria University Press.

Duncan, I. and Bollard, A. (1992) *Corporatisation and Privatization: Lessons From New Zealand* Auckland: Oxford University Press.

Harbridge, R. (1997) *Recent Industrial Disputes and their Impact on Future Industrial Relations Management*, discussion paper at the 11th Industrial Relations Conference, Auckland: Institute for International Research.

Harbridge, R. and Crawford, A. (1998a) "The Impact of the Employment Contracts Act on Industrial Relations," *California Western International Law Journal*, **XXVIII**(1).

Harbridge, R. and Crawford, A. (1998b) "The Employment Contracts Act and Collective Bargaining Patterns: A Review of the 1997/98 Year," in Harbridge, R., Crawford, A., and Kiely, P. (eds.), *Employment Contracts: Bargaining Trends and Employment Law Update 1997/98*, Wellington: Victoria University, Graduate School of Business and Government Management.

Harbridge, R. and Hince, K. (1994) *A Sourcebook of New Zealand Trade Unions and Employee Organizations*, Wellington: Victoria University, Industrial Relations Center.

Harbridge, R. and Honeybone, A. (1996) "External Legitimacy of Unions: Trends in New Zealand," *Journal of Labor Research*, **XVII**(3).

Henderson, A. (1990) *The Quest for Efficiency: The Origins of the State Services Commission*, Wellington: State Services Commission.

Keating, E. (1974) "Trade Unionism in State Organizations," in Howells, J., Woods, N., and Young, F. (eds.), *Labor and Industrial Relations in New Zealand* Melbourne: Pitman Pacific Books.

Kiely, P. (1997) "Employment Law Update," in Harbridge, R., Crawford, A., and Kiely, P. (eds.) *Employment Contracts: Bargaining Trends and Employment Law Update 1996/97* Wellington: Victoria University, Graduate School of Business and Government Management.

Lister, P., Rivers, M. J., and Wilkinson, A. (1991) "The Management of Change – The Social and Personnel Perspective," in Boston, J., Martin, J., Pallot, J., and Walsh, P. (eds.), *Reshaping the State: New Zealand's Bureaucratic Revolution*, Auckland: Oxford University Press.

Mcgiee, D. (1992) *No Right to Strike: The History of the New Zealand Police Service Organizations*, Wellington: New Zealand Police Service Organizations.

Ministry of Education (1992) *Devolution in the New Zealand Education System* Wellington: Ministry of Education.

Pallot, J. (1991a) "Financial Management Reform," in Boston, J., Martin, J., Pallot, J. and Walsh, P. (eds.), *Reshaping the State: New Zealand's Bureaucratic Revolution*, Auckland: Oxford University Press.

Pallot, J. (1991b) "Accounting, Auditing and Accountability," in Boston, J., Martin, J., Pallot, J. and Walsh, P. (eds.), *Reshaping the State: New Zealand's Bureaucratic Revolution*, Auckland: Oxford University Press.

Palmer, G. (1988) "Political Perspectives", in Martin, J. and Harper, J. (eds.) *Devolution and accountability. Studies in Public Administration* (34).

Powell, I. (1995a) "The Experience of Collective Bargaining for Salaried Doctors Under the Employment Contracts Act," *New Zealand Journal of Industrial Relations*, XX(2).

Powell, I. (1995b) "Alumnus View 1," in Hince, K. (ed.), *Industrial Relations in New Zealand: Where Now?*, Wellington: Victoria University, Industrial Relations Center.

Schick, A. (1996) *The Spirit of Reform: Managing the New Zealand State Sector in a Time Change* Wellington: State Services Commission.

Scott, G., Bushnell, P., and Sallee, N. (1990) "Reform of the Core Public Sector: The New Zealand Experience," *Governance*, III(2).

Smith, T. (1974) *The New Zealand Bureaucrat*, Wellington: Chesire Publishing.

Smith, V. (1997) *Reining in the Dinosaur: The Story Behind the Remarkable Turnaround of New Zealand Post*, Wellington: New Zealand Post.

State Services Commission (1989) *Report of The State Services Commission for The Year Ended 31 March 1989*, Wellington: State Services Commission.

State Services Commission (1997a) *Six-Monthly Staffing Survey (SMOSS): Public Service Departments and Selected Crown Entities as at 30 June 1997*, Wellington: State Services Commission.

State Services Commission (1997b) *Strategic Human Resource Capacity Issues in the Public Service: Full Project Report with Recommendations*, Wellington: State Services Commission, Strategic Human Resource Development Branch.

State Services Commission (1998a) *Six-Monthly Staffing Survey (SMOSS): Public Service Departments and Selected Crown Entities as at 30 June 1998*, Wellington: State Services Commission.

State Services Commission (1998b) *Annual Report of the State Services Commission for the Year Ended 30 June 1998*, Wellington: State Services Commission.

Statistics New Zealand (1997a) *New Zealand Official Yearbook 1996*, Wellington: Statistics New Zealand.

Statistics New Zealand (1997b) *Labor Market 1996*, Wellington: Statistics New Zealand.

Walsh, P. (1988) "The Struggle for Power and Control in the New Corporations: The First Year of Industrial in the State-Owned Enterprises," *New Zealand Journal of Industrial Relations*, XIII(2).

Walsh, P. (1993) "Managerialism and Collective Bargaining in the New Zealand Public Sector," in Gardner, M. (ed.), *Human Resource Management and Industrial Relations in the Public Sector*, Melbourne: Macmillan – now Palgrave.

Walsh, P. (1994) "Has the Evil Been Remedied? The Development of Public Sector Unionism in New Zealand," in Walsh, P. (ed.), *Pioneering New Zealand Labor History: Essays in Honour of Bert Roth*, Palmerston North: Dunmore Press.

Walsh, P. and Wetzel, K. (1993) "Preparing for Privatization: Corporate Strategy and Industrial Relations in New Zealand's State-Owned Enterprises," *British Journal of Industrial Relations*, **XXXI**(1).

9
Employment Relations in the Australian Public Sector

Russell D. Lansbury and Duncan K. Macdonald

Introduction

The public sector has long been a significant part of the Australian political economy. The Commonwealth of Australia was formed in 1901 from six separate British colonies and now comprises one federal and eight state or territory-based governments. Although the Australian constitution established a division of powers between the commonwealth or federal and state governments, each has a series of administrative departments covering areas such as education, health and transport, which provide public services. There are numerous statutory authorities and government business enterprises, which provide services such as electricity supply, railways, broadcasting and telecommunications. There are also important judicial bodies, including courts and tribunals at both state and federal levels. Finally, there is a layer of government at local or municipal level responsible for a range of services. Together, these comprise the public sector which has been defined as "the institutional framework of government administration, public commercial activities and state-run utilities" (Davis et al., 1993). Hence, the Australian public sector includes employees in a wide range of work and employment settings.

By the 1990s, general government outlays in Australia accounted for 33 percent of gross domestic product (GDP), although this compares with an OECD average of around 40 percent. The level of public sector employment, around 28 percent of employed persons, is reasonably consistent with OECD averages, although Australia has a comparatively high level of employment in government business enterprises (GBEs) compared with many other industrialized market economies (EPAC 1990). The number employed by government, excluding employees in

GBEs, is about 17 percent of the workforce. Approximately 67 percent of these are in state employment and 10 percent in local government. Female employees comprise 48 percent of the public sector workforce (ABS, Cat 62030).

During the last decade there was a greater decline in the size of the Australian public service than in most other OECD countries. This began with the Labor government (from 1983 to 1996) and has continued under the Liberal National Party Coalition government. A wide range of factors, operating over the past two decades, has been responsible for the decline in public sector employment (see Gardner and Palmer, 1997). Governments from both sides of the political spectrum have sought to deploy a limited pool of financial resources more effectively in order to meet the simultaneous demands for less government expenditure and yet improved quantity and quality of services to the public. In particular, governments have sought to limit pay rises in the public sector and were successful in actually reducing the level of real wages by 9 percent between 1985 and 1990 (EPAC, 1990). However, governments at all levels have also sought to reduce costs in other ways, including: increased targeting of social welfare payments, greater use of cost recovery from government services, and a variety of efficiency measures (which are explored in greater detail later in this chapter).

Organizational structure, employment and wages

Organizational structure

Until the 1980s, the federal public service was divided into four divisions. The fourth, the lowest paid, included clerical assistants and many others in lower level white- and blue-collar occupations while the first division consisted of departmental heads or chief executive officers in three grades (see Corbett, 1996). The rationale behind this bureaucratic structure was that there needed to be a system whereby those with higher levels of skill and responsibility would receive higher pay. Promotion between the ranks was based on merit and people were appointed by competitive application for more senior positions. This meant that there had to be precise, formal job descriptions so that the most able of the competing applicants could be fairly selected. Hence, considerable time and effort was spent by public service departments on the classification of jobs and monitoring of systems in use. Unions also became involved in disputes over how particular jobs ought to be classified and appeal rights were written into public service acts and industrial awards.

In the late 1980s, the Australian public service underwent a process of office work restructuring in line with award restructuring, which was occurring in the wider industrial relations system. As a result, the number classifications and grades were reduced: some 93 separate classification structures were reduced to eight levels in one structure (Selby Smith, 1993). The change affected approximately 115,000 staff across not only federal government departments but also some 38 other federal bodies required by statute to confirm to public service board classification rulings. Sweeping changes to the organizational structure, such as these, were possible because the federal public service was still highly centralized.

One of the most significant examples of restructuring for greater flexibility in management was the establishment of the senior executive service (SES) at the federal level in 1984. This reform was intended to create an elite corps of senior, experienced managers who were expected to be both flexible and mobile between departments. The underlying notion of the SES was that ministers needed to have a management team of broadly experienced executives capable of enthusiastically implementing government policy. However, various inquiries reached the conclusion that this, in fact, had not occurred.

Quantitative composition of employees in the public sector

The decline of employment numbers in each of the three levels of government (federal, state and local) in Australia for the years 1990 to 1997 is shown in Table 9.1. It is evident that the reduction of employee numbers has been much greater at the federal level than at the other two levels of government, with a very substantial decrease in 1995–96. During much of this period, the Labor government was in office but the extent of reductions since the Coalition took office indicate that it is even more determined to reduce government employment than its predecessor.

As shown in Table 9.2, the number of total employees in the Australian public service (more narrowly defined) has declined from 165,000 in 1988 to 134,000 in 1997. However, the composition of public sector employment has also changed as a greater proportion of the workforce are now in temporary and part-time employment than was previously the case. In 1989 approximately 6,000 employees were classified as part time while 153,000 were full time. By 1997, the number of part-time employees exceeded 7,000 while full-time employees were 126,500. Similarly, the number of employees classified as temporary has increased from 145,000 in 1988 to 15,000 in 1997 while the number

Table 9.1 Changes in numbers of government employees, 1990–1997

Year (August)	Federal		State		Local	
	Number (000s)	Percent change	Number (000s)	Percent change	Number (000s)	Percent change
1990	403.3		1170.1		159.8	
1991	408.8	+1.36	1146.0	−2.06	161.0	+0.75
1992	392.7	−3.94	1121.9	−2.10	159.7	−0.81
1993	374.4	−4.66	1106.0	−1.42	160.8	+0.69
1994	355.2	−5.13	1057.1	−4.42	158.2	−1.62
1995	347.6	−2.14	1061.6	−0.43	155.3	−1.83
1996	305.4	−12.14	1053.6	−0.75	146.5	−5.67
1997	285.6	−6.48	1047.3	−0.63	143.3	−2.18

Note: This is the number of employees regardless of status and number of hours worked. Unfortunately the ABS does not keep data on the breakdown of all employees in each sector according to whether they are full time, part time or casual. This means that changes in status may magnify or reduce the changes indicated here.

Source: Australian Bureau of Statistics, *Catalogue* 6248.0.

Table 9.2 Employment in the Australian public service (in thousands), 1988–1997

	1988	1990	1992	1994	1996	1997
Male	93	86	82	77	75	69
Female	72	73	67	67	69	65
Permanent	128	134	128	142	142	119
Temporary	14	25	21	18	17	15
Full time	N/A	152	142	136	138	127
Part time	N/A	7	7	7	6	7
Total	165	159	149	144	143	134

Note: N/A is not available.

Source: Australian Public Service, *Statistical Bulletins* (1988–97).

of permanent employees has declined from 128,000 in 1988 to 118,500 in 1997.

Taking the Federal Department of Health as an example, it can be seen in Table 9.3 that although the total number of employees increased between 1990 and 1997, the composition of the workforce has changed considerably. The most significant increase was in the category of temporary employees (from 601 in 1990 to 1,037 in 1997). The number of female employees also increased (from 3,537 to 3,656) while

Table 9.3 Employment in the Federal Department of Health, 1990–1997

	1990	1992	1994	1996	1997
Male	2,279	2,337	2,480	2,590	2,035
Female	3,537	3,712	4,285	4,942	3,656
Permanent	5,215	5,424	5,973	6,703	5,691
Temporary	601	625	792	829	1037
Part time	5,517	5,708	6,196	7,131	5,376
Full time	301	341	569	401	315
Total	5,817	6,049	6,765	7,532	6,728

Source: Australian Public Service, *Statistical Bulletins* (1990–97).

Table 9.4 Employment in the State Department of Education in New South Wales, 1988–1996

	1988	1990	1992	1994	1996
Male	24,220	22,472	21,567	21,437	21,268
Female	42,093	42,899	42,825	43,963	48,923
Part time	6,338	7,685	6,433	5,450	8,164
Full time	59,975	57,686	57,959	59,950	62,027
Total	66,313	65,371	64,392	65,400	70,191

Source: Australian Bureau of Statistics, *Schools Australia*, Catalogue No. 4221.00.

the number (and proportion) of male employees declined, from 2,279 to 2,035. This is consistent with a broader trend in the public sector which has seen a high proportion of female employees in the part-time and temporary area of the labor market.

Almost half the total federal public service cuts for Australia as a whole have occurred in New South Wales (NSW), the most populous state. The changing pattern of employment in the Department of Education in NSW can be seen in Table 9.4. Although the number of teachers and other staff employed by the Department increased from 66,313 to 70,191 between 1988 and 1996, the proportion of part-time employees grew markedly. In 1988 there were 59,975 full-time employees compared with 6,338 part-timers. By 1996, the number of part-timers had increased to 8,164 while full-time employees had grown to 62,027. The gender balance also shifted more towards women during this period, with an increase of almost 7,000 female employees being appointed while the number of males declined by 3,000. Not surprisingly, women appear to be taking up most of the increased number of part-time positions.

Qualitative characteristics of the public sector labor market

Public servants are appointed under various public service Acts, often to a specific position. These are "career" positions which enjoy access to promotion, tenure or substantial employment security and various merit protections such as appeal rights on promotion and disciplinary matters. Employees of statutory corporations or government business enterprises (for example, Australia Post) have employment conditions specified by the Act establishing the corporation. Typically these conditions are modeled on public service Acts. However, as these organizations become more like private corporations, their employment conditions are also changing. According to McCarry (1994), the concept of security of tenure, which once characterized many areas of public sector employment, has been steadily eroded and the differences between job security in the private and public sectors have become less discernible.

There has been both change and continuity in employment practices within the public sector in recent years. Points of entry to the public service have expanded and recruitment is no longer dominated by entry from school on the basis of competitive examination, although entry to the "base grade" of the public service is still mainly through selection following open examination. Merit remains the central selection tool for entry and promotion. Although job security is less guaranteed than in the past, the long-held notion of the "career service," as described by Caiden (1965), still exists in some respects and received a boost from award restructuring in the 1980s. However, the continuing relevance of career service was challenged in the 1990s, particularly in relation to government business enterprises and for senior staff such as the heads of public service agencies. It has become increasingly common for chief executive officers of agencies to be removed when there is a change of government in line with the practice in the US, although without the same connotations of political patronage.

Wages and salaries

In the past, there were strong pressures towards uniformity in wages and salaries across the public sector. Furthermore, although the rather centralized industrial relations system which existed in Australia for much of this century tended to reinforce comparability between private and public sector wage levels for similar work, public sector employees traditionally "traded off" somewhat lower wage levels in exchange for greater job security. The differences between the private and public sector in terms of wages, however, has diminished in recent years. The current federal government's policies to align public sector employment practices closer to the private sector will strengthen the similarities between the two sectors. It was during the tenure of the previous Labor government, especially since the early 1990s, that many of the current trends were initiated. The Labor government pressed ahead with devolution of pay setting in the public service to the enterprise or agency level to make industrial relations in public service departments more "flexible," even in the face of resistance by the public sector unions. By 1995, decentralized arrangements had spread much further in the public sector than the private sector with 77 percent of workplaces in the federal public service covered by agency/enterprise agreements compared with 61 percent of private sector workplaces (DIR, 1996). With the passage of the Workplace Relations Act 1996, enterprise bargaining was enshrined as the principal means of wage fixation in the public sector. By 1998, approximately 80 percent of employees within the Australian public service were covered by agency agreements.

Despite the determination of both Labor and Coalition governments to render wages and salaries systems in the public sector identical to those of the private sector, there is still a tendency towards greater equity in wages outcomes within the public sector. Public sector agreements have tended to grant lower wage increases than those in the private sector and to be set for longer periods. Furthermore, the requirement for attention to overall equity was written into the 1992 framework agreement for the Australian public service. This was via a "foldback" mechanism which provided for all agencies to contribute to a pool which would provide compensation for those agencies that could not fund a particular base level of increase up to that level.

It can also be argued that agency bargaining in the public sector is not genuine enterprise bargaining in that the usual unit for negotiation is not a single workplace but rather a whole department or agency. The model adopted thus far by the Australian public service retains service-wide bargaining over a core of conditions and terms of employment, and has been described as a "medial devolution model." In addition to the service-wide agreement, there can be agency agreements on supplementary terms and conditions. The proposed Public Service Bill would still retain general concepts of engagement, promotion, and transfer within the Australian public service employment framework, even though wages and conditions would be set at the level of the individual agency. However, the current "watchdog" role of the Department of Workplace Relations and Small Business ensures high degrees of procedural, if not substantive, uniformity across all federal government employment.

The role of employers in the public sector

State policies and practices in relation to public sector regulation

For many, the changes to the organization and administration of the public sector both in Australia and overseas, is encapsulated in terms such as "New Public Management" (NPM), but, as Considine and Painter (1997) point out, while NPM may be an accurate depiction of developments during the 1980s, such terms cannot be so readily applied to the changes that have been implemented in more recent years. The new era, rather than emphasizing the necessity for managerial authority, discretion and accountability, lauds the superiority of the market; that is, market forces, rather than managerial judgment and discretion, should be the motivators for the allocation of resources and the utilization of those resources. In place of the 1980's catch-cry of "let the managers manage" (see, for example, Yeatman, 1997:13), the public sector management credo of the 1990s is more one of "let the market direct." Thus Considine and Painter (1997) argue that there have been two waves of reform through the Australian public sector since 1980, "managerialism" and "marketization" (p.10).

Post World War II reform of the Australian public sector began with the introduction of the Public Service Reform Act 1984 by the Hawke Labor government. This was seen as the first major step towards the "creation of a technocratic, managerial state" as a "key condition for enhancing and sustaining an internationalized economy" (Fairbrother et al., 1997). The Labor government was convinced of the necessity for increased efficiency in the public sector based on the adoption of private sector practices as well as much improved policy advice and program development.

The essence of managerialism is captured by Davis (1997:212) when he sets out its supposed advantages as "emphasizing results over conformity, management over administration, flexibility over tenure and, perhaps most significantly in retrospect, performance measures and service agreements over traditional command and control mechanisms." The new information technology was critical to the new approach because of its need to monitor activity. It introduced the concepts of program budgeting, performance indicators and corporate planning, and the widespread adoption of "risk management" was a critical development. In place of absolute compliance in respect of regulation and maximum reliability and quality in service provision, there was now an attempt to apply a type of cost-benefit approach whereby the costs involved are weighed against the benefits obtained.

With respect to the regulation of the employment relationship one of the critical developments was the introduction of the Senior Executive Service, mentioned earlier. This symbolized the fracturing of the internal labor market and challenged the concept of the career service (Considine, 1997). No longer were the majority of government employees expected to progress along extended career paths. Indeed, layers of middle management disappeared as the principle of devolution was implemented. Instead, management performance measures and improvement techniques were introduced along with performance payment systems, and reclassification and redeployment of staff was freed from the previous statutory constraints. Public Service Boards, which had played a critical role in the employer function for Australian public servants and many government employees, disappeared in a number of states such as Queensland, South Australia and Tasmania and from the Commonwealth system while, in other jurisdictions, such as New South Wales, their structure and role was significantly modified.

Because one of the driving forces for reform was dwindling resources, there was a strong emphasis on "doing more with less." Workplace reforms involving increased flexibility, that were implemented in many cases with the full co-operation of the relevant unions, often resulted in greater work intensity which reflected badly on the unions involved and alienated much of the membership (see O'Donnell, 1995).

Marketization, as the second wave of reform, was to see even more significant changes to the relationship between the state in Australia and its employees. To begin with, the number of employees, which had been reduced drastically under managerialism (see above), was to fall even more rapidly as outsourcing and contracting out took over increasingly from increased managerial prerogative as the key to economic efficiency in the public sector. Despite the continued resistance from sections of the labor movement, the federal Labor government (under the leadership of both Hawke and Keating) sold off a number of government-owned enterprises including Australian National Railways, Qantas Airways, the Commonwealth Bank, the Commonwealth Serum Laboratories, and AUSSAT (see Fairbrother et al., 1997). This was accompanied by growing levels of contracting out (or outsourcing), and according to Harman (1993), by the early 1990s contracting out already accounted for $1 billion or 5 percent of total expenditure on goods and services by government departments and agencies.

The momentum of all these trends increased further under the Liberal National Party Coalition government. Operating from the premise that, as far as possible, all services should be provided by the private sector, with government confined to the functions of policy development and implementation, the provision of IT services to government departments was placed in private hands (Davis, 1998). Labor market and employment services also became the responsibility of private providers and a corporatized remnant of the original Commonwealth Employment Service, retitled Employment National (Horin, 1998). The industrial relations implications of these changes were substantial, with Employment National demonstrating a propensity to adopt a more extreme version of managerialism in relation to its dealing with the workforce and trade unions.

The employer in the public sector

The nature of the employer in the Australian public sector varies across the three types of organization: public service, government authority and government business enterprise, and across the various jurisdictions. In the case of the public services and many authorities, public service boards have historically played a very significant role at both state and federal levels. However, this has changed significantly in recent years. At the federal level, the Commonwealth Public Service Board was abolished in 1987 when the Public Service Commission was established. However, the newly established Commission only took over some of the functions of the original Board, such as training, EEO and the Senior Executive Service, with others being allocated to departments such as Finance and Industrial Relations (Gardner and Palmer, 1997). In 1995 the Public Service Commission was combined with the Merit Protection and Review Agency to form the Public Service and Merit Protection Commission (PSMPC). The Department of Industrial Relations was given the important role of overseeing sector-wide industrial relations and the role of this department in public service management has been continued and strengthened under the Howard Government.

In 1997 the Coalition government introduced a Public Service Bill into federal parliament in which it is envisaged that 'employment powers (will) rest predominantly with Secretaries (or Chief Executives) and that the primary employment relationship (will be) between the employer and employee at the agency level (PSMPC, 1998). Under the new system, only general concepts of engagement, promotion and transfer will be retained within the APS employment framework, and the duties of employees and their work location will be determined by departmental secretaries. As noted in a background paper to the Bill: "the government has abandoned a service-wide approach to the setting of wages and conditions in favor of a greater emphasis on workplace relations at the level of individual agencies" (PSMPC, 1998).

Yet, despite the Howard government's professed ambitions to create a more decentralized (if not deregulated) approach to industrial relations in the public sector, the Department of Workplace Relations and Small Business (DWR&SB) has been given the important "watchdog" role to ensure high degrees of procedural, if not substantive, uniformity across all federal government employment (even though there appears to be no role for the department in the new legislation). In the case of Public Service agencies, Certified Agreements must receive both "first stage" (that is proposal stage) and "second stage" (that is pre-endorsement stage) approved by the department before they can go to be voted on by the union membership and/or the staff (DWR&SB, 1998). To be approved, they must comply with at least 12 policy parameters that include funding, classification structures, performance management and relationship to awards, other agreements, and legislation. Government authorities and GBEs are not required to have agreements approved by the department but have to comply with certain guidelines which, in the case of authorities, are quite detailed.

Furthermore, despite differences in rhetoric and ultimate purpose, the Howard government appears to be pursuing a similar strategy to some of its Labor predecessors (particularly governments led by Gough Whitlam and Ben Chifley) in using the federal public service to set in place industrial relations policies which it seeks to have adopted more widely. Thus, while it has subscribed officially to the advantages of devolution, and has gone to some lengths to implement it via proposed legislation, the government has found that it needs to have an interventionist approach to ensure compliance, particularly within the public service. Moreover, due to limitations on the ability of the federal government to exercise industrial powers beyond the APS, its approaches have not been necessarily followed at the state and municipal levels, even when governments of the same parties are in power. Hence, the Howard government may continue to find it difficult to implement many of its industrial relations reforms beyond the limits of the Australian Public Service, over which it is able to exercise direct control, to broader areas of the public sector.

The status and roles of managers in the public sector

Within the Australian Public Service, the most senior officers are the departmental secretaries or agency heads, now increasingly referred to as CEOs. According to the Public Service Act 1992 (as cited by Weller and Wanna, 1997)

> The Secretary of a Department shall, under the Minister, be responsible for its general working, and for all the business thereof, and shall advise the Minister in all matters relating to the Department.

These officer holders do not enjoy tenure in their positions nor in the public service itself. Indeed, as Weller and Wanna (1997) point out, "The appointment can be terminated at any time by the Governor-General and, unless the person is given another job, they cease being a member of the APS when they leave the position of secretary" (p.16). This was demonstrated in March, 1996 when, on the change of government, six departmental secretaries lost their positions and a seventh subsequently retired to be replaced by people with demonstrated sympathies to the incoming government.[1]

Different management structures are to be found in public education and health which are largely controlled, but only partly funded, by the state governments. In primary and secondary government education, the structure is still highly bureaucratic with recruitment to managerial positions largely from within, although the role of seniority has all but disappeared in the last decade. Day-to-day employment matters are controlled by the school principals but within guidelines laid down by bodies at the state level such as the NSW Department of School Education. Negotiations with the unions are largely conducted at the state level with some regional negotiations from time to time. While most schools have a union representative and often a management committee in the case of secondary schools, these institutions are largely ignored by the school principals and others in the management role and management is still highly autocratic and paternalistic.

In public health the management role has been very much affected by the reduced funding by governments at both state and federal level and the need to "do more with less" (O'Donnell, 1995). This reduced funding has seen the introduction of initiatives such as casemix, a form of output-based funding and an increasing number of services for which a "user-pays" policy applies. In addition, an intensification of competitive tendering has seen more services provided by private contractors which "introduces a purchaser/provider relationship which ostensibly separates out the role of government as purchaser of health services from that of provider of health services" (Stanton, 1998). This has implications at a number of levels. At the shopfloor level, managers become inspectors rather than supervisors with responsibilities to ensure that the terms of the contract are fulfilled with the actual role of labor management, or the immediate extraction of surplus value, being carried out by someone else. At higher levels there can be serious concerns about controlling the reliability and the quality of supply especially when this is critical to patient care and possibly survival.

According to Stanton (1998) the ultimate employer in the health sector is still the government because it supplies the all critical funding. Citing Fox (1996), Stanton draws the distinction between the legal employer (the hospitals) and the effective employer (the government). This virtually replicates the situation in higher education with the universities being the legal employers but with the federal government, supplying the vast majority of the funding, being the effective employer in that its decisions have an immediate impact on the determination of wages and other aspects of the employment relationship. Thus managers in the public sector, and certainly in those areas such as health and education where the majority of funding comes from the government rather than the consumers of the services, do not enjoy the autonomy or authority that their legal status might indicate.

Employer associations and the public sector

Unlike some other countries, there are no employer bodies within Australian government employment proper that bargain with unions on behalf of individual organizations. Within government departments (at both federal and state levels) the chief executive (usually known as the permanent head) reports to a minister who is responsible for those working in the department. As there is often a need to coordinate and monitor employment terms and conditions offered within individual departments (even in an era of decentralization and enterprise bargaining) governments have created statutory bodies, such as public service commissions, to perform this role.

This pattern of public administration, as noted previously, was established in the late nineteenth century within the separate colonies when public service boards were given responsibility to determine rates of pay, staffing levels and personnel policies. Public service boards were later established by the federal public service and they became very powerful, particularly when led by chief executives who sought to exercise their considerable authority within the public service. However, as noted previously, a wave of reforms during the 1980s led to the abolition of most public service boards (at both state and federal levels) and their replacement by public service commissions or commissioners with more restricted roles. As formal power and responsibility for industrial relations and other matters have been increasingly devolved to individual departments and agencies, public service commissions (or other central bodies) have been confined to setting policy parameters and assisting departments with their implementation.

However, within areas such as public education and health there are to be found a few employer associations. Universities, which with only a few exceptions operate under an Act of Parliament and are funded principally by the federal government, belong to the Australian Higher Education Industrial Association (AHEIA) which is registered as an employer organization under the Industrial Relations Act 1988 (Commonwealth). AHEIA was established on January 2, 1990 as an amalgam of two older organizations, the Australian Universities Industrial Association, and the Australian Advanced Education Industrial Association and is responsible for protecting the industrial relations interest of its members at state and federal levels. It advises members on award and general industrial matters and represents them, on either an individual or collective basis, before industrial tribunals and internal disciplinary and appeal committees. In addition, AHEIA formulates policies in consultation with its members and negotiates with industrial unions, such as the National Tertiary Education Industry Union, in accordance with such policies.

It should also be noted that some of the larger government business enterprises are members of the Business Council of Australia (BCA). While the BCA does not bargain on behalf of employers with unions, it has pursued a policy of activity supporting enterprise-based bargaining and individual employment contracts. The BCA was formed in 1983 and represents some 80 major companies. During the late 1980s, it had considerable influence on the federal Labor government in reshaping the structures of bargaining in Australia to a more decentralized model. The BCA's reform agenda for industrial relations has also helped to shape the current Coalition government's policy both at the wider national level as well as in regard to the public sector (Sheldon and Thornthwaite, 1996).

Trade unions

Public sector unionism in Australia has a long history. While they tended to remain apart from the general trade union movement for much of their history and, in many cases, did not engage in strike action until recent decades, most unions of government employees are now very similar to their private sector counterparts (Gardner and Palmer, 1997:541). Union density has always been higher in the public sector than the private sector with the respective figures for 1996 being 60 percent and 24 percent (ABS, Cat. 6325).

As in the private sector, amalgamations have been a highly significant feature of public sector unionism in the last decade (see Table 9.5). The Community and Public Sector Union (CPSU), for example, is by far the largest union covering government employees in Australia and resulted from the amalgamation of the Public Sector Professional Scientific Research, Technical Communications Aviation and Broadcasting Union, itself an amalgam of various commonwealth employees' unions, and the State Public Services Federation. It claims to represent 250,000 workers (CPSU, 1998) and is divided into two principal groups, the Public Sector Union (PSU) group which represents workers in Commonwealth Government departments, statutory authorities and business enterprises and the State Public Services Federation (SPSF) group which has members in state government agencies, authorities and business enterprises. Management and decision making in the union is largely devolved to these groups and to the state branches, such as the Public Service Association of NSW which are relatively autonomous bodies largely operating independently of the federal body.

Another very important public sector union especially in government authorities, business enterprises, and local government is the Australian Services Union (ASU) which represents mainly administrative, supervisory and technical workers although it has been able to expand its coverage of more varied occupations in recent years, especially within the energy industry (ASU, 1998). It grew out of a series of amalgamations, the last being finalized in 1993. Within NSW and Australian Capital Territory the unions that amalgamated to form the branch include: Australian Transport Officers Federation, the Municipal Officers Association, the Water and Maritime Industry Union, the Australian Social Welfare Union, the Australian Shipping and Travel Officers Association, the Technical Services Guild, and the Local Government Clerks Associations.

Coverage in the ASU, however, is not confined to government employees, with most of the industry-based divisions of the union covering private sector enterprises as well government organizations. Another large union that spans both private and public sectors is the Communications, Electrical and Plumbing Union (CEPU). However, given that its principal base in the public sector is Telstra (Communications), the increasing privatization of that organization will see the public sector membership of that union shrink dramatically.

National unity arising from amalgamation and a federation style of government is also to be found in pubic education. The Australian Education Union (AEU) has coverage of virtually all employees in the government or publicly funded education sector apart from higher education. The institutions comprising this sector range from pre-school kindergartens, through primary and secondary schools, to vocational and further education colleges. In addition it covers a wide range of employees including teachers, support staff, principals and administrators. The AEU has its origins in the Australian Teachers' Federation which was formed in 1922 as a loose federation of the state unions (Spaull and Mann, 1985). The main period of development for teachers' unions was the first two decades of this century when the growing influence of the compulsory arbitration system and the presence of Labor governments provided a highly supportive environment for the growth of unionism (Spaull and Mann, 1985:14). For example, the NSW Teachers' Federation was formed in 1919, and in 1920 represented 78 percent of the teachers in the state's government schools (NSW Teachers' Federation, 1998). The other major union in the publicly funded education system is the National Tertiary Education Union (NTEU) which covers academic staff and, in some states, non-academic staff from Australia's 40 universities. Thus, at the present time the NTEU has some 25,000 members in universities, TAFE colleges, research institutes, adult education providers, student organizations, university and college companies and commercial arms and independent post-secondary education providers. Their occupations range from academics, to general and research staff to student union employees.

As result of amalgamations since 1990, there are only three major unions in the health sector representing medical staff, nurses and related workers. They are, respectively, the Australian Salaried Medical Officers Federation, the Australian Nursing Federation and the Health Services Union of Australia. Each are federations of relatively autonomous state branches with the Nursing Federation and the Health Services Union representing employees in privately owned organizations as well as in public health.

Another area that has seen a dramatic reduction in the number of unions since 1990 is public transport. From a situation in which there were over 20 unions in NSW State Rail alone there is only one, the Public Transport Union (PTU). It has two divisions, the Bus and Tram

Division which was previously the Australian Tram and Motor Omnibus Employees Association (AT&MOEA) and the Locomotive Division.

Each state has a union of police force members, an example of which is the Police Association of South Australia (PASA). The membership of the PASA is drawn from all ranks of the South Australian Police and in 1998 the membership comprised approximately 3,500 police officers and aides. The PASA is affiliated with the Police Federation of Australia and New Zealand, the United Trades and Labor Council of South Australia, and the ACTU (PASA, 1998). Another emergency service which is strongly unionized is fire-fighting. At the national level there is the United Fire-fighters' Union of Australia (UFUA), a federation of much older states-based unions, which was registered in 1969 and currently has a membership of approximately 11,000. From the outset there was the question of whether the officers, that is the supervisory staff in the brigade, should be members of the union. On the union's formation, officers were excluded and in 1931 they formed their own union in the face of opposition from the employees' union. In 1948 the two unions formally amalgamated, but a year later an independent Senior Officers' Association was formed and it was not until 1975 that it was formally absorbed into the main union.

Public sector industrial relations

Outline of the present situation and main features

The Australian public sector has been swept up into the wider changes which have occurred in industrial relations in general during the past decade or so. Between 1983 and 1996, there was a brief period of centralized wage determination after the Hawke Labor government was elected and the Accord between the unions and the Australian Labor Party (ALP) was implemented. This meant that in the public sector, as in the broader economy, wages were fully adjusted to reflect increases in the consumer price index. Following a balance of payment crisis and other economic problems in the mid 1980s, the Hawke Labor government abandoned its centralized approach and adopted a policy of "managed decentralism." Full wage indexation was abandoned and a two-tier wage system was introduced which took account of productivity increases at both the industry and enterprise levels, but maintained a system of national wage adjustments. The 1988 National Wage Case Decision by the Australian Industrial Relations Commission (AIRC) established a "structural efficiency principle" designed to encourage the parties to reach collective agreements on the introduction of multiskilling, broad-based work classifications and a reduction of demarcation disputes within industries, including the public sector. This ushered in significant increases in labor market flexibility while retaining the broad institutional framework.

After its surprise election victory in March, 1993, the Labor government (now led by Paul Keating) introduced further reforms to extend enterprise bargaining with the Industrial Relations Reform Act 1993. Although the new Act incorporated a number of ILO conventions and recommendations, which strengthened worker protection and granted a wider range of minimum entitlements, it also included provisions which facilitated bargaining without unions. Hence, the period from 1991 to 1996 was one of transition towards more individualized forms of industrial relations, as some employers sought to take full advantage of the more flexible bargaining arrangements which were permitted under the new legislation, and the AIRC found its role significantly diminished.

The most recent phase of industrial relations reform, which we have entitled "fragmented flexibility," began with the election of the Liberal–National Party Coalition government, led by John Howard, in 1996. The Workplace Relations Act 1996 signaled a more radical decentralization of industrial relations to the enterprise level, with broader scope for non-union agreements and further diminution in the role of the AIRC. A key element of the Workplace Relations Act 1996, embodied in the new Australian Workplace Agreements (AWAs), seeks to enable (and encourage) employers to enter into either a non-union agreement or an individual contract with their employees. While AWAs have so far played only a relatively minor role in regulating wages and conditions, and are unlikely to become the main form of agreement between employers and employees, they are part of a broader trend towards a more individualized and flexible approach to labor market arrangements.

Collective bargaining structures in the public sector

The development of industrial relations in the public sector has followed the general trend across all industries. Prior to the early 1990s, the wages and conditions of government employees not determined by legislation and associated regulations were set out in awards of the federal and state arbitration tribunals. In 1992, enterprise level bargaining replaced service-wide arbitration for Commonwealth government employees and similar changes took place at the state level at about the same time. While the Commonwealth agreement at that time introduced the concept of agency bargaining, service-wide pay and classification structures remained in place. Furthermore, a high degree of uniformity in pay and conditions was maintained by an elaborate arrangement whereby a proportion of productivity gains were pooled to enable those agencies unable to achieve such gains to draw on the pool and thus provide supplementary wage increases to their employees (Elliott and Bender, 1997). Enterprise bargaining spread rather slowly across the federal public service but, by the end of 1994, at least half of all agencies employing more than three-quarters of the APS were signatories to agreements that had been certified by the federal commission (Elliot and Bender, 1997:465). This led to some diversity of outcomes but the second wave of enterprise bargaining that took place during 1995–96 saw a return to uniformity with three pay increases of the same amount to be paid to all public servants on the same dates.

The election of the Coalition government saw a new approach to reform. The Howard government has consistently argued that reform of industrial relations is the key to improving efficiency in the public sector, particularly within the public service. The Minister of Workplace Relations and Small Business has been critical of employment arrangements in the public service which "derive from a legislative and procedural framework which envisaged a Commonwealth-wide public service with strong centralized control, regulation of uniform conditions and permanent employment to a life time career" (Reith, 1996). Under the previous Labor government, the formerly highly centralized organizations of the public service had begun to change, but there remained an important role for unions. The Howard government, by contrast, has made a concerted attack on collectivism. Under the government's policy guidelines, for example, all certified agreements must contain a provision allowing for the introduction of AWAs at any time for any staff under the agreement. There have been examples where management, unable to reach agreement with the relevant union, has taken the draft agreement directly to staff for approval under the Workplace Relations Act (Section 170 LK). Such a tactic can only work in a situation of relatively weak unionism and it seems the context of declining union membership is encouraging the government to vigorously pursue its anti-collectivist agenda in the public sector.

In other sectors a variety of arrangements exists with varying degrees of centralization. Wage determination in Australian education, for example, reached an unprecedented degree of centralization in 1990 when the Australian Industrial Relations Commission handed down a decision based on the Structural Efficiency (award restructuring)

Principle which led directly to the adjustment of awards determining wages and conditions for all school staff, including those in private schools, right across Australia. Previously wages and conditions were determined at state level with the public and private systems operating independently. The commission was persuaded that education should be one of the five industries to have priority in the award restructuring process (Ashenden, 1991:66) and the resulting decision introduced national salary benchmarks which were intended to attempt to redress the relative decline in teachers' salaries that had occurred in the previous five years. The salary increases were well above those being received by wage earners generally and, in addition, a new grade of teacher, the Advanced Skills Classification, was introduced. To engage in this centralized wage determination process, the employer side was also coordinated to an unprecedented extent. The Commonwealth and State Ministers for Education had formed a standing committee which carried the imprimatur of the Australian Education Commission, but its decisions were not binding on its constituents as was demonstrated by the initial refusal of the Tasmanian government to recognize the salary benchmarks (Durbridge, 1991:99).

Industrial disputes

Public sector employees have shown a relatively greater propensity than their private sector counterparts to engage in industrial action. This is shown very clearly by AWIRS 95 (Morehead et al., 1997) and also by the ABS statistics but, unfortunately, the trends are not as evident from that source as there is no public sector/private sector breakdown within the relevant series. However, some industry classifications used by the ABS are either exclusively public sector, such as government administration and defense, or are dominated by the public sector, such as electricity, gas, water supply, education, health and community services. Thus it is possible to gain some idea, from these statistics, of the manner in which disputation in the public sector compares with that in the private sector and changes over time in that comparison.

Table 9.6, based on AWIRS data, shows the public sector being much more conflict prone that the private sector, at least in terms of occurrence of any industrial action in two 12-month periods; that is, the 12 months prior to the conduct of 1990 and 1995. In 1990, 43 percent of public sector workplaces with five or more employees reported industrial action whereas only 7 percent of private sector workplaces from the same survey population reported any action

Table 9.5 Major public sector unions in Australia[a]

	1995	1998[b]
Community and Public Sector Union (including Australian Public Service Federation)	225,000	250,000
Australian Services Union (including Federated Municipal and Shire Council Employees)	163,300	
Australian Education Union	152,600	153,370
Health Services Union (including Health and Research Employees Association)	68,400	
Australian Nursing Federation	62,300	
NSW Nurses' Federation	42,510	46,380
Police Federation of Australia and New Zealand	36,900	42,000
Public Transport Union (including Australian Railway Union)	33,500	
National Tertiary Education Union	22,000	25,000
Communications, Electrical and Plumbing Union (includes Australian Postal and Telecommunications Union and Australian Telecommunications Employees' Association)	161,700	137,700
United Fire-fighters' Union of Australia	10,990	11,000

Notes:
[a] Taken in large part from Gardner and Palmer (1997:540).
[b] These figures, where available, have been taken from union websites and from information provided by the unions themselves.

Table 9.6 Industrial conflict in Australia: comparison of public and private sectors

	Any industrial action		Strikes		Overtime bans or restrictions	
	1990	1995	1990	1995	1990	1995
Public sector	52	45	50	42	76	69
Private sector	19	13	52	45	79	72

Percentage of workplaces experiencing industrial action in the 12 months prior to the conduct of the 1990 and 1995 AWIRS surveys.

Source: Morehead, 1997, Tables A4.12a and A4.12b.

(Morehead et al., 1997:614–15). In 1995 the figures were 29 percent for the public sector and 4 percent for the private sector. In terms of the traditional forms of industrial action, strikes and overtime bans or restrictions, however, there is little difference between the sectors. Thus it is necessary to look further, and the AWIRS tables that are the basis for Table 9.6 show that it is in respect of "work to rule" and "other bans" that public sector workplaces are more conflict prone than those in the private sector. Moreover, certain areas of the public sector, such as education, electricity, gas, and water supply exhibit much higher instances of industrial action than other areas. Education stood out in both years but particularly in 1995 when the number of workplaces reporting action was at least double that of all but one other industry classification.

Turning to the ABS statistics (Cat. 6322.0) it is found that education again shows out as being highly prone to disputation. In 1996, for example, working days lost per 1,000 employees through industrial disputes, which include strikes and lockouts, totaled 239 for the industry classification, Education, Health and Community Services, which was the second highest figure behind only Construction (334 days lost). The picture was similar for 1997 although numbers of days lost were lower throughout and the total for Education and so on, 94, was not only below Construction (107) but was also below manufacturing (145) and mining (97). Nevertheless, it certainly rated very highly and while the classification is not restricted to public sector organizations, it seems that, at least in terms of disputation, it is dominated not only by education, but by public education.

Table 9.7, based on AWIRS data, compares three public sector or predominantly public sector industries with mining, a predominantly private sector industry which is recognized internationally as traditionally conflict prone. While there is the same pattern of reduction in conflict from 1990 to 1995, the table shows that education has been almost as conflict prone as mining while government administration and electricity, gas, and water are not far behind. Thus certain significant industrial sectors, wholly or almost wholly within the public sector, are almost as conflict prone as mining. However, Government Administration and Electricity, gas and water supply, rated very low in terms of working days lost, according to the ABS. Any apparent contradiction with the AWIRS findings can be explained in terms of the type of action and numbers of workers involved. Electricity, gas, and water rated high in AWIRS which looked at the number of workplaces experiencing industrial action of any kind, and it emerges that stop work meetings and overtime bans were more common than strikes. Thus this industry classification is revealed as being prone to certain types of industrial action but did not figure prominently in terms of working days lost.

Table 9.7 Industrial conflict in Australia: selected industries

	Any industrial action		Strikes		Overtime bans or restrictions	
	1990	1995	1990	1995	1990	1995
Mining	58	37	73	89	98	69
Electricity, gas and water supply	48	41	34	39	94	64
Government administration	42	30	65	11	85	76
Education	59	55	70	56	70	72

Percentage of workplaces experiencing industrial action in the 12 months prior to the conduct of the 1990 and 1995 AWIRS Surveys.

Source: Morehead et al., 1997, Tables A4.12a and A4.12b.

Apart from the influence of education, the Australian public sector tends to be more prone to industrial action because of two underlying characteristics: size of workplace and union density. Public sector organizations are, on average, larger than private sector organizations (Morehead et al., 1997:31) although the difference did narrow a little between 1990 and 1995. Also, union presence is much higher in the public sector, as is the presence of delegates (Morehead et al., 1997:140). Thus, it is not surprising that industrial action is more prevalent in the public sector.

Information, consultation and participation rights and institutions

The concept of employee participation in workplace decision making has been popular at various times within the public sector. One of the longest established formal systems which has provided for consultation about organizational decisions with employees and unions in the public sector dates from 1945. The Chifley Labor government established a joint council comprised of representatives from government departments, the public service board and unions (or staff associations as they were often called) in the early post World War II period. The joint council still operates as a consultative forum in which senior management meets with public sector union leaders to discuss matters such as grievances, allowances, leave, superannuation rules, and other matters of general interest. It does not deal with rates of pay or industrial disputes. When both sides of the joint council agree on a matter, it is almost always adopted as policy by the relevant government authorities, but management can avoid this by simply withholding its agreement at the council's sessions. The joint council's scope does not include statutory authorities whose employees are not subject to the Public Service Act. Formal centralized mechanisms for consultation have also become a less favored means of providing employee participation by the current federal government, which has emphasized a more decentralized and informal approach to employee involvement in decision making.

The emphasis on employee participation was enshrined in the Hawke government's Public Service Reform Act 1984 which extended the rights of employees in the federal public sector to information and consultation and obliged government departments to create "industrial democracy action plans." By the end of the 1980s, however, the Hawke government's support for a centralized approach to industrial relations and a strong emphasis on industrial democracy as an agency of reform had declined, particularly with regard to the public sector. The disbanding of the Public Service Board in 1987 saw its important responsibilities for fostering and monitoring employee participation in the public service transferred to the Department of Industrial Relations. While devolution of management responsibilities did not automatically mean the abandonment of employee participation, it did tend to be associated with a reassertion of managerial rights. Furthermore, more direct forms of employee participation, which did not rely on a formal representative structure, had not developed within departments. According to Teicher (1989), the Hawke government's emphasis shifted from support for employee participation initiatives, with union involvement, to the adoption of private sector management practices, particularly strategic management and human resources management (HRM), which tended to focus on managerial prerogatives.

The Howard Coalition government has shown little interest or support for formal systems of employee participation or consultation in either the public or private sectors. It would appear that the momentum for employee participation and industrial democracy that was building in the 1980s, particularly in the public sector, had largely dissipated by the mid 1990s. While formal consultative committees have spread, especially in the public sector, their impact has been questionable in terms of management practices. This is confirmed by Gardner and Palmer (1997:567) who commented that the history of consultative committees in the public sector is of "patching implementation and short-lived experiments." This correlates with the findings of a Federal

Taskforce on Management Improvement (1992) which reported that "the process towards implementation of industrial democracy plans and consultative mechanisms has been uneven."

Conclusions

There has been a significant decline in employment within the Australian public sector during the past two decades, particularly in the federal public service, under both Labor and Coalition governments. Faced with a declining pool of financial resources to meet increasing demands for expenditure, government has sought to reduce costs by various means. These have included greater use of cost recovery from government services, targeting of social welfare payments, and limitation on wage rises for public sector employees. Since the mid 1980s, public sector administration has also been subjected to a number of reforms variously labeled as "New Public Management," "managerialism," and "marketization." Underpinning the last mentioned was the principle that market forces should determine the allocation and utilization of resources in the public sector with the New Zealand experience being cited by conservative governments, at both the federal and state levels, as the appropriate model. Thus "marketization" saw also privatization of a number of public enterprises and a growing level of contracting out.

Employment relations in the public sector have reflected changes in the broader economy from "managed decentralism" in the late 1980s towards "fragmented flexibility" in the late 1990s. Under the previous federal Labor government, decentralized wage setting arrangements spread much further in the public sector than the private sector, but service-wide bargaining over core conditions and terms of employment was retained as was a prominent role for unions. The Coalition government, on the other hand, has made a concerted attack on collectivism and trade unionism and has undertaken a more radical devolution of industrial relations with wages and conditions being set at the level of the individual government department or agency. Furthermore, "partnership" programs, such as employee participation/industrial democracy, as well as "equity-based" programs, such as Affirmative Action, have been downgraded because they do not fit easily with the more managerialist approaches of and are inconsistent with the principles of, "marketization". Hence, employment relations in the public sector are likely to be subject to continuing changes in the foreseeable future.

Notes

1. Weller and Wanna (1997) point out, however, that the business appointments held by these people took up a relatively short period in their careers, which had been based for the most part on the Federal government bureaucracy.

References

Australian Bureau of Statistics (Cat. no. 6203.0) *The Labor Force Australia*, Canberra: Australian Bureau of Statistics.
Australian Bureau of Statistics (Cat. no. 6322.) *Industrial Disputes Australia*, Canberra: Australian Bureau of Statistics.
Australian Bureau of Statistics (Cat. no. 6325.0) *Trade Union Members Australia*, Canberra: Australian Bureau of Statistics.
Ashenden, D. (1991) "Award Restructuring and Productivity in the Future of Schooling," in Riley, D. (ed.), *Industrial Relations in Australian Education*, Australia: Social Science Press.
ASU (1998) *About us*, Australian Services Union, NSW and ACT Branch, http://auservices.labor.net.au/about/whos.html
Caiden, G. (1965) *Career Service*, Melbourne: Melbourne University Press.
Considine, M. (1997) "The Corporate Management Framework as Administrative Science," in Considine, M. and Painter, M. (eds.), *Managerialism: The Great Debate*, Carlton South: Melbourne University Press.
Considine, M. and Painter, M. (1997) "Introduction," in Considine, M. and Painter, M. (eds.), *Managerialism: The Great Debate*, Carlton South: Melbourne University Press.
Corbett, D. (1996, 2nd edn.), *Australian Public Sector Management*, St. Leonards: Allen & Unwin.
CPSU (1998) *Delegates Manual*, http:www.cpsu.org/delegate.htm
Davis, G. (1997) "Toward a Hollow State? Managerialism and its Critics," in Considine, M. and Painter, M. (eds.), *Managerialism: The Great Debate*, Carlton South: Melbourne University Press.
Davis, G., Wanna, J., Warhust, J., and Weller, P. (1993, 2nd edn.), *Public Policy in Australia*, Sydney: Allen and Unwin.
Davis, I. (1998) "Federal IT outsourcing contract 'delights' local industry," *Australian Financial Review*, March.
DIR (1996) *Annual Report 1995: Enterprise Bargaining in Australia*, Canberra: Australian, Government Publishing Service
Durbridge, R. (1991) "Towards Enterprise Education? in Education Reform," in Riley, D. (ed.), *Industrial Relations in Australian Education*, Australia: Social Science Press.
DWR&SB(1998) *Workplace Relations Advice* (4).
Elliott, R. and Bender, K. (1997) "Decentralization and Pay Reform in Central Government: a Study of Three Countries," *British Journal of Industrial Relations*, **XXXV**(3).
EPAC (1990) *The Size and Efficiency of the Public Sector*, Canberra: AGPS.
Fairbrother P., Svensen, S., and Teicher, J. (1997) "The Withering Away of the Australian State: Privatization and its Implications for Labor," *Labor and Industry*, **VIII**(2).

Fox, C. (1996) *Enterprise Bargaining and Health Services: A Special Case?*, Melbourne: Monash University, National Key Center in Industrial Relations.

Gardner, M. and Palmer, G. (1997, 2nd edn.) *Employment Relations: Industrial Relations and Human Resource Management in Australia*, Melbourne: Macmillan – now Palgrave.

Harman, E. (1993) "The Impact of Public Sector Reforms on Australian Government," in Weller, P., Forster, J., and Davis, G. (eds.), *Reforming the Public Service: Lessons from Recent Experience*, Melbourne: Macmillan – now Palgrave.

Horin, A. (1998) "Jobless Sold to the Lowest Bidder," *The Sydney Morning Herald*, November.

McCarry, G. (1994) "The Demise of Tenure in Public Sector Employment," in McCallum, R., McCarry, G., and Ronfeldt, P. (eds.), *Employment Security*, Sydney: Federation Press.

Morehead, A., Steel, M., Alexander, M., Stephen, K., and Duffin, L. (1997) *Changes at Work: The 1995 Australian Workplace Industrial Relations Survey*, Melbourne: Addison Wesley, Longman.

NSW Teachers' Federation (1998) "History of the NSW Teachers' Federation," http://www.nswtf.org.au/history.htm

O'Donnell, M. (1995) "Empowerment or Enslavement?: Lean Production, Immigrant Women and Service Work in Public Hospitals," *Labor and Industry*, VI(3).

PASA (1998) *The Organization*, http://www.pasa.asn.au/org

PSMPC (1998) *The Public Service Act 1997: Accountability in a Devolved Management Framework*, Canberra: PSMPC.

Reith, P. (1996) *Towards Best Practice Australian Public Service*, Canberra: PSMPC.

Selby Smith, C. (1993) "A New Career Service?," in Gardner, M. (ed.), *Human Resource Management and Industrial Relations in the Public Sector*, Melbourne: Macmillan – now Palgrave.

Sheldon, P. and Thornthwaite, L. (1996) "Re-Evaluating the Impact of Employer Associations on the Accord: An Analysis of Changes to Bargaining Structures, 1983–94," in Fells, R. and Todd, T. (eds.), *Current Research in Industrial Relations*, Perth: AIRAANZ Conference.

Spaull, A. and Mann, S. (1985) "Teacher Unionism in Australia: The Case of Victoria," in Lawn, M. (ed.), *The Politics of Teacher Unionism: International Perspectives*, London: Croom Helm.

Stanton, P. (1998) "Changing Employment Relationships in Victorian Public Hospitals," discussion paper at the conference "Public Sector Restructuring and Industrial Relations," Melbourne: Monash University, National Key Center in Industrial Relations.

Teicher, J. (1989) "Industrial Democracy and Employee Participation in Australian Government Employment: Progress and Prospect," in Corbett, D., Selby Smith, C., and Smith R. F. I. (eds.), *Public Sector Personnel Policies for the 1990s*, Melbourne: Monash University, Public Sector Management Institute.

Weller, P. and Wanna, J. (1997) "Department Secretaries: Appointment, Termination and their Impact," report to the Institute of Public Administration Australia, ACT Division, *Australian Journal of Public Administration*, LVI(4).

Yeatman, A. (1997) "The Concept of Public Management and the Australian State in the 1980s," in Considine, M. and Painter, M. (eds.), *Managerialism: The Great Debate*, Carlton South: Melbourne University Press.

Subject Index

Notes: 'n.' after a page reference indicates the number of a note on that page.
Index entries appear in their expanded forms. Abbreviations are listed on pp. xiv–xvii.

accountability, USA 104
Administrative Reform Council (Japan) 157
Administrative Reform Plan (Japan) 157
Advisory Council of Economy and Finance (Japan) 170
Agenzia per la Rappresentanza Negoziale della Pubblica (ARAN, Italy) 60, 62, 77
age of employees, USA 99
air controllers, USA 119
Alcohol Monopoly (Japan) 156
Amalgamated Transit Workers Union (USA) 114
American Federation of Government Employees 112
American Federation of State, County and Municipal Employees (AFSCME) 113, 114
American Federation of Teachers (AFT) 113–14
Amtrak 100
Angestellte (Germany) 53, 62
appraisal of staff 10, 27
Arbeiter (Germany) 53, 62
Arbetsgivar Verket (AgV, Sweden) 62, 77
arbitration
  Canada 141, 142, 145, 148, 149
  Japan 179, 180
  New Zealand 210
  USA 118–19, 120
Arbitration Commission (New Zealand) 210
Area Health Boards (AHBs, New Zealand) 206
armed forces, Western Europe 53
assessment of staff 10, 27

Association of County Councils (UK) 93n.1
Association of District Councils (UK) 93n.1
Association of Metropolitan Authorities (UK) 93n.1
Association of Salaried Medical Specialists (ASMS, New Zealand) 201, 210
Association of Staff in Tertiary Education (ASTE, New Zealand) 201
Association of University Staff (Australia, New Zealand) 201
Association of X-ray Workers (New Zealand) 212n.1
AUSSAT 224
Australia 22, 216–17, 240
  collective bargaining 16, 233–5
  competitive tendering 6
  employer associations 74, 75, 83, 228–9
  employers 223–8
  industrial relations 232–40
  labor cost reduction 9
  labor market characteristics 221
  levels of government 13
  new public management 11
  organization structure 217–18
  output-based funding 6–7
  privatization 5
  public employment trends 8, 218–20
  trade unions 18, 20, 85, 229–32
  wages and salaries 221–3
Australian Advanced Education Industrial Association 229
Australian Council Trade Union (ACTU) 232

243

Australian Education Commission 235
Australian Education Union (AEU) 231, 236
Australian Higher Education Industrial Association (AHEIA) 229
Australian Industrial Relations Commission (AIRC) 232–3, 234–5
Australian National Railways 224
Australian Nursing Federation 231, 236
Australian Postal and Telecommunications Union 236
Australian Public Service (APS) 226–7
Australian Public Service Federation 236
Australian Railway Union 236
Australian Salaried Medical Officers Federation 231
Australian Services Union (ASU) 230, 236
Australian Shipping and Travel Officers Association 230
Australian Social Welfare Union 230
Australian Teachers' Federation 231
Australian Telecommunications Employees Association 236
Australian Tram and Motor Omnibus Employees Association (AT & MOEA) 231
Australian Transport Officers Federation 230
Australian Universities Industrial Association 229
Australian Workplace Agreements (AWAs) 233, 234
Australia Post 221
Authority Commission (Japan) 165
aziendalizzazione (hospitals run as companies) 6, 81

Bank of Japan 156
Basic Law (Germany, 1949) 63
Basic Law to Reform Central Ministries (Japan) 157
Beamte (German civil servants)
 collective bargaining 14, 53–4, 61–2, 63
 employer associations 74, 79–80
 legal rights and obligations 28
 New Public Management 10, 28
 trade unions 85
bonuses
 Canada 135
 Japan 166, 178
 New Zealand 193
Bureau of Administrative Service (Japan) 171
Bureau of Employee Relations (Japan) 172
Bureau of Equity (Japan) 172
Bureau of Recruitment (Japan) 171
Bureau of Remuneration (Japan) 171–2
Business Council of Australia (BCA) 229

Cabinet Office (Japan) 170
Canada 127–9, 150–2
 collective bargaining 16, 144–5
 compensation 145–6
 employers and employer associations 73, 135–8
 labor conflict and regulation of strikes 146–9
 labor cost reduction 7, 8, 9, 127–8
 labor management cooperation 149–50
 labor relations 140–4
 levels of government 13
 new public management 11, 12
 organizational structure 129–31
 privatization 5
 public employment trends 8, 131–3
 trade unions 20, 138–40
 wages and salaries 133–5
Canadian Labor Congress (CLC) 139
Canadian Union of Public Employees (CUPE) 139, 140, 141
Centers for Disease Control (CDC, USA) 100
central government
 decentralization, administrative 13

central government – *continued*
  Japan   157–8, 162, 163–4, 165–6, 167, 168
  New Zealand   186–8, 198, 208
  United Kingdom   36
  see also federal government
centralization
  collective bargaining   51, 57–62, 66, 144–5
  employer associations   74–8
  trade unions   84, 92
Central Labor Relations Commission (CLRC, Japan)   178, 179, 180
Central Ministries and Agencies (Japan)   157
charters   2
Chifley, Ben   226, 238
Civil Servants Act (Denmark, 1969)   54–5
civil servants/civil service   28, 32, 85
  Canada   132, 133, 137, 149
  Denmark   34, 54–5, 80
  France   19, 28, 34, 80
  Germany *see Beamte*
  Italy   80
  Japan   163, 164
  Netherlands   57
  Spain   37, 57
  United Kingdom   16, 37, 38, 55, 59
  United States   101, 103, 109–10, 121
Civil Service Commission (CSC, USA)   109
closed-shop agreements
  Japan   174
  New Zealand   199
collective bargaining   13–17, 27
  Australia   233–5
  Canada   129, 132, 134, 136–8, 140–5, 149–50
  Japan   155, 159–61, 166, 178, 179–80
  New Zealand   197, 198, 202, 204–8, 210
  United States   101, 102, 107–8, 111–22
  Western Europe   48–50, 65–7: centralization v. decentralization   57–62;

comparative analysis framework   50–2; coordination   62–5; unilateral v. joint regulation   52–7
Combined State Service Organization (CSSO, New Zealand)   201
Commonwealth Bank (Australia)   224
Commonwealth Employment Service (Australia)   225
Commonwealth Public Service Board (Australia)   225
Commonwealth Serum Laboratories (Australia)   224
Communications, Electrical and Plumbing Union (CEPU, Australia)   230–1, 236
Community and Public Sector Union (CPSU, Australia)   230, 236
competitive tendering   6
  Australia   227–8
  Europe   37–8
Confederation Française Du Travail (CFDT, France)   89, 90
Confederation of Economic Organizations (Japan)   156
conciliation, New Zealand   210
Conservative governments   22
  United Kingdom: collective bargaining   59; employer associations   75; New Public Management   36, 42; trade unions   18, 90
consultancies
  Europe   81–2
  United States   106
consultation economy, The Netherlands   89
consumer councils, Denmark   38
contingent work   18, 86
  United States   106
contracting out   6
  Australia   224–5
  Canada   127
  Europe   38
  United States   106–7
convergence theory   22
cooperative relationships
  Canada   144, 149
  United States   99, 122

corporate management techniques   2
corporatization, New Zealand   187–8, 192
Council of Trade Union (CTU, New Zealand)   201
Crown corporations, Canada   128
Crown Health Enterprises (New Zealand)   189, 206
Customs Department (New Zealand)   200

decentralization, administrative   2–3, 12–13
  Canada   128–9, 130, 134, 144
  collective bargaining   15–17, 51, 57–62, 66
  employer associations   74–8, 82–3, 92
  trade unions   82, 94
Defense Agency (Japan)   170
Denmark
  collective bargaining   15, 66–7: coordination   64, 65; unilateral v. joint bargaining   53, 54–5
  Economic and Monetary Union   92
  employer associations: centralization v. decentralization   74, 75, 76, 77; initiating change and modernization   80, 81, 82
  labor cost reduction   9
  New Public Management   34, 36, 38–9, 43
  public employment trends   8
  trade unions   20, 88, 92
Department of Corrections (New Zealand)   206
Department of Industrial Relations (Australia)   225, 239
Department of Social Welfare (New Zealand)   200
Department of Workplace Relations and Small Business (DWR&SB, Australia)   222–3, 226
Deutscher Gewerschaftsbund (DGB, Germany)   62
devolution   7

employer associations   75–6, 81, 82, 92
New Public Management   11–12
trade unions   92
dismissals
  Japan   164
  United States   103–4
Dokoh, Toshio   156
Durafour agreement (France, 1990)   61

Economic and Monetary Union (EMU)
  challenge   92–3
  collective bargaining   48, 54
  employer associations   78
  New Public Management   24
Economic Planning Agency (Japan)   170
Education Act (New Zealand, 1989)   196
educational attainment of employees, USA   99
education sector
  Australia: collective bargaining   234–5; employer associations   229; employment   220, 227, 228; industrial disputes   237, 238; trade unions   231
  Canada   128: employers and employer associations   136, 137; employment   131, 133; industrial relations   141, 142; organization   130–1; strikes   147; trade unions   139, 140
  Denmark   81
  France   81
  Italy   37, 81
  Japan   158, 161, 162, 169
  New Zealand   7: collective bargaining   205, 206–8; employers and employer associations   196–8; employment   189; trade unions   199, 200–1, 203
  United Kingdom   81
  United States   101, 113–14
  Western Europe   37, 81
effectiveness improvements   2, 10–11

efficiency improvements   2, 10–11
élite   28
employer associations
  Australia   228–9
  Canada   135–8, 141, 144, 149
  Japan   173–4
  United States   110
  Western Europe   71–4:
    centralization v.
    decentralization   74–8;
    initiating change and
    modernization   78–83; outlook
    91–3
  see also professional associations
Employment Contracts Act (ECA,
  New Zealand, 1991)   18, 195
  labor relations   204, 205, 206, 208,
    209–10
  trade unions   199–200, 201, 202,
    203
Employment National (Australia)
  225
Equal Employment Opportunity
  Commission (EEOC, USA)   120
Equal Pay Act (USA)   108
ethnicity of employees, USA   98
evaluation of staff   10, 27

Fair Labor Standards Act (USA)
  126n.20
Federal Civil Service Reform Act (USA,
  1978)   102, 103, 104
federal government   12–13
  Australia   15: collective bargaining
    234; employee participation
    239; employers   226;
    employment   218, 219;
    organizational structure   218;
    wages and salaries   222–3
  Canada   15, 128: collective
    bargaining   144–5;
    compensation   146; employers
    and employer associations
    135; employment   131;
    industrial relations   141,
    142–3; organization   129, 130;
    strikes   147, 148; trade unions
    139; wages and salaries   133,
    134

  United States   14, 15, 97–8: civil
    service   109; contracting out
    107; organizational structure
    100–1; recent policies   99;
    trade unions   112; wages and
    salaries   107
  see also central government
Federal Labor Relations Authority
  (FLRA, USA)   111, 112, 113, 118
Federal Law Enforcement Agencies
  (USA)   100
Federal Public Health Service (USA)
  100, 101
Federated Municipal and Shire Council
  Employees (Australia)   236
Federation de l'Education Nationale
  (FEN, France)   89, 90
Federation of All Trade Unions in
  Japan (Zenrokyo)   175, 177
Federation of Labor (FOL, New
  Zealand)   201
Federation of National Public
  Employee Unions, Zenroren
  (Kokko Roren, Japan)   177, 182
Federation of National Public Service
  (Japan)   175
Federation of Unions of Local
  Government Employees (Japan)
  167
Fédération Syndicale Unitaire (FSU,
  France)   84, 90
feminization of labor force   83
  New Zealand   189–90
  see also women employees
Finland   8, 9, 12, 20
fire-fighters
  Australia   232
  New Zealand   207
  United States   114
Fiscal Law (Japan)   165
fiscal policy   1
fixed-term contracts   18, 86
  New Zealand   191, 198
France
  collective bargaining   14, 15, 66,
    93: centralization v.
    decentralization   61, 62;
    coordination   63; unilateral v.
    joint bargaining   53, 54, 57

France – *continued*
  employer associations   73, 74: centralization v. decentralization   74, 77; initiating change and modernization   80, 81
  health sector   6
  labor cost reduction   7, 8, 9
  New Public Management   12, 43: devolution of managerial responsibilities   36; EMU   24; market-type mechanisms   38; professional management development   34–5; traditional organization and practice   27, 28
  public employment trends   8
  trade unions   19, 84, 87, 89–90, 91
Franco, Francisco   35

gainsharing, USA   105
Germany
  collective bargaining   14, 15, 66: centralization v. decentralization   61; coordination   63–4; unilateral v. joint bargaining   53–4
  decentralization, administrative   13
  employer associations   73, 74: centralization v. decentralization   74, 75, 77; initiating change and modernization   79–80, 82
  labor cost reduction   9
  New Public Management   10, 12, 28, 43: devolution of managerial responsibilities   36, 37; market-type mechanisms   38; professional management development   34, 35
  public employment trends   8
  trade unions   19, 84, 85, 87: coping with change   89; outlook   92
  works councils   175
Gewerkschaft Oftentiche Deutsch, Transport und Werker (OTV, Germany)   19, 62, 89

Gore, Al   109
government, relations between different levels of   12–13
government business enterprises (GBEs), Australia   216–17, 226

Hashimoto, Ryutaro   157
Hawke administration   223, 224, 232, 239
Health and Research Employees Association (Australia)   236
health sector
  Australia   6–7: employer associations   229; employment   220, 227–8; trade unions   231
  Canada: employers and employer associations   136, 137; employment   131, 133; industrial relations   141, 142; organization   130, 131; strikes   147, 148; trade unions   139, 140; wages and salaries   134
  Europe   6, 35, 37, 80–1
  France   6, 35, 81
  Italy   6, 37, 81
  Japan   161
  New Zealand: collective bargaining   205, 206; employers and employer associations   196, 197–8; employment   189; trade unions   200, 201, 203
  United Kingdom   6, 81
  United States   100–1
Health Services Union (Australia)   231, 236
Higher Salaries Commission (HSC, New Zealand)   197, 207
Howard administration   225–6, 233, 234, 239
human resources management (HRM)   2, 10–12
  Australia   239

identity, staff   26
Incorporated Societies Act (New Zealand, 1908)   199
industrial action   85
  Australia   229–30, 235–8
  Canada   141, 142, 143, 146–9

Index 249

industrial action – *continued*
  Japan 155, 159–61, 166, 178, 180–1
  New Zealand 209–10
  United States 102, 112, 116, 118, 119–21
industrial relations 13
  see also collective bargaining; employer associations; trade unions
Industrial Relations Act (New Zealand, 1973) 212n.4
Industrial Relations Act (Commonwealth) (Australia, 1988) 229
Industrial Relations Reform Act (Australia, 1993) 233
inflation 1
information technology
  Australia 223, 225
  United States 99
Inland Revenue Department (New Zealand) 200, 206
internal markets 6, 37
  Europe 38–9: United Kingdom 81
Internal Revenue Service (USA) 100
International Association of Fire Fighters (IAFF, USA) 114
International Brotherhood of Police (USA) 114
International Brotherhood of Teamsters (USA) 114
International Labor Office (ILO)
  Australia 233
  Japan 156, 174, 181, 182n.1
International Union of Police Associations, AFL-CIO (USA) 114
Internet 99
Ireland 8, 9, 12, 15
Ishikawajima Harima Industries (IHI) 156
Italy
  aziendalizzazione (hospitals run as companies) 6
  collective bargaining 15, 66–7: centralization v. decentralization 60–1, 62;
  coordination 63; unilateral v. joint bargaining 54, 56, 67n.2
  employer associations 74, 76, 77, 80, 81
  labor cost reduction 7, 8, 9
  New Public Management: devolution of managerial responsibilities 37; EMU 24, 42; market-type mechanisms 38; professional management development 33–4
  public management trends 8
  trade unions 19, 84, 88–9, 91, 92

jail services, USA 101, 118
Japan 22, 155–7, 181–2
  collective bargaining 14, 15
  employers and employer associations 169–74
  employment 157–63
  internal labor market 163–4
  labor cost reduction 8
  labor relations 178–81
  New Public Management 12
  privatization 5
  trade unions 19, 174–8
  wages and salaries 164–9
Japanese Federation of Employers Associations 174
Japanese Institute of Labor (JIL) 156
Japan External Trade Organization (JETRO) 156
Japan Railways (JR) 155, 157, 181
Japan Teachers Union 169
Japan Tobacco and Salt Monopoly 155, 157
Jichiro (Japan) 167
judges, exclusion from collective bargaining 53

Keating administration 224, 233
Keidanren 156
Keizai Zaisei Simon Kaigi (Japan) 170
KL (local government employers, Denmark) 82
Kokko Ren (Japan) 175
Kokko Roren (Japan) 177, 182
Kokuru (Japan) 175, 181

250 *Index*

Kommunale GemeinSchaftstelle (KGSt, Germany) 82, 89
Labor–Alliance coalition, New Zealand 211
labor cost reductions 4, 7–9, 17
 Canada 127–8, 143
 Japan 156, 162
labor flexibility, trade unions' response to 17–21
Labor Party
 Australia: collective bargaining 234; consultation 238; employees 218; employer associations 229; employers 223, 224, 226; industrial relations 232, 233; organization structure 217; trade unions 231; wages and salaries 222
 New Zealand 186, 192, 195, 196
 United Kingdom 38, 42, 65, 90
Labor Relations Act (New Zealand, 1987) 198, 202, 209
Labor Relations Adjustment Law (Japan, 1946) 180
Labor Standards Law Amended (Japan, 1998) 183n.3
legal issues 13, 25
 Canada 147–8, 149
 Japan 157
 New Zealand 202, 204
 United States 109
length of service
 Canada 133
 Japan 167–8
 New Zealand 190–1
 United States 99
Liberal Democratic Party (LDP, Japan) 169, 180
Liberal–National Party Coalition (Australia) 217
 collective bargaining 234
 employee participation 239
 employer associations 229
 employment 218, 225
 industrial relations 233
 wages and salaries 222
Liberal Party (Canada) 152

local government 13
 Australia 218, 219
 Canada 128, 131–2
 Japan: employment 157–8, 159–61, 162–3; internal labor market 164; wages and salaries 167–9
 New Zealand 186, 200
 United States 97, 98: civil service 109–10; contracting out 107; organizational structure 101–2; recent policies 99; trade unions 112–13; wages and salaries 107
 see also municipal government; provincial government
Local Government Association (LGA, UK) 75, 90
Local Government Clerks Association (Australia) 230
Local Government Management Board (LGMB, UK) 82
Local Government Utility Labor Relations Law (Japan) 159, 167
Local Public Service Law (Japan) 164, 167, 171
lock outs, New Zealand 209

Maastricht Treaty 48, 54
MacArthur, General 180
Management and Coordination Agency, Prime Minister's Office (Japan) 156
managerialism 11
 Australia 223–4, 225
 New Zealand 202
 see also New Public Management
managers
 Australia 218, 227–8
 Canada 133, 135, 137–8, 149
 Europe 30, 32–7
 New Zealand 198
 United States 103, 108
marketization, Australia 224–5
market mechanisms, introduction of 2, 37–9, 78
Massachusetts Commission Against Discrimination 120

Index 251

mediation
  Canada 149
  Japan 179, 180
  New Zealand 210
  United States 118, 120
mental health care, USA 100
merit pay, Italy 61, 76
Merit Protection and Review Agency (Australia) 225
Merit Systems Protection Board (MSPB, USA) 109
mining, Australia 237
Ministry of Agriculture, Forestries and Fisheries (Japan) 162, 170
Ministry of Education (New Zealand) 196, 206
Ministry of Finance (Japan) 170, 171, 172–3, 177–8, 179
Ministry of Foreign Affairs (Japan) 162, 170
Ministry of Health and Welfare (Japan) 170
Ministry of Home Affairs (Japan) 167, 169, 171, 173
Ministry of International Trade and Industry (Japan) 170
Ministry of Justice (Japan) 170
Ministry of Labor (Japan) 170
monetary policy 1
motivation, staff 26–7
municipal government, Canada 128
  employers and employer associations 135, 136
  industrial relations 141
  organization 130–1
  strikes 147, 148
  trade unions 138, 139
Municipal Officers Association (Australia) 230

Naikaku Fu (Cabinet Office, Japan) 170
National Association of Government Employees (USA) 112
National Education Association (NEA, USA) 113–14
National Federation of Federal Employees (USA) 112
National Health Service Confederation (UK) 75
National Labor Relations Act (USA) 101
National Park Service (USA) 100
National Partnership for Reinventing Government (USA) 109
National Performance Review (NPR, USA) 109
National Personnel Authority (NPA, Japan) 156, 158, 163, 171–2
  labor relations 178, 179
  wages and salaries 165, 166, 167, 169, 182
National Public Safety Commission (Japan) 170
National Public Service Law (Japan) 164, 165, 171, 178–9, 180
National Tertiary Education Industry Union (Australia) 229
National Tertiary Education Union (NTEU, Australia) 231, 236
National Treasury Employees Union (USA) 112
National Union of Provincial and General Employees (NUPGE, Canada) 139, 140
National Union of Public Employees (New Zealand) 201
National Union of the Japanese National Railway 181
neo-Taylorist reform 18, 21
Netherlands, The
  collective bargaining 15, 56, 57
  labor cost reduction 8, 9
  New Public Management 11
  public employment trends 8
  trade unions 89
Neue Steuerungsmodelle (NSM, Germany) 82
New Democratic Party (NDP, Canada) 140, 143, 144
New Public Management (NPM) 9–12
  Australia 223
  Europe: challenges and problems 24–5; comparative evidence 32–7; employer associations 79, 82; management practice 28–32; market-type

New Public Management (NPM) – *continued*
  Australia – *continued*
    mechanisms 37–9; national variations 39–44; trade unions 92; traditional organization and practice 25–8
New South Wales Nurses Federation 236
New Zealand 22, 185–6, 210–12
  collective bargaining 16
  competitive tendering 6
  decentralization, administrative 13
  employer associations 73, 75, 78, 79, 83
  employment 186–91
  labor cost reduction 9
  labor market characteristics 191–2
  labor relations 204–10
  neo-Taylorist reform 21
  New Public Management 11, 12
  privatization 6
  public employment trends 8
  regulation of public sector 193–8
  trade unions 18, 84, 85, 86, 198–203
  user element of public service management 7
  wages and salaries 192–3
New Zealand Educational Institute (NZEI) 201
New Zealand Nurses Organization (NZNO) 201
Nihon Broadcasting Corporation (NHK) 156
Nikkeiren (Japan) 174
Nippon Telegraph and Telephone (NTT) 155, 157
Norway 87
NSW Nurses Federation 236

Obuchi, Keizo 157
Occupational Safety and Health Administration (OSHA, USA) 120
Office of Personnel Management (OPM, USA) 109, 118

Organization for Economic Cooperation and Development (OECD) 30–1
  PUMA 2, 9–10, 12, 21, 24, 30–1
overtime, New Zealand 208

part-time working 18, 86
  Australia 218, 219, 220
  Japan 161
  New Zealand 189, 190
patronage, USA 103
pay *see* wages and salaries
pay differentials 17
pay individualization 17
pay merit 17
pensions, Canada 135, 142
performance, USA 104
performance-related pay 17
  Canada 135, 137
  Denmark 20
  France 35
  Germany 35
  New Zealand 193
  Spain 35
  United Kingdom 20, 32
  United States 104–5
Personnel Bureau, Prime Minister's Office (Japan) 156
Police Association of South Australia (PASA) 232
Police Federation of Australia and New Zealand 232, 236
police forces, USA 101, 114, 118
Postal Service (Japan) 175, 177
Post-Primary Teachers Association (PPTA, New Zealand) 201
Prime Minister's Office (Japan) 156, 171, 172, 181
prison services, USA 101, 114, 118
private sector 22
  Australia: industrial action 235–7, 238; trade unions 230; wages and salaries 221–2
  Canada 134, 139, 140, 141–2: compensation 145–6; strikes 147, 148, 149
  change, pressures for 1
  collective bargaining 50, 51, 58, 67

private sector – *continued*
  decentralization, administrative 12, 13
  employer associations 72, 73
  Japan 156: trade unions 174, 175, 176, 177; wages and salaries 165, 166, 167, 169
  New Public Management 11, 24, 25, 26
  New Zealand: employment 190; industrial disputes 209–10; trade unions 200, 203; wages and salaries 204–5, 207–8
  and public sector, changing boundaries between 2
  trade unions 17, 83, 84, 86, 87
  United Kingdom 58
  United States 100, 101: contracting out 106, 107; temporary employment 106; trade unions 111; wages and salaries 108
privatization 4–7
  Canada 127
  Europe: collective bargaining 49, 53, 55, 63; employer associations 78–9; New Public Management 29, 37; trade unions 88–9
  Japan 155, 156–7, 183n.1
  New Zealand 188
  United States 99, 107
professional associations 27, 28
  New Zealand 186, 200
  United States 110–11
  see also employer associations
Professional Fire-Fighters Union (New Zealand) 207
promotions 10, 27
  Australia 221
  Canada 132, 133
  New Zealand 191–2
provincial government, Canada 128
  collective bargaining 144–5
  employers and employer associations 135, 136, 137
  employment 131–2, 133
  industrial relations 141–2, 143
  organization 129–30, 131

strikes 147, 148
trade unions 139
wages and salaries 133
Public Corporation and National Utility Labor Relations Law (Japan) 157
Public Employee Relations Boards (PERBs, USA) 102, 111, 112, 113, 118
Public Employee Relations Commissions (PERCs, USA) 102, 111, 112, 113, 118
Public Finance Act (New Zealand, 1989) 194, 195
Public Health Service (PHS, USA) 100, 101
Public Management Service (PUMA) 21
  New Public Management 9–10, 12, 24, 30–1
  reform proposals 2
public safety sector, USA 101, 114, 118
Public Sector Professional Scientific Research, Technical Communications Aviation and Broadcasting Union (Australia) 230
Public Sector Union (PSU, Australia) 230
Public Service Act (Australia, 1992) 227, 239
Public Service Act (New Zealand, 1912) 191
Public Service Alliance of Canada (PSAC) 139, 148
Public Service and Merit Protection Commission (PSMPC, Australia) 225
Public Service Appeal Board (New Zealand) 192
Public Service Association (PSA, New Zealand) 200, 201, 203, 205
Public Service Bill (Australia) 222, 225–6
Public Service Boards (Australia) 224, 225, 228–9, 239
Public Service Commission (Australia) 225, 229

public service ethos 27
Public Service Personnel System Council (Japan) 157
Public Service Reform Act (Australia, 1984) 223, 239
public transport, Australia 231–2
Public Transport Union (PTU, Australia) 231–2, 236

Qantas Airways 224
quality of public services 2
United States 99
quasi-governmental organizations, Japan 156

race of employees, USA 98
ranges of rates system, New Zealand 193
Reagan administration 119
recruitment see selection, staff
redundancies, New Zealand 192
Registrar of Trade Unions (New Zealand) 202
regulation, market 29
Remuneration Law (Japan) 158, 159, 160, 161, 165
Rengo (Japan) 175, 177
reprofiling, UK 36
Resident Doctors Association (New Zealand) 201
review bodies, UK 55–6, 59, 64–5

salaries see wages and salaries
Sato administration 156
Scandinavia
  New Public Management 43
  privatization 5, 78
  trade unions 19–20, 87, 88, 91
  see also named countries
schools see education sector
selection, staff 27
  Australia 221
  Canada 132
  Japan 163–4
  New Zealand 191, 192, 194, 197
  United States 102–3
Senior Executive Service (SES, Australia) 11, 218, 224, 225
Senior Executive Service (SES, New Zealand) 11, 195
Senior Executive Service (SES, USA) 103
Senior Officers' Association (Australia) 232
Service & Food Workers Union (New Zealand) 201
Service Employees International Union (SEIU, USA) 113, 114
Sindacato Nazionale Autonomo Lavoratori della Scuola (SNALS) 84
skill-based pay incentives, USA 105
Sohyo 180
Solidaires, Unitaires et Démocratique (SUD, France) 90
Spain
  collective bargaining 14, 15, 53, 57
  employer associations 73, 74, 77, 80
  labor cost reduction 7, 8, 9
  New Public Management 34, 35, 36–7, 38, 43
  public employment trends 8
  trade unions 84, 90
Stability and Growth, Pact on 48
staff councils 87
State Administrative Organization Law (Japan, 1949) 170
State Financial Control (Sweden) 44
state government 12–13
  Australia 218, 219, 227
  United States 97, 98: civil service 109–10; contracting out 107; organizational structure 101–2; recent policies 99; trade unions 112–13; wages and salaries 107
state-owned enterprises (SOEs, New Zealand, 1986) 11, 186
  collective bargaining 206
  employment 187, 188
  trade unions 200
State Owned Enterprises Act (New Zealand, 1986) 186, 194
State Public Services Federation (SPSF, Australia) 230

State Sector Act (New Zealand) 11, 16, 192, 193
  collective bargaining 205
  employers and employer associations 194–5, 196, 197
  trade unions 198, 199
State Services Act (New Zealand, 1962) 191, 192, 210
State Services Commission (SSC, New Zealand) 185
  collective bargaining 207
  employers and employer associations 194, 195, 196, 197–8
  employment 191, 192
State Services Conditions of Employment Act (New Zealand, 1977) 205
strategic incentive plans (SIPs, New Zealand) 198
strategic management, Australia 239
strikes *see* industrial action
supervisors, USA 103
Sweden
  collective bargaining 56–7, 62, 66
  decentralization, administrative 13
  Economic and Monetary Union 92
  employer associations 76, 77
  labor cost reduction 7, 9
  New Public Management 11, 12, 43–4
  public employment trends 8
  trade unions 20
Switzerland 12

taxation 1
  New Zealand 192
team incentive programs, USA 105–6
Technical Services Guild (Australia) 230
Telstra (Communications) (Australia) 231
Temporary Administrative Research Commission (Japan) 156
Temporary Deliberation Councils on Administrative Reform (Japan) 156

Temporary Study Committees on Administration (Japan) 156
temporary work 18
  Australia 218, 219, 220
  Canada 133
  Japan 159, 160, 161
  United States 106
Thatcher, Margaret 42
Trade Union Federation (TUF, New Zealand) 201
Trade Union for Education and Science (GEW, Germany) 84
Trade Union Law (Japan) 174
trade unions
  Australia 227, 229–32, 234, 236
  Canada 136, 138–40, 141–2, 149–50
  collective bargaining *see* collective bargaining
  Japan 156, 174–8, 182n.1: labor relations 180; wages and salaries 169
  New Zealand 185–6, 198–203
  responses to increasing flexibility 17–21
  United States 111–14, 125n.11
  Western Europe 71, 83–7: coping with change 87–91; New Public Management 27, 28; outlook 91–3
transfer payments 2
Transport Workers Union (TWU, USA) 114
Treasury (Japan) 170, 178
tribunals, Canada 138
Tsujimura, Kotaro 157

unemployment 87
Union of the Japanese National Railways 175
UNISON 92
United Fire-fighters' Union of Australia (UFUA) 232, 236
United Kingdom 22
  collective bargaining 14, 15, 16, 50, 66: centralization v. decentralization 58–9; coordination 64–5; unilateral v. joint bargaining 55–6

256 *Index*

United Kingdom – *continued*
  competitive tendering 6, 37–8
  decentralization, administrative 13
  Economic and Monetary Union 92
  employer associations 73:
    centralization v. decentralization 74, 75;
    initiating change and modernization 78, 80, 81, 82
  internal markets 6
  labor cost reduction 7, 8, 9
  neo-Taylorist reform 21
  New Public Management 11, 41–2:
    devolution of managerial responsibilities 35–6; market-type mechanisms 37–8; professional management development 32–3; traditional organization and practice 27
  privatization 5, 6
  public employment trends 8
  trade unions 18, 20, 84, 87:
    coping with change 90; outlook 92
United Nations International Women's Year (1975) 163
United States of America 123–4
  bargaining and negotiations 114–21
  civil service systems 109–10
  collective bargaining 14, 15, 16
  employer associations 73, 110–11
  labor cost reduction 7, 8, 9
  levels of government 13
  New Public Management 11
  organizational structure 100–2
  privatization 5
  public employment trends 8, 97–9
  qualitative employment and wages 102–8
  recent policies 99
  reform efforts 121–2
  trade unions 20, 86, 111–14
United Trades and Labor Council of South Australia 232
US Postal Service (USPS) 100

wages and salaries
  Australia 221–3, 232, 234–5
  Canada 128, 133–5, 137–8, 142–3, 145–6
  collective bargaining *see* collective bargaining
  Europe 76, 77, 88, 89
  Japan 164–9
  New Zealand 192–3, 197, 204–5, 207–8
  performance-related pay *see* performance-related pay
  restraints 8
  United States 107–8
Water and Maritime Industry Union (Australia) 230
welfare state 91
  Spain 35
Western Europe
  collective bargaining 48–50, 65–7:
    centralization v. decentralization 57–62;
    comparative analysis framework 50–2; coordination 62–5; unilateral v. joint regulation 52–7
  employer associations 71–4:
    centralization v. decentralization 74–8;
    initiating change and modernization 78–83; outlook 91–3
  New Public Management:
    challenges and problems 24–5; comparative evidence 32–7; management practice 28–32; market-type mechanisms 37–9; national variations 39–44; traditional organization and practice 25–8
  privatization 5
  trade unions 71, 83–7: coping with change 87–91; outlook 91–3
  see also named countries
Whitlam, Gough 226
women employees 83, 86
  Australia 217, 219–20

Canada 132–4
Japan 161, 163–4
New Zealand 189–90
United States 98
Workplace Relations Act (Australia, 1996) 222, 233, 234

works councils
   Denmark 34
   Germany 175

Zenrokyo (Japan) 175, 177
Zenroren (Japan) 175, 177, 182